THE MOST
EVIL
MEN AND
WOMEN
IN HISTORY

THE MOST
EVIL
MEN AND
WOMEN
IN HISTORY

Miranda Twiss

BARNES
&NOBLE
BOOKS
NEW YORK

First published in Great Britain in 2002 by
Michael O'Mara Books Limited
9 Lion Yard
Tremadoc Road
London SW4 7NQ

This edition published by Barnes & Noble, Inc.,
by arrangement with Michael O'Mara Books Limited

2002 Barnes & Noble Books

M 10 9 8 7 6 5 4

ISBN 0-7607-3496-8 (hardcover)
ISBN 0-7607-3495-X (paperback)

Designed and typeset by Design 23

Printed and bound in Singapore by Tien Wah Press

CONTENTS

INTRODUCTION

Evil. 1. Morally wrong or bad; wicked: an evil ruler. 2. Causing harm or injury; harmful: an evil plan. 3. Marked or accompanied by misfortune; unlucky: an evil fate. 4. (Of temper, disposition, etc.) characterized by anger or spite. 5. Not in high esteem; infamous: an evil reputation. 6. Offensive or unpleasant: an evil smell. 7. The quality or an instance of being morally wrong; wickedness: the evil of war. 8. A force or power that brings about wickedness or harm: evil is strong in the world.
OXFORD ENGLISH DICTIONARY

Power tends to corrupt and absolute power corrupts absolutely.
JOHN DAHLBERG, FIRST BARON ACTON,
letter to Bishop Mandell Creighton, 3 April 1877

The only unifying factor between the sixteen men and women who appear in these pages and the evil acts they committed is that they all wielded unlimited power over other people's lives. As a group their own lives span nearly 2,000 years – from the birth of Caligula in the Roman Empire of 12AD to the genocide of the Cambodian people during the 1980s. Motivated by power, religion, lust and political belief, these men and women have all become bywords for terror throughout the world.

Evil is a fact of life. We can see it, not only in the reigns of Stalin and Hitler, but also in everyday crimes such as murder, rape and battery; not to mention the millions of lives brutalized by poverty, disease and starvation.

John Stuart Mill said that 'the dictum that truth always triumphs over persecution is one of the pleasant falsehoods which men repeat after one another till they pass into commonplaces, but which experience refutes. History teems with instances of truth and goodness put down by persecution'. How many times have you heard someone say, 'What goes around comes around'? In the grand scheme of things we often choose to believe that human goodness will prevail, and that the evil-doers will get what's coming to them. But justice for the sixteen men and women in this book is only occasionally meted out – the good may suffer but the wicked may also flourish. Ivan the Terrible, Stalin, Pol Pot, Torquemada and Pizarro all died in old age and, of the sixteen, only six died as a result of their actions. Various dictators, like Amin, live out their lives in comfort, continuing to wield power, whilst good causes supported by good people continually lose out. Sadly, the most obvious lesson to be learnt from comparing the sixteen's heinous crimes is that they all show us just how very little we have learnt from our mistakes. The ability of people to 'see no evil, hear no evil' was just as prevalent during Idi Amin's reign of terror as it had been in Hitler's and even further back to Nero. All three were giving a large section of the population exactly what they wanted and, in exchange for this, the people chose to ignore the cruelties perpetuated on their fellow citizens.

Power draws people towards the centre from which it emanates. None of the people in this book have committed their acts of atrocity by themselves – all have had very willing and able accomplices. Elizabeth Bathory may only have had a few like-minded sadists to help her along the way, but whole sections of Cambodian, German, Russian and Ugandan society mobilized behind Pol Pot, Hitler, Stalin and Amin in conducting mass killings. When Ivan the Terrible created his army of henchmen, the *Oprichniki*, he had no shortage of volunteers. Attila's bloodthirsty army drew people from throughout the civilized world and, for many Ugandans, Amin's promise of wealth and unlimited power over life and death led hundreds to join his State Research Bureau. Men and women followed these evil leaders because they knew that complicity was the path to influence, money and power. Despite having to deal with the unpredictability of their leaders, people followed their baser instincts.

In mitigation it should be pointed out that many 'evil' people's reigns of horror were mercifully short. Pol Pot, Bloody Mary and Caligula only attained supreme power for four years, Amin for eight. However, this was not always the case. Stalin remained in power for over thirty years and, when he died, there were mass outpourings of grief at the passing of 'Uncle Joe' and, despite the fact that he had been directly responsible for the destruction of millions of people's lives, his image was kept intact for some years after his death. Indeed, most of the evil people within these pages still have their apologists who choose to ignore the reports of these people's atrocities as propaganda.

Of course, the portrayal of people as evil has its benefits. If your enemy is seen in a bad light, then any means to stop them becomes acceptable and your own evil acts can be justified. When Vlad the Impaler was captured by the King of Hungary, a series of forged letters were produced showing how Vlad's evil had corrupted him from God's true path, and extensive use was made of the sensationalist German horror stories in blackening his name. The political reality was that Vlad was just too successful and uncontrollable for Hungary's liking. Rasputin provided the perfect scapegoat with which to undermine the Russian Tsar and Tsarina. It was his power over them that was seen at the time as a malevolent force. He was corrupting the Tsarina by his licentious ways, and corrupting the Tsar by isolating him from his advisers. Rasputin was a vehicle through which to attack the worst excesses of the royal family, and hasten the end of the Romanov dynasty and, thereby, the monarchy in Russia. Many of the stories attributed to the likes of Caligula, Nero and Attila portray them as the Antichrist – conjuring up the Devil in various forms to assist them in their malevolent acts. Cannibalism regularly emerges in popular myth as one of the foul deeds perpetrated by many of the sixteen. That is not to say that some did not partake of human flesh, but the image was used with monotonous regularity, probably to illustrate how far from the path of righteous behaviour they had strayed.

Is evil ever justified? With two of the sixteen there is a point to be made in their favour. It is extremely doubtful whether Attila the Hun would have forged such a large empire if not for his infamy. Town after town fell to him without a fight, simply because the tales of his evil had preceded him. And Stalin took Russia from the wooden plough to a superpower in thirty years. He may have lost sight of the fact that human dignity and well-being lay at the heart of all progress, but I do not believe that a nation so used to the absolute power of the Tsarist state would have responded so quickly to a kindly leader. The very fact that Russia was used to an autocratic style of leadership made it possible for Stalin to implement his monstrous reforms without any regard for human life. Even the relatively benevolent Lenin appreciated the need for force and intimidation when it came to forging a new nation.

We do not really understand evil – often taking it as an absolute rather than as a comparative word. Our concept of evil in the twenty-first century is dramatically different from previous centuries. Can you imagine going to the Albert Hall today to watch Muslims being eaten by lions, or attending a burning of heretics outside Westminster Abbey? It may seem a ridiculous concept, but the fact is that thousands of people in their time actively participated in and enjoyed these gruesome ceremonies.

In many cases, religion seems to have provided the sixteen with either a reason for inflicting their barbarity, or a tool for receiving forgiveness for their evil acts. If they felt that God was on their side, their enemies were not only against them but also against their God and therefore any acts committed could be justified. After each killing spree, Ivan the Terrible would spend weeks purging himself before the altar; Torquemada dressed in his monk's habit, and ordered the torture and executions of the supposed 'heretics'; and Elizabeth Bathory and Vlad the Impaler both regularly attended church services. Francisco Pizarro conquered and ravaged the Inca Empire in the name of Christ, and Bloody Mary had hundreds of Protestants burnt in the name of the Catholic Church. God may represent love and forgiveness, but the history books are full of terrible deeds committed in the name of religion.

Of the people included, only three are women. Elizabeth Bathory reputedly killed over 600 girls in her castles, and Ilse Koch turned Buchenwald into her own private amusement park, but they did not have access to the troops or the political power that is required if you are to employ large numbers of people to do your dirty work for you. On the other hand, Mary I was the first English queen in her own right, but her reign was short and the number of people killed as a result of her policies pales into insignificance when compared to the number killed under the reign of her father, King Henry VIII. Maybe the very fact that she was a woman made her more vulnerable to accusations of evil-doing. You only have to look at the vast numbers of women accused of witchcraft and burnt at the stake during this time to see how conveniently women could be used as scapegoats.

Human vice is often at the root of most evil-doing: envy, pride, vanity, greed – they are all evident in the lives of the people discussed. But where does evil begin? I find it impossible to believe that a child is born evil and yet there can be little doubt from the evidence provided that Ivan the Terrible was a malicious child and that Caligula's boyhood experiences fed the dark side of his nature, rather than drawing out the best.

We try to ascribe reasons for evil. With some of the people in this book, it is easier to see clear delineations – before they were evil and after they became so – as a result of childhood experiences, or the death of a spouse or of a mother or father. King John was bought up amid a court rife with treachery and double-dealing, so it is hardly surprising he was chronically insecure and weak. But sometimes it is just not possible to draw such simplistic conclusions. In addition, evil acts are not comparable because the circumstances in which the acts are committed vary according to each situation. Without the right circumstances, none of the sixteen would have been able to gain the power needed to accomplish their deeds. If the Americans had not withdrawn all funding to Cambodia, Pol Pot would not have risen to the heights he attained; if the Tsar and Tsarina had been less removed from reality and the needs of their people, Rasputin would never have gained such a strong foothold; and if Ilse Koch had been married to someone else and not gone to Buchenwald concentration camp, she may well have lived out her life as a provincial German *hausfrau*, indulging her passion for pain in private.

What makes evil so fascinating? Glancing through the pages of history, it is difficult to find any subject that has puzzled the intelligence of mankind more than the subject of evil. A book outlining the history of man's inhumanity to man is somehow more gripping than one detailing people's good deeds. Evil destroys the integrity, the happiness and the welfare of a 'normal' society, yet we are absorbed by it, maybe in the hope that we will learn from our mistakes, but more likely from a perverse desire to hear of others' misfortunes whilst we comfort ourselves with the thought that it could never happen to us.

MIRANDA TWISS
January 2002

CALIGULA

THE SCHIZOPHRENIC EMPEROR

There was never a better slave or a worse master.
TIBERIUS, EMPEROR OF ROME

There was relief and rejoicing throughout the Roman Empire when the Emperor Tiberius died in 37AD. Tiberius, who had spent years of self-imposed exile on the island of Capri, had become feared and despised because of the cruel executions of his critics in the Roman army.

His young successor appeared to promise a new Golden Age. The people were dazzled by Gaius Caesar and his family connections, and the Senate handed him unprecedented powers. For the next four years, the schizophrenic Emperor would use these powers to terrorize, rape and murder, with sadistic delight. Two thousand years on, his sex life is still a watchword for depravity. He revelled in torture, demanding slow and painful executions to be carried out as he dined. Men, women and even the Empire were treated as his personal toys, as he embarked on a series of ever more bizarre schemes to boost his ego. Finally, Caligula would declare himself a God.

Gaius Julius Caesar was born in 12AD into the most powerful family in the Roman Empire. His father, Germanicus, was a war hero, posted on the Empire's northern frontier. His mother, Agrippina, was the granddaughter of Emperor Augustus and was ambitious and outspoken. His father had often taken the infant Gaius on Roman army campaigns, and the legionnaires had doted on the child, adopting him as a lucky mascot. He

Gaius Julius Caesar – 'Caligula' – 'tall and spindly, with sunken eyes and thinning hair'. Cruel beyond barbarity, capricious and perverse, and not a little mad, his brief reign as Emperor was marked by tyranny and mass slaughter. (STAPLETON COLLECTION/CORBIS)

was dressed in a tiny uniform, complete with hand-crafted boots, called *caligae* from which he earned his nickname, Caligula, a name he grew to despise.

His father Germanicus was more charming than talented, in contrast to the increasingly austere Tiberius. Minor military victories in Germany had won Tiberius huge popular support. But Germanicus's glittering reputation made him a threat to the Emperor. In May 17AD Germanicus was recalled from the front. It was a glorious return to Rome complete with captives and the spoils of war. Germanicus led a triumphant procession and, riding alongside him in his chariot, four-year-old Caligula lapped up the adulation being showered upon his father. The family had little time to enjoy their glory, because two years later Germanicus died. His painful and lingering death displayed all the symptoms of poisoning – and Germanicus believed that the Emperor Tiberius was responsible. Agrippina believed this too and, encouraged by the massive display of public grief, accused Tiberius of her husband's murder, claiming that her whole family had been marked out for extermination. She was not far off the mark, but the arrogant and outspoken personality of Agrippina brought about her own downfall.

Agrippina and her two eldest sons, Nero and Drusus, were arrested and charged with being enemies of the state. Nero was forced to slit his own throat, while Drusus and Agrippina were left to starve to death. In childhood, Caligula saw an entire catalogue of murders, exiles and bestial humiliations inflicted on those around him.

However, for the youngest son, there was a reprieve. Caligula was sent to live with his grandmother Antonia. Antonia's years at the heart of the imperial court had taught her diplomacy and cunning, in contrast to the volatile Agrippina. The impressionable teenager, however, was initiating an incestuous relationship with his two sisters, although it was the youngest, Drusilla, who became the primary focus of his sexual obsession. In 31AD, Caligula's life took a dramatic turn. At the age of nineteen, he received an imperial summons to join the ageing Tiberius on the island of Capri. Tiberius had retired to Capri in 26AD and during his time there, the island had become notorious for cruelty and debauchery, with people being thrown off the cliffs to their deaths when he tired of them.

Caligula was to live as a house guest for six years with the man responsible for the eradication of his family, and yet he displayed no evidence of any malice. Caligula was playing the survival game and, besides, he found plenty with which to entertain himself. Caligula had a wild streak of youthful extravagance and an appetite for sexual adventuring, and if his elders thought he would eschew such behavior as he adopted the mature responsibilities of Emperor, they were sadly mistaken. His youthful excesses merely masked a depraved insanity that only surfaced when he began to revel in the full power of his new office. His biographer, Suetonius, noted that: 'He was not able to control his savage and reprehensible nature. Indeed, he showed the keenest interest in witnessing the sufferings and torments of those condemned being tortured. At night he was in the habit of going out, disguised in a wig and a long cloak, to indulge in gluttony and adultery.'

Nevertheless, Caligula was also using his time in Capri to form strong political links. He created a powerful strategic alliance with the head of the Praetorian Guard, Macro. Macro was a veteran of the politics of violence. As Tiberius's right-hand man, he had overseen the notorious trials and executions of his reign. Now he saw a kindred spirit in Caligula. The alliance was cemented by an agreement between the two men that Caligula could sleep with Macro's wife, Ennia.

Tiberius had no doubts about the character of his long-term guest. He predicted bloodshed. In 35AD Caligula was named the joint successor with Gemellus, Tiberius's grandson. Embracing the child, Tiberius said to Caligula, 'You will kill him and another will kill you.'

But the Emperor's hands were tied. As Germanicus's son, Caligula was hugely popular and, with Macro behind him, he also had the support of the imperial forces. Tiberius had no choice but to promote him. Germanicus's untimely end had concentrated resentment against Tiberius and created a legend of Germanicus's superhuman qualities, which was now transferred to his only surviving son, Caligula.

Tiberius died, unmourned, on 16 March 37AD. Guided by Macro, the Senate threw out the Emperor's will on the grounds that he had been of unsound mind. The Empire was handed over to Caligula, who then underlined Gemellus's youth by adopting him. Gemellus was to have no share in the Empire, and within a year he was murdered.

To the delight of Rome, the son of Germanicus now had sole control of the entire Roman Empire. It is said that, in the first three months of his rule, more than 160,000 people were sacrificed in his honour throughout the Empire. The City of Rome was celebrating the end of a reign that had been hated by the upper classes for its taxation and by the lower classes for its dullness.

The new Emperor was tall and spindly, with sunken eyes and thinning hair. It was forbidden for anyone to look down from any height as Caligula passed by, and men with thicker hair were often made to shave it off. He had a liberal covering of body hair, however, and the very mention of goats in his presence became a crime punishable by death.

But Caligula's tyrannical megalomania had yet to show itself fully. For now, the Senate was as charmed as the people. Within hours of arriving in Rome, the young Emperor was awarded 'power and authority in all things.' In fact Caligula's powers were so wide that only the great Augustus had amassed as much authority.

The first six months of Caligula's reign were a spectacular 'honeymoon' period for the citizens of Rome. Caligula quickly won their affection by giving away most of Tiberius's treasury in generous tax rebates and cash bonuses for the soldiers of the garrison in Rome. He paid small fortunes to the soldiers he trusted most, namely the broad-shouldered German mercenaries who made up his personal bodyguard.

With reckless disregard for the worried senators who warned him he would bankrupt himself and the office of Emperor, Caligula also began to lavish unheard-of expense on the bloodletting rituals of the circuses in the Roman amphitheatres. From

A nineteenth-century representation of Caligula buying a gladiator. He bankrupted himself in presenting circuses, the bloodletting rituals that pitched men against men or wild animals. When he was booed for staging a feeble spectacle in an attempt to save money, he had the chief jeerers mutilated and sent into the arena to face the half-starved animals, and delightedly applauded their gruesome deaths. (CORBIS)

all parts of the Empire, a sinister menagerie of lions, panthers, elephants and bears was captured in the forests and deserts, to be brought to Rome and butchered in staged 'hunts' in the arenas, to the delight of the spectators.

Prize money for gladiators and charioteers was doubled and trebled to encourage them to fight each other to the death. The shows were breathtaking extravaganzas, wildly acclaimed by their audiences, and they made Caligula an Emperor to be admired and applauded.

Furthermore, the Roman elite was also reassured that Tiberius's treason trials would stop and, in an apparently heroic gesture, Caligula tore up Tiberius's records. To the Senate's relief, Caligula also declared that he would not punish those involved in the deaths of his mother and brothers and declared an amnesty for all Romans imprisoned or exiled under Tiberius. A skilled orator, he outlined a programme of co-operation with the Senate that was received with rapturous applause.

But Caligula's family was not forgotten entirely, and honours were heaped on both his dead parents. In addition, his grandmother and three sisters were all made Vestal Virgins (particularly ironic considering that he used to indulge in incest with his sisters on a regular basis) and, in an unprecedented move, he had coinage minted with their images. It was an early warning sign of Caligula's ego – one that went unheeded by an enraptured Rome.

In less than a year, Caligula ran through the two-and-a-half billion sesterces left by Tiberius's years of careful economy. But the golden period had taken an even greater toll on his mental health. The strains of power and adulation had stretched

Caligula to breaking point and, before the summer was over, he suffered a physical and mental breakdown. For a month, he hovered between life and death. Caligula's condition sent shockwaves through Rome, and sympathetic Romans gathered in their thousands day and night, outside the palace. All traffic of chariots and handcarts and the noise of music and trade in the street were banned within half-a-mile of the palace, while the citizens prayed for his recovery. High-ranking Romans offered to fight as gladiators, or even to sacrifice their own lives, if the Emperor could be spared.

Finally, Caligula regained full consciousness – weakened, but growing stronger each day. Calling his friends and family around him, he confided: 'I wasn't really ill, I was just being reborn a God.' From now on, Caligula's reign began to take a very different course. He became increasingly tyrannical and erratic, as he realized just what he could get away with, and, for the first time, Caligula became frightened of assassination, and his fear bred cruelty. For the rest of his life, the Emperor would suffer from nightmares and insomnia, often wandering through his palace until daylight.

Upon his recovery, Caligula sought out the men who had offered to sacrifice themselves for him. The man who had promised he would fight as a gladiator was obliged to fulfil his vow. Caligula looked on as he struggled in combat and did not give him a reprieve until he had won his fight and pleaded repeatedly for delivery. Another man was handed to his slaves who were to drive him, wearing sacred wreaths, through the streets, demanding fulfilment, and then, finally, hurl him from the ramparts. Caligula also ordered a series of games to celebrate his recovery. Roman trade and commerce almost ground to a halt as day after day was declared a public holiday, but the constant bloody carnival finally took its toll on Caligula's purse. Prize money fell, and when one circus featured mangy, underfed lions and middle-aged gladiators, Caligula was booed by the audience.

The mad Caligula reacted swiftly. Those who had led the jeering were seized by his guards and dragged away to the cellars under the arena. Their tongues were cut out, and, choking on their own blood, they were forced into the arena to do battle with the wild animals. The Roman people were stunned, but Caligula enjoyed the scene immensely, clapping until the last of the hecklers was eaten. The spirit of goodwill had come to an end and, as he regained his strength, Caligula now began striking out at close relatives and former friends. Gemellus was accused of making plans in anticipation of Caligula's death. The eighteen-year-old was handed a sword and shown how to commit suicide. Next, Caligula turned on his father-in-law, Silanus. The old man was accused of treason, after he refused to accompany Caligula on a boat trip. Silanus was forced to cut his own throat with a razor. And even Caligula's henchmen fell foul of his new mood. Macro's advice had been increasingly resented by his protégé. Now Macro was charged with prostituting his wife, Ennia, the woman who had been Caligula's mistress. Both were ordered to commit suicide.

With Macro gone, no one remained to influence Caligula's behaviour. The Roman elite may have believed they could mould the young Emperor to their wishes, but it was fast becoming clear that Caligula had his own agenda. The deaths of

Gemellus, Silanus and Macro were followed by a wave of executions amongst Macro's supporters. People suspected of any type of disloyalty were put to death immediately. A supervisor of games and beast fights was flogged with chains in Caligula's presence for days on end, and was only executed when Caligula became offended by the smell of gangrene.

Under Caligula, the law became an instrument of torture. When one man claimed he was innocent, Caligula had the execution halted and ordered his tongue to be cut out before he was put to death. Caligula demanded that the victim's families watch the killings and when one father excused himself on the grounds of ill health, Caligula sent a litter to his house to collect him. Another father was ordered to dine with Caligula, hours after watching his own son's death.

But the Emperor also ordered executions for financial motives – his most effective money-making schemes involved the use of fear. He issued a series of trumped-up charges against some of the wealthiest citizens of Rome, and their vast estates and fortunes were seized as punishment. The paid informers who gave perjured evidence were rewarded with a few gold coins.

Caligula drank pearls dissolved in vinegar and loved to roll on piles of gold. His self-indulgent and depraved lifestyle was funded by new taxes on food, lawsuits and prostitution. Visitors were lent money with interest, and he would force people to amend their wills in his favour, and then murder them. He also declared wills null and void if they weren't made out in his name, on the grounds of ingratitude. Once, when a supposedly rich man had finally died, but turned out to be penniless, Caligula commented, 'Oh dear, he died in vain.' Suetonius records how Caligula slept with prisoners, senators and members of his own family. 'He habitually indulged in incestuous relations with all his sisters and at a crowded banquet he would make them take turns in lying beneath him, while his wife lay above.'

Caligula's 'sense of humour' showed just how obsessed he was with the dark potential of his power. When kissing the neck of his wife or mistress, he would comment that he could have it cut whenever he wanted. When asked why he was laughing out loud during a meeting of the consuls, Caligula replied that with a single nod from him they would be killed on the spot. He also insisted that his favourite horse, Incitatus, be made a consul and gave the animal jewelled necklaces, a marble stable with furniture and made him a priest of his temple.

The limitless extent of his power had left him and his office open to ridicule, but in June 38AD, shaken by the death of his youngest sister, Drusilla, Caligula embarked on an even more bizarre campaign, that of turning his sister into a goddess. Whilst it was common practice to worship an Emperor when he was dead, Drusilla was a woman of no importance to anyone but Caligula. During the enforced period of public mourning, it was an offence throughout the Empire to laugh, wash or dine with one's family. Caligula ordered a golden statue of Drusilla to be set up in the Senate itself and a special priesthood, of both sexes, was appointed to preside over her cult.

Within days, the bereaved brother threw himself into his third marriage. Caligula was irresistibly attracted to women he could not possess. Caligula's first wife had died in childbirth, but his second, Livia Orestilla, stolen from her groom at her own wedding, had been quickly divorced. Now he had chosen again.

Lollia Paulina was an extremely wealthy woman, and already married. Caligula forced her husband to give her away. Once again, he was soon tired of her, divorcing her within weeks, and ordering that she remain celibate for the rest of her life.

Only in his fourth wife, Caesonia, whom he married in 39AD, did Caligula find a soulmate. She was promiscuous, with a reputation for extravagance, and Caligula's delight with her was so intense that he paraded her naked in front of his friends. She was to bear him his only child, Drusilla, named after his dead sister, although it is doubtful that Caligula was actually her father.

Less than two years after becoming Emperor, Caligula's autocratic behaviour was causing alarm in the Senate. As hopes for a peaceful and stable reign vanished, there were early stirrings of resistance to the Emperor's rule. His brother-in-law, Lepidus, schemed with Agrippina, the mother of the future Emperor Nero, and a commander of the imperial forces. But their plans came to nothing. Rumours abounded of a series of plots hatched in the Senate. Caligula's response was ruthless. In early 39AD, he marched into the chamber and delivered a dramatic and savage denunciation of its members.

Labelling his senators hypocrites, he revealed that he had lied about destroying the evidence surrounding the deaths of his mother and brothers. All those present were accused of being informers. He had realized that they could betray him, just as they had Tiberius. Now he promised that if there was nothing to be gained in trying to please them, he might as well rule by fear. Knowing that Caligula was highly strung, the terrified Senate was forced to agree to a resumption of the treason trials instigated by Tiberius. From now on, the threat of accusation and summary execution would hang over them all.

Caligula's humiliation of his senators would become a pattern for the remainder of his reign. Some who had held the highest offices now had to run for many miles in their togas alongside his military chariot. Others were invited to dine with the Emperor, only to be made to wait as Caligula took the wife of one of his guests to an adjoining room. On his return, he would comment on her sexual prowess to the rest of his guests.

Caligula's behaviour in the Senate had left no doubt about who was in power. But, later in the year, he embarked on a grandiose scheme designed to impress the rest of Italy.

As a boy, Caligula had been told by a soothsayer that he had as much chance of becoming Emperor as crossing the Bay of Naples and keeping dry. Now he decided to prove the soothsayer wrong. Five kilometres of water separated Puteoli and Baiae, over the Bay of Naples, and Caligula built a temporary floating bridge across it. For two days, Caligula, dressed in the breastplate of Alexander the Great, and a cloak of gold studded with jewels, rode backwards and forwards, followed by a retinue of soldiers and prisoners. The calm seas convinced him that even the god Neptune held him in awe.

On the second day, Caligula climbed onto a platform on the middle of the bridge to boast of his achievement. Celebrations continued into the night and a number of revellers drowned. By this time, the Treasury was almost bankrupt, and Caligula threw all caution to the wind in his lust for gold. His guards rounded up ordinary citizens off the street and forced them to contribute every coin in their purses to the Emperor. Holding back a single coin could mean instant death. Then Caligula announced he was to open a brothel in the palace. Eminent senators were ordered to turn up at the enforced sex orgies and pay an entrance fee of 1,000 gold pieces, and to bring their wives and daughters, so they could be put to work as prostitutes.

In the first three years of his reign, Caligula's impact was only felt in Rome, but by late 39AD, he had widened his net. The Emperor started to believe that he could eclipse his father's military successes. He decided that he would extend the boundaries of his Empire in Germany and into Britain. For the first time in over fifty years, an Emperor would leave Italy – he planned to return covered in glory.

In reality, his plans more closely resembled farce. Caligula's journey into battle was made in considerable comfort. With a vast retinue, each town he passed through was cleaned, and invitations to dine with the Emperor were sold to local dignitaries. There were reports that some were subsequently killed, and their property confiscated.

A chronicler reports that once Caligula was playing dice and, upon finding that he had no money, called for the census lists of Gaul to be brought to him. He then proceeded to order the wealthiest of his citizens to be put to death. Turning to his fellow players, he remarked: 'While you have been playing for a few denarii, I have taken in a good 150 million'.

Caligula arrived on the German border early in 40AD. But, despite the presence of the enemy nearby, he made no move into German territory. In one small skirmish, his legions captured about 1,000 prisoners. Caligula picked out 300 men to be sent back to Rome and ordered for the remainder to be lined up against a cliff, with a bald man at each end. Satisfied that he had enough prisoners for a swaggering triumphant entrance back into Rome, he ordered his legions to '…kill every man from bald head to bald head.' Meanwhile, back in Rome, the Senate received reports that Caligula was '…on campaign and exposed to great dangers'.

From Germany, Caligula moved onto Britain, and the most extraordinary episode of his reign.

Camping outside the port of Boulogne, he ordered his dispirited and nervous army to line up on the beaches. Roman archers formed ranks at the water's edge. Huge catapults and slings were dragged onto the sand dunes, massed troops of cavalry waited on the flanks. All eyes were set to the horizon, watching for the appearance of some distant enemy.

Then Caligula rose with imperial majesty and rode into the shallow water. With blood-curdling oaths, he unsheathed his sword and swore revenge on the sea god,

The forum at Pompeii, with the arch of Caligula that still stands today. The pleasure-loving city exactly reflected the Emperor's perverse tastes, and paid, as many saw it, a heavy price in divine retribution; badly damaged by an earthquake during the reign of Nero, it was overwhelmed sixteen years later by the great eruption of Vesuvius in 79AD. (BETTMANN/CORBIS)

Neptune. The soldiers watched as Caligula began to slash the foam with his sword, the infantry charged and the shallow waters were pierced with spears as the cavalry rode in and out of the surf.

'Now for the plunder,' shouted Caligula, and each man had to begin looting the sea – gathering piles of seashells in their helmets, which were taken back to Rome as spoils of his heroic victory. The mighty Roman Legions had been reduced to clowning for their insane Emperor.

Caligula's dreams of conquest had been frustrated and he was furious. He had inflicted greater havoc on his subjects and soldiers than on the enemy. Caligula returned to Rome, bringing the straggling German prisoners and a handful of Britons he had captured from a trading boat in Boulogne, together with tons of seashells. Upon his arrival, in May 40AD, he was met by a delegation sent by the Senate, led by his uncle, Claudius. They had come to offer congratulations, but Caligula was in no mood to listen. Slapping his dagger, he replied, 'I'm on my way, and so is this.'

Now he offered his own proclamation to the shocked delegation – he was only returning to those who wanted him – the people – but not the Senate. Caligula was looking for scapegoats and the senators were the obvious choice. Testing their loyalty to the utmost, he demanded their recognition, not just as Supreme Leader, but also as a God. However, the plots against Caligula were growing apace.

From the onset of his illness, Caligula had taken great delight in the wearing of elaborate costumes. A frequent cross-dresser, he would also appear as demigods like Hercules, Apollo, Bacchus, Castor and Pollux. But as his madness progressed, Caligula moved onto the major gods: Hermes, Apollo and Mars. He was often to be seen with a gilded beard, holding a thunderbolt, a trident and sometimes even dressed in the regalia of the goddesses Venus, Juno and Diana.

By the middle of 40AD, Caligula's delusions of divinity were uncontrollable. As a sun god, he courted the moon and claimed fellowship with the gods. He would have conversations with Jupiter, calling him his brother. The powerless Senate could only watch, as he ordered a temple to be built to himself in the heart of Rome. Wealthy nobles, including his uncle, Claudius, were forced to pay vast sums towards the construction. Caligula then extended part of his palace right into the forum, incorporating the temple of Castor and Pollux as his own. He drew up plans for all the heads of statues of gods in Rome to be remade with an image of his own head.

He spent the entire summer of 40AD rigorously preparing himself to be a God. He sent for the most adept magicians from every corner of the Empire, and they spent several weeks in a darkened room with the Emperor, revealing every last secret of their art to him. In a final ceremony, they formed a circle around him, and chanting strange invocations in many tongues, they infused his naked body with all their arcane powers.

By the end of the year, Caligula's exploitation of his power was threatening the security of the Empire. He provoked outrage with a demand that the Temple of Jerusalem be converted into an imperial shrine containing a huge statue of himself. He took the refusal as an act of grave disloyalty and ordered the deaths of those who had opposed him. Only the tact and diplomacy of the local governor prevented major riots from breaking out. Understanding that the desecration would cause fury, Publis Petronius stalled the sculptors. It was an action that could have cost him his life, but by the time he received his death sentence, Caligula was already dead.

On 24 January 41AD, on the last day of the Palatine Games, Caligula was stabbed to death while returning from the theatre. Amongst the assassins were members of his own family and the Praetorian Guard who had been assigned to protect him. The fatal blow was struck by Casius Chaerea, a man whom Caligula had openly mocked at court for his effeminacy. It was a brutal and frenzied murder, and the corpse was left with more than thirty stab wounds.

The conspirators then obliterated all traces of their Emperor. His wife, Caesonia, was hunted down, and stabbed to death. Drusilla, their two-year-old daughter, was picked up by a soldier and smashed repeatedly against a wall. When Claudius was found shaking behind a curtain, he was convinced that he, too, was on the hit list. Instead he was marched into the Praetorian camp, where he was solemnly proclaimed Emperor. Once again there was rejoicing in the Senate.

Caligula had reigned for just three years and eleven months. In the great annals of atrocity, the reign of the Emperor Caligula stands out with brilliance and splendour. Unlike the acts of almost every other autocrat in the black history of mass slaughter, Caligula's tyranny was executed with a supreme deviance and caprice, staged as a vast performance of bestiality, brutality, sexual excess and perversion.

NERO

FIFTH EMPEROR OF ROME

'What an artist dies with me!'
SUETONIUS, *LIVES OF THE CAESARS*

When Nero became Emperor in 54AD, Rome was at the zenith of its power. The Imperial legions had carved out an empire which stretched from the banks of the Rhine to the deserts of the Sahara. Over 60 million people, a fifth of the world's population, lived under the banner of the Roman eagle. But Nero's tyrannical fourteen-year reign would bring to an end Rome's Golden Age. He was a perverse, cross-dressing exhibitionist who murdered his mother, brother and wife and anyone else who stood in his way. His cruelty, violence and grotesque appetite for self-indulgence brought the Roman Empire to the brink of political and financial ruin. He viciously persecuted the Christians and they would remember him as the ultimate embodiment of evil: the Antichrist.

Nero was born on 15 December 37AD in Antium. He was named Lucius Domitus Ahenobarbus. His father, Ignatius, who was from an old Roman aristocratic family, died when Nero was three years old. He had been a cruel, hard drinking man, who once deliberately ran over a child in his chariot, and gouged out the eye of a knight in the Roman forum for offending him.

Nero's grandmother had become a fanatic, his father was a hopeless debauchee, his uncles were either licentious or lunatic, or both, and one of his aunts had been compromised by agreeing to leave her husband to enter an incestuous relationship with her brother, the Emperor. But it was from his mother, Agrippina, that Nero learnt about the realities of life in the royal household, and how to get what he wanted, whatever the cost.

Raped by her brother Caligula when she was twelve, Agrippina was banished two years after her son's birth and Nero was sent to his aunt, Domita Lepida, who left him alone and neglected, in conditions of terrible squalor. However, in 41AD Claudius became Emperor and one of his first acts was to recall Agrippina from exile. Agrippina arrived back in Rome, and married the immensely wealthy Passienus Crispus, who died within a few years, leaving her all his money and estates. Now she was free to pursue her ultimate goal.

Emperor Claudius was married to Messalina, who was debauched and unfaithful to Claudius. Messalina eventually took her own life, and then Agrippina moved in and consolidated her position. She had plotted to replace Messalina as Claudius's wife, and succeeded. They were married in 49AD. Agrippina was already the Emperor's wife; all that remained now was to ensure that she became the Emperor's mother. But caution was required. Nero was only eleven and, for the time being, Claudius was of more use to Agrippina alive than dead.

Nero received an education fit for a prince. Seneca was recalled from exile and given the Praetorship. Seneca's political acumen would prove invaluable to mother and son in their later plots against Claudius.

In 50AD Agrippina persuaded Claudius to adopt Nero. There were precedents for this and Claudius only had one son, Britannicus. But Claudius went even further than Agrippina had hoped, and granted Nero precedence over his own son. Agrippina then took steps to ensure that Nero would receive a superior education and continue to be favoured over Britannicus by removing Britannicus's tutors and replacing them with her spies.

When Nero was sixteen, his mother engineered his marriage to the Emperor's daughter, Octavia, Nero's stepsister. One by one, the Emperor's allies fell by the wayside as Agrippina plotted their destruction, and now she could turn her attention to the ageing Claudius himself. She summoned the expert poisoner, Locusta, who prepared a dish of poisoned mushrooms. But the poison was slow in working. Agrippina was wracked with nerves, and called the physician Xenophon who inserted a feather smeared with a fast-working poison, into Claudius's throat on the pretext of inducing vomiting. On 12 October 54AD the Emperor Claudius died. The next day, the Praetorian Guard declared Nero Emperor.

At the age of seventeen, Nero had become ruler of the biggest empire the world had ever seen. But while the Romans celebrated in the streets, their new Emperor was already showing a disturbing tendency towards violence.

Disguised as a slave, Nero trawled the street brothels and taverns with his friends. They pilfered goods from shops, and assaulted wayfarers. When it became known that the hoodlum was the Emperor, attacks on distinguished men and women multiplied – since disorderliness was tolerated, indeed condoned, pseudo-Nero gangs proliferated and behaved similarly. Rome, by night, became a lawless city.

Despite his delinquent behaviour, the start of Nero's reign was greeted with great enthusiasm. The young Emperor was seventeen, and it was believed, perhaps naively, that he was not yet old enough to have been corrupted. His first official apperance was at the funeral of the Divine Claudius – he addressed the crowd with a speech written by his tutor, Seneca. He proposed to restore to the Senate the judicial powers that it had enjoyed under Augustus; he was not going to make the same mistakes that Claudius had made of confusing the administration of the Empire with that of his own household. It was a masterstroke, since it ensured that the Senate left him alone to pursue his own pleasures. Roman government went on as before and Rome looked forward to enjoying a long era of gentle and kindly rule. But, as so often in Imperial Rome, political calmness and moderation were cloaks for domestic upheaval and intrigue.

Desperate to consolidate her position, Agrippina fostered Nero's paranoia towards

Nero gives the thumbs-down signal at the circus, so ending the life of some wretched defeated gladiator. Vicious and merciless – among a huge list of crimes, he had his mother and his wife murdered – he took his own life when even the people of Rome turned against him. (BETTMANN/CORBIS)

his older brother, Britannicus. She reminded Nero that Britannicus was Claudius's true son so Nero soon came to believe that it would be much better if Britannicus were dead. He needed to find a method that would not arouse suspicion, but to achieve this, he would need help. He chose poison, which he obtained from Locusta, and then ordered that the substance be brought into the dining room and given to Britannicus. When Britannicus collapsed, Nero rewarded Locusta with immunity from prosecution and an ample estate. He even sent her pupils.

With Britannicus now out of the way, Nero and his mother reigned with impunity. They passed laws and appeared on Roman currency together, with Agrippina acting as the young Emperor's self-styled regent. She was determined to maintain absolute control over her son and would go to any lengths to do so.

His mother had put supreme power into Nero's hands, but, in so doing, she had also given Nero the one thing that he had previously lacked – the authority to do what he liked without consulting her first. Failure to realize this was Agrippina's one fatal mistake because when, at the beginning of 55AD, Nero had begun to tire of her, his supreme power guaranteed that his rejection of her would be absolute throughout the Empire.

Meanwhile, Nero's wife, Octavia, who had lived for so long in the shadows, was also put in danger, for Nero had become infatuated with Poppea, the wife of a Roman soldier. Nero quickly dispatched Poppea's husband to a far-flung corner of the empire, and settled down to a life of debauchery. However, Poppea, well aware that Nero could not divorce Octavia whilst Agrippina was still alive, further fuelled his desire to rid himself of his demanding mother.

As Nero's thoughts turned from devotion to murder, he banished Agrippina and started to hatch a bizarre plan with the Admiral of the Fleet. He ordered the construction of a booby-trapped boat, designed to fall apart when under sail. When the boat was completed, he invited Agrippina to join him at the resort town of Biyi, for a festival. After a pleasant evening together, Nero kissed his mother farewell and left by land, while she left by sea. Midway across the bay, the concealed lead weights crashed through the boat's roof and it began to sink. But the injured Agrippina managed to swim to safety.

When Nero heard that his mother had survived, he was terrified of what reprisals she might take and immediately dispatched assassins to her villa. As the murderers closed around her, she bared her abdomen, imploring her assailants to strike the womb that had borne Nero.

It is rumoured that when Agrippina's corpse was brought before him, Nero and his gloating circle examined the dead body for its good and bad points, remarking, between drinks, on the virtues of the legs, hips, arms and vagina, whilst handling the corpse as if appraising a potential lover.

But his mother was not yet finished with Nero. He was haunted with guilt for killing her, and she invaded his dreams. Nero complained that he was being pursued by the Furies, and, unable to free himself from their menacing presence, he employed Persian occultists to conjure up the ghost and exorcize it. However, the guilt that he felt over his mother's death did not diminish Nero's thirst for blood, and shortly afterwards he murdered his aunt, Domita, who had sheltered him during his earliest years. Her estates at Baiae were the inducement. Nero had expensive tastes and they needed to be paid for. Top of the list was his love of chariot-racing and the staging of lavish spectacles and games. Nobles from the aristocratic Roman families were forced to take part in front of the rabble of Rome and the ever-increasing foreign contingent in the city. In the sideshows surrounding the amphitheatre, every kind of vice was catered for. The climax of the shows was the appearance of Nero himself. He recruited a claque of five thousand supporters, called the Augustans, to lead the applause, which they did with deafening conviction, so that all the audience joined in and Nero's delight was unalloyed.

When he was singing, no one was permitted to leave the theatre, even for the most pressing of reasons. It was alleged that a woman gave birth during one of his shows, and many people who were tired of listening and applauding, either jumped furtively off the walls when the entrance gates closed or else pretended to be dead and were carried out for burial.

It was considered undignified and shocking for a Roman Emperor to show an interest in the composition of poetry: it was an unthinkable affront for him to proclaim it in public and it was the height of profligacy, debauchery and dissipation to act in drama. But if his antics made Nero an object of hatred to the aristocrats, it is by no means certain that the general populace saw it in the same way.

In the year 60AD there were the first rumblings of discontent, emanating from the murder of Agrippina. A comet appeared in the sky, a portent normally held to foretell a change in dynasty. But, by now, Nero was drunk on his own omnipotence, even urinating on the statue of Atargatis, a Syrian goddess he had previously worshipped, as a gesture of his superiority.

Now that Agrippina was out of the way, Nero was planning to take Poppea as his wife; however, several problems presented themselves, the most obvious of which was that Octavia was held in very high regard by the Roman people and she also had the protection of Burrus, commander of the Praetorian Guard. Conveniently, Burrus died the following year, but while his death opened the way for Poppea to become Empress, it also had far greater implications for Nero's tutor, Seneca. Burrus and Seneca had acted as brakes on Nero's worst excesses and Seneca now found himself replaced by others in Nero's counsels. The stage was clear for a new manager of Rome's affairs – he was Ofonius Tigellinus and he would prove to be the very worst of influences on an already dissipated Emperor.

Tigellinus's first act was to take complete control of the Praetorian Guard – his next would be to obtain mastery of Nero. He reckoned that the best way to make himself indispensable was to find out whom Nero really feared. A conversation with the Emperor revealed that Sulla and Plautus were two such men. Within six days, Sulla's head had been brought before Nero, whose only comment was to note that his hair had turned grey. Plautus's took a little longer to arrive, having come all the way from Asia, and Nero remarked what a very big nose he had. Knowing that he would be held accountable, Nero wrote to the Senate as though both victims were still alive, complaining of their ambitious designs and expressing anxiety for the safety of the state. When their deaths were reported Nero was applauded for his vigilance.

Nero now divorced Octavia, calling her a barren woman and banishing her to Campania in Southern Italy, after which he married the scheming Poppea. But they had both underestimated the popularity of Octavia. Public fervour was such that recently erected statues of Poppea were smashed and replaced with those of Octavia. Poppea convinced Nero that the mobs would butcher them both and reminded him that if Octavia were to marry again, her husband could become the people's champion against Nero. The threat was obvious, Octavia must be murdered – and quickly. Octavia was moved to Pandtaria, a barren and dismal island, where she soon received news that she was to die. Nero concocted a story that she had been unfaithful with his Admiral of the Fleet (who was rewarded in secret) and her fate was sealed. Octavia was tightly bound and her veins were opened, but terror made her blood congeal and flow too slowly. She was killed by being placed in a searingly hot bath. Her severed head was sent to Rome for Nero and Poppea to gloat over. The Senate, in all their hypocrisy, ordered a day of thanksgiving.

But the gods had not forgotten Nero's deeds. In the same year as Octavia's murder, a statue of Nero, cast in bronze, was struck by lightning and reduced to a molten mass. Pompeii, the pleasure-loving city, was largely destroyed by an earthquake and the volcano Vesuvius was beginning to rumble. Nero and Poppea's first child, Augusta, died and Nero, from all accounts, was genuinely wracked with grief.

On the night of 18 July 64AD Rome started to burn. It is uncertain whether it was due to chance or to the treacherous designs of the Emperor. The fire began at the Circus Maximus and the wind soon ensured that it spread far into the city. The speed of the fire and the narrowness of the streets made it impossible for people to escape. No one dared to extinguish the flames, for there were people throwing oil onto them, insisting they were acting under orders. Nero was at Anzio, and returned when the fire started to threaten his own palace. Two sources of the time record that Nero was reciting his poem 'The Fall of Troy' against the backdrop of a burning Rome, but this has never been proved. A second fire then started on the property of Nero's favourite, Tigellinus, and this lent substance to the growing belief that Nero wanted Rome obliterated, to build a new and more glorious city. The great Roman fire left hundreds

When, in July 64AD, a great fire destroyed much of Rome and killed many of its citizens, it seemed that Nero was the only person to have benefited. As a result, he made the Christians the scapegoats, fabricating charges against them and then condemning them to die – in this case, by facing the starving, maddened wild animals at the circus, a depraved public spectacle of which Romans were only too fond. (BETTMANN/CORBIS)

of thousands of Romans destitute and the Roman economy in such crisis that the currency had to be devalued.

One man alone seemed to benefit from the carnage. As land became available, the Emperor took advantage and started to build a new palace. He began construction in various parts of the city, giving the citizens the impression that he was taking over the city and riding roughshod over the sufferings of the people who had lost so much. Nero cleared an area the size of London's Hyde Park in the centre of Rome. Here he built a sprawling new palace complex called 'The Golden House', after the plates of gold that were set to cover its ceilings and walls. It contained an enormous lake and expansive grounds, which were populated with all manner of exotic animals. The banqueting halls had inlaid ceilings fitted with panels of ivory, which revolved, scattering flowers, and the halls were fitted with pipes, which sprayed perfume on those beneath. The principal banqueting chamber had a dome, which revolved continuously both day and night, like the heavens. When the house was brought to completion, Nero said nothing more to indicate his approval than to declare he had at last begun to live like a human being, or the God he believed himself to be.

Whether or not Nero was actually implicated in the fire of Rome will never be fully proved, but what is important is that many people at the time believed he was guilty. After all, he had murdered his mother, and wife; with such a man, anything was possible and, in such an atmosphere, Nero had only one choice and he took it. He looked for scapegoats.

The scapegoats to hand were the Christians. Nero fabricated charges of his own, by spreading rumours that it was they who had started the fires. It was a cunning move because, to the Romans, the Christians presented a threat to the new and struggling *Pax Romana*, established after a century of bloodshed. Nero also realized that anyone would believe the Christians capable of any crime, in addition to which there was a wonderful way of getting them to confess because if you were a Christian, you could not deny the fact. So, if Nero announced that the Christians had started the fire, anyone who confessed to their Christianity was assumed to have confessed to arson.

Tacitus tells us that he had them 'brunted up, dressed in animal skins and attacked by dogs.' He had some crucified and many burnt. In the evening, he lit up his palace gardens, using Christians as human torches.

Nero's attack on the Christians was the first persecution of Christianity under the Roman Empire. It's believed that both the disciple Peter and the apostle Paul were tortured and killed during Nero's reign. In the Bible's Book of Revelation, John described the end of the world and warns of a beast with two horns. Was it Nero that he had in mind?

In 64AD Nero's one-time adviser and tutor, Seneca, retired from public life – there were rumours that Nero had tried to poison him, but failed. However, the final withdrawal of Seneca was a clear signal to others. Was this the time to rid themselves of the despotic tyrant? Nero had been Emperor for ten bloody years and the promise of his early years had long been forgotten. Though the imperial government had been carried out efficiently, and without serious interference, the inner circle of Empire in Rome had become bedevilled by Nero's absurd whims and delusions of grandeur.

The Roman public were now prepared to give credence to any story about Nero, asking only that it should be bad enough to be credible. The discontent was not confined to any particular class, and the conspiracy that followed involved knights, senators, soldiers and ordinary men and women. They had no successor in mind – their only objective was to rid themselves of Nero.

In 65AD Nero came to hear of this plot, when his Admiral of the Fleet, Proculus, told him the conspirators had tried to recruit him. However, the woman who had approached Proculus had given no names. Nero was therefore powerless to act and could only keep his informant in custody. Meanwhile, the conspirators had found the perfect opportunity to kill Nero. They chose the Festival of Ceres in April, when a series of games would be held in Rome. Nero was a great enthusiast for the games and would be out of the confines of his palace, where he was spending an increasing amount of time. The secret was kept until the eve of the proposed assassination, when one of the conspirators, Scaevinus, deciding to free all his slaves, asked one of them, Milichus, to sharpen his dagger and prepare a bag with first-aid equipment. Milichus viewed this with the deepest suspicion, and daybreak saw him hurrying into Nero's palace. It took him a while to get through the guards, but when he did, he presented the Emperor with evidence of the treachery that was afoot. Nero immediately issued orders for Scaevinus to be arrested and brought to him. The conspiracy had been uncovered.

One by one, the conspirators confessed and implicated their friends. Nero acted quickly. A state of emergency and martial law were declared in Rome. The wrath of Nero knew no bounds and senators, soldiers and advisers were put to death. Even Seneca, whom many people believe was not involved in the plot, was sentenced to death by Nero.

Nero soon saw that the conspiracy could be very useful to him. It would enable him to rid himself of those people whom he most distrusted or disliked, whether they were accomplices or not. One of these was Vestinus who had once been a close friend of Nero, but who had made the mistake of telling Nero the truth, especially about his vices. Nero waited in vain for Vestinus to be named as a conspirator, and when he saw that his chance of disposing of him was slipping away, he resorted to his favourite device as absolute ruler – a display of naked force, unsupported by a shred of legal or moral justice. Vestinus had his veins opened.

After his narrow escape, Nero began to see enemies everywhere. Each year, he murdered more and more senators, aristocrats and army officers. The final death toll will never be known. Nero ensured that the conspiracy provided a convenient excuse for political murder for some time to come. However, in the midst of the celebrations that followed the routing of the conspiracy, the Emperor became aware of a new emotion – he was frightened. In the past, it had been he who had plotted against others, now the plot had been against him. He knew that some Roman would soon strike again.

Aware that the aristocracy and most of the wealthy classes in Rome were against him, Nero now suffered a personal loss. In a fit of rage, he had lashed out at his beloved wife Poppea, after she had chided him about coming back late from a chariot race. She was pregnant and, after suffering a miscarriage, she died.

It was a murderous act that Nero bitterly regretted. In a fit of remorse, he took a boy called Sporus who reminded him of Poppea. The boy was castrated, dressed and made up to look like the dead Empress and married to Nero in an extravagant ceremony.

Nero's private behaviour was becoming increasingly debauched. 'He prostituted his body to such a degree that when virtually every part of his body had been employed in filthy lust, he devised a new game and then pressed it into use. Disguised in the pelt of a wild animal, he would rush out of a dam and attack the private parts of men and women who were attached to sticks.'

After Poppea's death, Nero also embarked on another period of senseless and unprovoked killings. He chose as his victims some of the most respectable members of the aristocracy, inflamed as he was by their apparent distaste for him and his pleasures. The year ended with violent storms in southern Italy, and a plague that swept through Rome. The elements seemed to be joining Nero in the work of destruction, and those who died were envied by those left behind to endure Nero's vindictive caprice.

The Emperor now decided to wed again. He first chose Antonia, daughter of Claudius. When she refused to marry him, he had her put to death. Finally, in 66AD he married Messalina, who had long been a favourite of his. He then determined to visit Greece with his new bride, and left Rome in the hands of Helius, a man with almost as much of a passion for blood as himself. However, while Nero was cavorting around the Mediterranean, rumblings of dissatisfaction began to grow at home. The citizens of Rome were chafing under the yoke and the soldiers in the provinces were preparing to act. The Roman rabble might love Nero for the lavishness of his entertainments, but the Roman soldiers despised him for his indolence. Generals throughout the Empire suddenly realized the necessity of securing the loyalty of their own armies against the capricious wrath of the Emperor.

After briefly returning to Rome, Nero set off to sample the delights of Naples, and it was here that he heard news of a revolt in Gaul, under the leadership of Julius Vindex. Vindex had issued a proclamation, calling for the Imperial army to rise against the tyrant Nero, adding a taunt that he was a second-rate lute player. Vindex proposed that Servius Galba replace Nero.

Nero immediately had Galba declared an enemy of the state and confiscated all his property, whereupon Galba retaliated by taking Nero's Spanish possessions. Ironically, Vindex was then killed before anything really occurred. However, there was no shortage of contenders to the Imperial throne amongst the Imperial forces, as the events in 69AD were to prove.

The anti-Nero forces in Rome saw their saviour in Galba. Even though, at seventy-two, Galba was an old man, they figured that he would provide them with enough time to train a suitable successor to run the Empire if, indeed, an Emperor was needed at all.

The forces that rallied behind Galba were enough to inflate a minor provincial military uprising into a successful *coup d'état*. Nero was taking steps to end Galba's life, but it was he who lacked friends, not Galba. When Nero dispatched his troops to attack Galba, they were in no mood to fight and spent their time wandering around Gaul, rather than searching for Nero's enemy. Even his faithful henchman, Tigellinus, deserted him, and Nero knew he was really alone. It was alleged that he conceived a plan to poison all the senators in Rome, burn Rome to the ground and then slip away to Egypt.

One more blow was to fall. The Roman populace as a whole had enjoyed Nero's reign, but, at last, the ordinary people were beginning to turn against him, following a drastic corn shortage, and the head of the Praetorian Guard came out in favour of Galba. The armies, the Senate and now the people had deserted him. Nero's options were now extremely limited, and the only practical plan was to find somewhere he could hide out. He put on old and shabby clothing and, with one or two companions, among them his eunuch Sporus and his secretary Epaphroditus, he made his way to the villa Phaon which belonged to one of his freedmen. Hurrying through the streets, and despite being saluted by a soldier who recognized him, Nero made it to the villa. He drank a little water, which he now contrasted ironically with the water cooled in snow that was served to him in the palace.

In Rome, the news of Nero's departure had spread quickly, and the populace was wild with excitement. In his last years, Nero had displayed more of his vengeful caprices and less of the lavish entertainment that had fed their appetites. They were free, and the feeling was exhilarating.

But the Senate had something else in mind – the total destruction of Nero. A search was set in motion, and it was only a matter of time before the villa of Phaon came under scrutiny. As the sound of the guards drew near, Nero ordered a grave to be dug and, with the aid of Epaphroditus, drove a dagger into his own throat.

His two nurses saw that he was decently buried in his family tomb. The only other mourner was a mistress of long ago, a freedwoman called Acte. As she alone mourned, Rome jubilantly awaited the arrival of its new master.

It is one of the ironies of history that Nero would be remembered by the Roman people, not as the evil man he was, but as a benevolent provider of games and circuses, whose loss was something to be grieved over. Long after his death, flowers were put at his burial place and funerary busts of him were commissioned. Even his edicts were treated with special reverence, as though he was still alive and would soon return to take vengeance on his enemies.

Later emperors would try to eradicate the memory of Nero. They carved their own faces into Nero's statues and destroyed his golden palace, building bars over the ruins. An enormous arena was built, obliterating the great lake that once had reflected Nero's palace. The arena was called the amphitheatre of Titus, but became known as the Coliseum, because once a colossal statue of Nero had stood there.

ATTILA THE HUN

THE 'STORM FROM THE EAST'

A man born to shake the races of the world. The proud man's power was to be seen in the very movements of his body.

PRISCUS OF PANIUM

In the fifth century, one man brought terror and destruction to millions. Attila the Hun led thousands of bloodthirsty barbarians across the plains of Europe, bringing torture, rape, and death to all who stood in his way. He acquired a vast Empire that stretched across parts of Germany, Russia, Poland and much of southeast Europe. Known as the 'Scourge of God', he struck fear into the mighty Roman Empire with his savage methods of brutal destruction, razing cities to the ground and killing thousands in pursuit of gold and power. Legend has it that the Huns dipped their arrows in the juice of boiled embryos, drank women's blood and were descended from the unclean spirits of the wilderness.

Mass slaughter, rape and pillage had been an integral part of life for most of Northern Europe for centuries. Though the Greeks and Romans had established the Mediterranean as the cradle of civilization, it was constantly rocked by murderous incursions from barbarian hordes to the north. Greek historian, Herodotus, described savage Scythians who skinned opponents to make coats, sawed off the top of their skulls to make drinking cups and drank the blood of their victims. Wild Goths swept south from Sweden, and in 410AD sacked Rome in a six-day orgy of rape and killing. Vicious Vandals reached the city less than fifty years later, after storming through Germany, Gaul, Spain and North Africa, leaving death and destruction in their wake. Saxons, Franks and Vikings were other warlike and unmerciful raiders. But of all the brutal barbarians who terrorized Europe, none struck greater fear into men's hearts than that of the Huns; they rode as fast as the wind, and were as bloodthirsty as wolves.

The Huns first invaded Europe in the fourth century, descending from the borders of China. In the early centuries of the Christian era, a widespread movement of people was taking place throughout northern Europe. The climate was undergoing drastic changes, ensuring long winters and very short summers. The Huns, who lived a plain, hard existence in an area stretching from Siberia to Korea, found themselves unable to sustain themselves in the everlasting winter that descended.

Few accounts of their day-to-day lives exist – they did not keep written records, but what we do know, however, is that they were well used to migrating, taking everything they owned, including the yurts (tented houses), which were designed for mobility.

After a period of plundering the fertile Yellow River in China, the long migration began; an entire nation headed west and south for thousands of miles. Some invaded Persia and Asia Minor, but the majority moved through Russia toward Europe where native tribes were overrun. In their travels toward the Roman Empire, the Huns were confronted by a variety of peoples, with many of whom they did battle. Some people were more willing than others to accept the kind of dominion the Huns imposed. Some swelled the flood of refugees, and others provided valuable additional manpower to swell the ranks of the Hun armies. Finally, the vast exodus settled on the Hungarian plains, north of the river Danube, between the Volga and Don. The Roman Empire, on whose borders they now lived, initially fought them for a few years, and, from the year 410AD, chose to establish an uneasy détente with the Hun King, Ruga.

Unlike the earlier Roman Republic, the Roman Empire was not an aggressive, expansionist state. Its frontiers in Europe ran for over 2,000 kilometres. Frontier defence was not, for the most part, required; there were no threats from other major powers. For centuries, the only kingdom that the Romans had had any need to fear, or to respect militarily, was the Persian Empire of the Sassanids. However, all that would change with the coming of Attila.

Born in 406AD, Attila lost his father when he was very young. Like all Hun males, Attila was encouraged to ride before he could walk, and fight – using bow and arrow – by his fifth birthday. Brought up in a deeply superstitious society, amongst people who surrounded their camps with horses' heads on sticks to ward off evil spirits, Attila became well attuned to listening to prophecies, a trait that remained with him throughout his life, and served him well.

At the beginning of the fifth century, Rome bought peace for itself from King Ruga, Attila's uncle. They paid an annual tribute of 350 pounds of gold, and both sides took high-ranking hostages as a guarantee of good behaviour. Thus, Attila was exchanged with a young nobleman, Aetius, and sent to live in Ravenna, in the Western Roman Empire. Here, Attila learnt to speak, read and write Latin. He admired the Romans' strict organization, but quickly came to despise their decadent tendencies. In fact, Attila was witnessing the final glory days of the Empire, before its own decadence and corruption destroyed it, and these learning years would one day make him Rome's most dangerous enemy.

In his early twenties, Attila returned to his people. He was involved in several murderous Hun invasions, spurred on by King Ruga, who believed that 'everything the sun shines upon I can conquer'. However, when Attila was twenty-seven, King Ruga died and was succeeded by Attila's brother, Bleda. Attila was said to be furious, but he initially hid his frustration and carried on building his reputation as a lethally effective military leader.

By now, Attila was a striking figure, with a large head, swarthy complexion, small, deep-seated eyes, a flat nose and a few hairs in place of a beard. He had broad shoulders and a short, square body. Early on, he had realized the power of a ruthless image, and allowed his men freedom to inflict the worst possible atrocities on their enemies. He purposefully created an army of bloodthirsty sadists.

To the civilized Romans, the Huns were savages: they ate raw meat, lived and slept on horseback, didn't wash and were known to be untrustworthy. The Huns were also expert horsemen and known for their lightning attacks – the medieval equivalent of the twentieth-century *Blitzkrieg*. Surprise and terror were of the essence. The first a settlement would know of a Hun raid would be a cloud of dust, followed by the sky turning black under a hail of arrows, before the Horsemen of the Apocalypse unleashed hell. They could fire arrows forwards, backwards and sideways, whilst standing on horseback, and could kill a man at 150 metres. Whilst other empires only had bows that could draw a few centimetres, the Huns had developed ones that could draw up to thirty.

The secret behind the Huns' strength was an almost modern infrastructure. News could easily be relayed to far-away dominions by carriers who rode over thousands of miles, to deliver messages to every corner of the Hun world. Using reserve horses, they could ensure that no other message travelled as fast as theirs did. Many of the conquered people also became slaves of the Huns and when Hun nobles went to war, their retinues would consist equally of slaves and free men.

It wasn't surprising therefore that, after King Ruga's death (an event initially regarded by the Roman Empire as an excuse for suspending any agreements with the Huns), emissaries from Constantinople, cowed by the might of the Hun forces, signed the Treaty of Margus in 435AD and agreed to double their annual tribute to 700 pounds of gold. They also agreed not to enter into any alliances with enemies of the Huns, and to return all Hun prisoners.

A nineteenth-century engraving of Attila, King of the Huns, based on a sculpture dating from 1810, some thirteen centuries after the Scourge of God – and of Europe – had drowned in his own blood. (HULTON-DEUTSCH COLLECTION/CORBIS)

For the Huns, the treaty was an unqualified triumph and Bleda and Attila directed their attention away from the Balkans and started to consolidate their empire in the direction of the Alps and the Rhine. But in 439AD, a series of wars against the Roman Empire broke out on a number of fronts. Bleda and Attila now realized they could resume their plundering of the Balkans and, obtaining gold from the Bishop of Margus, who knew the Huns were not going to be deflected, they swept onwards.

In his late thirties, Attila attacked and decimated the city of Naissus; in fact, the riverbanks became so littered with human bones that for years after no one would enter the city because of the stench of death. Attila enjoyed the apocalyptic scenes his men caused. He had a habit of fiercely rolling his eyes, in order to inspire greater terror in his victims.

But a man of Attila's commanding and ruthless personality did not relish remaining second-in-command indefinitely, and in 445AD, frustrated at his lack of power, he murdered his brother, Bleda, in cold blood, and took the throne.

Becoming King in his early forties had given Attila time to plan his reign of terror. As a ruler, Attila was an originator, and in some respects a revolutionary. He knew that if the Huns were to be a great power, as he intended them to be, they must learn from other, more advanced, peoples. He was wary of creating a threat within Hunnick society, and discouraged literacy amongst his people, seeing the danger of having subjects with too much education and ambition. In consequence, his own intimate circle of advisers consisted largely of foreigners, and he purchased many of their services with gold. It has been suggested that one reason why Attila surrounded himself with foreigners is that, after Bleda's death, he no longer trusted prominent Huns. One of Attila's advisers, Orestes, was married to the daughter of the military commander of a Roman province. Bringing his wife with him, he came to the Hun court to offer his services. Attila's principal secretary, Constantius, came from Italy.

But Attila needed ever-increasing amounts of gold – the Hun Empire's main profession had been war and plunder and, with every territorial gain, further demands were made on Attila to provide for his new subjects. He also needed to consolidate his authority over the large number of tribes within the expanding Hun Empire. With this in mind, Attila, realizing the power of collaboration, galvanized not only the Hunnick tribes, but also the various barbarian groups – such as the Visigoths, Gepids and Vandals. United, they were a significant force – Attila now had up to half a million savage warriors at his disposal, enough fighting power to defeat an Empire. When an ancient sword was found by one of his tribesman, it was believed to be the sacred sword of Mars. Attila now believed he was invincible and that it was his destiny to lead his people to ultimate victory. Like crows snatching prey from an eagle, the Huns now threatened the Roman Empire.

The Roman Empire was divided into two halves – Eastern and Western Empires. Attila first set his sights on the East, which contained the largest city in the world, Constantinople (a city we know today as Istanbul). He instructed his forces to actively destroy the lands they conquered between the Black Sea and the Mediterranean, to heighten fear and suppress resistance.

The Huns pillaged churches and monasteries, slew monks and virgins, and desecrated the graves of saints. Attila captured more than a hundred cities and the death toll was so high that no one could count the dead.

However, Attila's ultimate objective was Constantinople, and his campaign was thus conducted with a thoroughness not shown previously by Hun armies although, from time to time, detours were made so that additional cities could also be captured and destroyed. One such was Sofia, on whose ruins a Slav people would later build a new city.

By March 447AD Attila's forces were approaching Constantinople; the citizens were in a blind panic at the impending hordes, and thousands fled. Attila, however, failed to launch an attack, because his army was incapable of using the siege techniques necessary to subdue a city as substantial and as well defended as Constantinople. His troops were also riddled with disease, principally malaria and dysentery.

But the army was only halted by sickness, it was not destroyed, and Attila remained a perpetual menace to the well-being and security of Constantinople and, indeed, to the whole of the Eastern Empire. Knowing this, he continually increased his demands. The annual tribute already stood at 6,000 pounds of gold and Attila sent one emissary after another, calling for new exactions. However, the war had seriously diminished the Eastern Roman Empire's treasury, and vast amounts of precious metals were melted down to meet Attila's demands.

Attila also repeated, more implacable than ever, that all Hun prisoners should be released and, in addition to this, he insisted on the handing over of men of any race who had transferred their loyalty from the Huns to the Empire. Many men chose death at the hands of imperial officers rather than return to the dreaded Huns. The prestige of the imperial army, unable to protect its own recruits, plummeted disastrously.

Every pound of gold that crossed the Danube made Attila more powerful and intimidating, and further humiliated the Romans. He had created so much devastation and fear that he was unopposed in the Eastern Roman Empire. Now he could plan his attack on the West. Finally, it all became too much for the Romans, and a plot was hatched to murder Attila. One of his allies, Edika, the Skirian king, offered to kill him for fifty pounds of gold, but Attila discovered the plot and dealt with its perpetrators.

Attila, although now king of a vast empire and millions of subjects, still kept his barbaric ways. Although he would entertain foreign dignitaries, serving them the finest food on silver plates and wine from golden goblets, he would only eat a lump of raw meat served on a wooden platter and drink wine from a wooden goblet. Rumours of his cannibalistic practices are not unfounded; he is believed to have eaten his own sons, Erp and Eitil, after his wife served them to him roasted in honey. The Hunnick practice of polygamy was also well suited to Attila's tastes. He is said to have fathered over a hundred children, with a vast number of wives.

In 450AD Theodosius II, Emperor of Eastern Rome, died and was replaced by Marcian. Theodosius's death deprived the Western Roman Emperor, Valentinian III,

Attila leading his horde. His name remains synonymous with death and destruction, and legends of his brutality survive in several European countries, even today. (BETTMANN/CORBIS)

of one of his most experienced statesmen. The Roman Empire was not the force it once was, with incursions becoming a regular occurrence and generations of complacency leading to political infighting. Then, in 450AD, Attila received an extraordinary offer.

Honoria was the sister of the Emperor of Valentinian III, but she had become an embarrassment and had been banished to Constantinople, after being caught having an affair with her chamberlain. Desperate to escape a regime of prayer and fasting, Honoria, entrusting a eunuch called Hyacinth, arranged to smuggle her gold ring to Attila as a proposal of marriage. Her mother had been married to a barbarian king, and she saw the advantage of a union between the powerful leader of the Huns and the sister of the Roman Emperor. Attila saw the benefits of the collaboration, too. He was already plentifully supplied with wives, but Honoria's advances fitted his own plans in a way he could hardly have hoped for. He accepted her proposal of marriage, adding, with splendid panache, that the dowry he expected to go with it was half the Western Roman Empire.

The Emperor Valentinian denounced his sister's actions and turned down Attila's demands. Attila declared war. With the excuse he needed, Attila unleashed the might of his combined barbarian armies into western Europe. In 451AD the Huns left their settlements in Hungary, and Attila's vast army crossed the Rhine through Germany and towards France. Attila claimed he was merely reclaiming his rightful lands, but this was simply an excuse to gain more riches.

His army of between 300,000 and 700,000 was the largest that Europe had seen since the expansion of the Roman Empire, over 200 years before. They were intent on wreaking havoc on a large scale, and did precisely that. Many of Europe's great cities were conquered, including Rheims, Strasbourg, Trier and Cologne.

While passing through Germany, Attila encountered St Ursula, the perpetual virgin. Attila was smitten and – putting his mission for Honoria to one side – proposed marriage to the chaste pilgrim. When she refused, he killed her with an arrow and slaughtered 11,000 of her pilgrim companions.

Attila's army tore into France, destroying everything in their path. When they entered Metz just before Easter, they 'gave the city to flames, and slew the people with the edge of the sword, and did to death the priests of the Lord before the holy altars.'

The destruction at Metz was a foretaste of much that was to occur as Attila's army advanced through France. City after city, we learn from the Christian chroniclers, suffered destruction as a punishment for the sins of the people. Where destruction and death were avoided, it was put down to divine response to the supplications and conduct of the pious. Nowhere, however, is it suggested that Attila's armies conquered through superior military skills.

Attila was a deeply superstitious man, who paid close attention to the pronouncements of his priests, soothsayers and shamans, and he allowed them to influence military decisions. As Attila approached Paris, he had a premonition that to attack the city would bring bad luck. Other cities would not be so lucky. But the tide was about to turn.

By May 451AD, Attila's army had reached Orleans. Here, they encountered heavy resistance. Orleans had been garrisoned by the now famous Roman commander, Aetius, who had spent his childhood with the Huns, and the city remained a fortress, however much Attila battered at its doors with his army. The city was saved by the arrival of Roman legions, allied to an army of Visigoths.

The successful resistance of the city of Orleans was a new and disturbing experience for Attila. In his campaigns in the Balkans and throughout Germany and France, he had become accustomed to cities that surrendered to him or which could be destroyed at his will. Only Constantinople, with its virtually impregnable walls, had been unattainable. Attila withdrew to the plains near Châlons-sur-Marne and prepared for battle.

The Battle of Châlons, or the Catalaunian Fields, became notorious for its brutality. The hand-to-hand fighting was so fierce that rivers of blood were formed and those thirsty from the fight had to drink water mingled with gore.

Attila was up against a formidable opponent – Aetius – a man who knew as much about the Hun mentality as Attila knew about the Romans. Aetius had arrived in France after a long trek over the Alps and had accumulated vast numbers of allies to fight by his side.

On the day battle commenced, Attila stood on the vast, flat plain surrounded by his army, with leaders of each tribe hanging upon his command, like slaves. 'When he gave a sign, or even a glance, they obeyed him without a murmur.' His army then began discharging a large number of iron-tipped arrows, guaranteed to penetrate leather battledresses, and a cavalry engagement followed. Attila and his allies gained an initial advantage by breaking through in the centre, after which they turned their attention to the Visigoths, who drove Attila back behind their defences. Suddenly, victory, although not decisive by any means, had gone to the armies of Rome and its allies.

Attila decided he must prepare for the worst. This was not death, but capture, and he had his own funeral pyre prepared. Wooden saddles and other cavalry accoutrements were piled up, ready to set ablaze if necessary. But all was not going well, either, for the Roman commander, Aetius. The Visigoths, under Thorismund's command, abandoned the Romans on the battlefield. Aetius knew that without their support, he would be in serious danger of defeat.

Attila, meanwhile, was astonished that Aetius had failed to exploit the advantage he had gained, and that the fighting had suddenly stopped. At first, he believed that the sudden retreat of the Goths was a stratagem intended to lure him into an injudicious attack, so he remained immobilized for some time, in the defensive position he had taken up. Then, when no action followed, he began to withdraw. Like Aetius, he could not be certain of victory.

The Battle of Châlons has been described as one of the fifteen most decisive battles in history. Had the Romans not won, Europeans today would be the direct line of descent from Attila and his Mongol hordes.

Further atrocities were committed by Attila's army. 'In retreat, they massacred their hostages as well as their captives; 200 young maidens were tortured with exquisite and unrelenting rage – their bodies were torn asunder by wild horses, or their bones were crushed under the weight of rolling wagons, and their unburied limbs were abandoned on the public roads as prey to dogs.'

Attila's campaign in France had been a disappointment to him. He had lost large areas of territory and was returning with considerably less booty than expected. Almost immediately after his return to Hungary, he was making further demands for large quantities of gold, and doing so without being in a position to back his demands with adequate force.

Theodosius's successor, Marcian, now began to exhibit both strength and statesmanship. He had refrained from attacking Attila's kingdom while he was away in France and Germany, but he had no intention of giving Attila any more gold.

Almost before his army's battle wounds had healed, Attila gave orders for them to fight again. Despite their arduous return to Hungary over the Alps, the Huns were still eager. War was their industry, and Attila's reputation had been largely unaffected by the defeat at Châlons.

Once again, Attila had asked for the hand of Honoria, the Emperor's sister, and had been refused. This time, he decided to take his demands straight to Rome. Attila believed that to invade Italy was a logical consequence of demanding half of the Western Empire as Honoria's dowry. He also knew that if he was going to achieve his ambition of conquering the world, then Rome would have to fall.

Attila set off for northern Italy in the spring of 452AD, once again commanding an international force of Gepids, Ostrogoths, Skirians, Swabians and Alemens. Because of the absence of the Hun forces in Armenia, it was certainly more Germanic than Hun in composition. The army moved towards Trieste, but was halted at Aquileia, a fortified town of major importance. Whoever held Aquileia was likely to command much of northern Italy. Attila decided to lay siege to the city, but at the end of three months, there was no indication that the garrison was considering either surrender or abandonment. Attila was on the verge of giving up the siege; however, legend tells us that, just as he was making the preparations to retreat, a single white stork rose from a tower on the city wall and, with his young upon his back, flew off away from the city. When the superstitious Attila saw this, he commanded the army to remain. Shortly afterwards, the section of wall containing the abandoned tower fell down, and Attila was able to storm the city.

The destruction inflicted upon Aquileia was total, and it never again became a city of importance. The news of what had happened spread like wildfire throughout Italy, and the rulers of other cities took note. From Aquileia, Attila's army then moved to Padua. This was a major city, supported by thriving agriculture and industry, with large numbers of important citizens. Attila's forces plundered it thoroughly, but before his arrival, a large number of people fled into the swamps, knowing that Attila's largely horse-driven army could not follow. The city they were to found was Venice.

As Attila's army advanced through Italy, they no doubt felt deeply content. Not only were they unopposed by any hostile army, but they increasingly found that the gates of the cities were opened to let them in. They were not so much made welcome, as recognized to be a force that it would be unwise to resist. The way was open to the former imperial capital, Milan.

Valentinian now fled from his temporary home in Ravenna to Rome, still hoping to find some effective means of resisting Attila's hordes. Meanwhile, Attila captured Milan, briefly occupying the royal palace. Here, he was reported to have asserted his power over Rome in a unique manner. A painting in which Caesars were depicted sitting on thrones, with Sythian princes prostrate at their feet, caught his eye and he ordered it to be changed. Now the Caesars were shown as suppliants, emptying bags of gold before the throne of Attila himself.

After Milan, Attila led his men deeper and deeper into Italy. The Horsemen of the Apocalypse had arrived – people fled in panic – but they had few places to hide. By the time he reached the River Po, Attila's army was having to deal with a new enemy – malaria – which was ravaging his troops. But luck was on his side, and once more, the terror that his name inspired had done its work for him. The Emperor Valentinian was truly intimidated; fearing an empire would be lost, he sent a delegation to appeal for a truce. Attila agreed to negotiations.

On the River Mincio he was confronted by Pope Leo I and two advisers: Trigetius, the Prefect of Rome and Gennadius Avienus, a rich and successful politician. Their job was to persuade Attila not to attack Rome. Attila received them, lying in his tent. He was certainly not overawed by them; they were the supplicants, not he. The contemporary historian, Priscus, relates that 'Attila's mind had been bent on going to Rome. But his followers took him away and reminded him that the last person to conquer Rome, Alaric the Visigoth, had not lived long after the event.' Attila's priests foretold disaster if he continued and so, faced with his disease-ravaged troops, polluted water, chronic heat and a shortage of food, he sensibly decided not to enter Rome. Instead, Attila and his barbarian hordes left, loaded down with great treasures, and headed home to the Hungarian plains.

Within a few months, Attila seemed to regret the peace and was vexed at the cessation of war. He sent ambassadors to Marcian, threatening to devastate the provinces because of what had been promised to him by Theodosius, saying that he would show himself crueler to his foes than ever, but those threats were never realized, as his reign of terror was soon to end.

By 453AD Attila was in his fifties. Despite his grand age, he retained his voracious sexual appetite. On 15 March 453AD, he married a young, beautiful German noblewoman, Ildrico. Legend has it that she had vowed to make Attila pay for the murder of so many of her countrymen. What is known is that after a wedding of great feasting and drinking, Attila retired to bed. By the morning, he was dead – an artery had burst and Attila had drowned in his own blood.

With his death, the now leaderless empire broke up. The Huns had ravaged Europe for almost two centuries. His men cut off their hair and disfigured their faces with deep scars so that Attila, their glorious hero, would be mourned, not by the tears of women, but by the blood of men.

His body was laid in state and his saddle and clothes burnt. Horsemen from the entire Hun population circled around, and a dirge was sung for one of history's most savage warriors. During the night, the body was secretly put into the earth. Within a year, the only two leaders who had successfully defied Attila, Aetius and Thorismund, were also dead.

A large number of the Huns who were scattered over half of Europe went back to the Mongolian steppes. By 476AD the Western Roman Empire came to an end, with the abdication of Romulus.

Attila the Hun had ruled for only eight years, but the terror that he brought to the population of fifth century Europe ensured his name is still synonymous with death and destruction to this day. Legends in which Attila was the central figure began to take shape soon after his death. Different countries and their legends have chosen to portray Attila in a variety of guises, some underplaying his brutality, while others revel in it.

KING JOHN

A CALLOUS, COLD-HEARTED MONARCH

*He was cruel and ruthless, violent and passionate, greedy and self-indulgent,
genial and repellent, arbitrary and judicious, clever and capable, original and
inquisitive.*

AUSTIN LANE POOLE, *From Domesday Book to Magna Carta*

D espite the fact that King John is guilty of many questionable acts, it is possible
that he was neither a bad king nor an evil man, but simply someone who
came to power in an age where violence was the norm, rather than the
exception. Born in 1167, John was the fifth son (the eighth and last child) of the
charismatic King Henry II and the formidable queen, Eleanor of Aquitaine. Together
Henry and Eleanor ruled most of England and a large part of France. It was the age
of the fighting man, and Henry epitomized the kind of vigorous, determined leader
that the people loved.

When John came into the world, Henry had been king for thirteen years. He was
a man of boundless energy who lived in a whirlwind of activity. He could not endure
a settled routine and dragged his court at breathless speed over the length and breadth
of England and his vast continental domains. Henry adored his sons, but
unfortunately he never educated them to government, trusting his justicars
(administrators) rather more than his blood. It was a recipe for disaster.

When Henry inherited the throne he quickly realized how omnipotent the barons
had become, and one of the main thrusts of his kingship was to reduce their power.
He made his own courts supreme and gradually reduced the sphere of influence in
which the baronial courts could act: he repressed private warfare and demolished the
castles of any barons who disregarded him; he brought law and order back into a land
of lawlessness.

John grew up in an atmosphere of treachery. A promise made today, whether
between father and son, or rulers, was often immediately broken as people constantly
changed sides according to which way the wind was blowing. Henry was renowned for
his incredible temper and it was a trait that John would inherit – with lethal
consequences.

Very little is known of John's life until he was three years old. Born on Christmas
Eve, he was given into the care of a wet-nurse and only returned to his parents when
he was bestowed the title Count of Mortain. Although it was an important title, it

conferred prestige more than power or lands, and in reference to it John received the nickname, Lackland, or Jean sans Terre.

Shortly afterwards, in 1172, John was betrothed to Alice, the Count of Maurienne's daughter. To match the proposed settlement, Henry planned to give John territories that he had already given to his son Henry. Henry was furious, and, joined by his brothers Geoffrey, Richard and Philip, King of France, they declared war on Henry. Discontented nobles and the King of Scotland joined them and Henry II was assailed from all sides. But they had reckoned without the English king's formidable fighting powers, and by the end of 1174, Henry had defeated his sons and his enemies.

In 1183, disaster befell the royal household when Henry and Eleanor's eldest son and heir, Henry, died. Now Richard, Eleanor's favourite, was heir to the throne. Richard was the most eligible man in Europe. He was handsome with reddish-gold hair, clear grey eyes and the strong, firm body characteristic of the men of the House of Anjou.

John was now one step closer to the throne and his father made an effort to provide him with more lands and security. Henry proposed to give him the already allocated Duchy of Aquitaine, a land that Richard coveted. As master of Lorraine, Richard had been tireless in subduing the rebellious nobles and making his authority felt throughout the area. The loss of Aquitaine would have been a bitter blow and Richard flatly refused to part with it. In order to avoid open conflict, Henry resolved the situation by giving the sixteen-year-old John permission ' …to lead an army into Richard's lands and get what he wanted by fighting him.' It was hardly a decision guaranteed to promote brotherly love. John and his brother Geoffrey collected an army, but Henry summoned all his sons to court and forced them to make peace.

By the age of seventeen, John was knighted at Windsor Castle and his father decided to send him to Ireland to subdue the restless nobles and to enforce the Papal Bull (an edict of the Pope), which sought to reform the Irish Church and bring it under the control of the Papacy.

John left England in April 1185 with 60 ships, 300 knights and 3,000 foot soldiers and horsemen. He landed at Waterford the following day and was greeted by his father's allies. Then he proceeded to Dublin and set about ruthlessly subjugating those who were not subordinate to Henry's rule. He took away their lands, giving them to more amenable candidates, and he installed a series of totally unsuitable governors, who were concerned only with collecting as much money as possible. Ireland was thrown into confusion and terror, but, finally, the King of Limerick defeated John's army. In addition to the loss of vast numbers of men in battle, a substantial percentage of John's troops had already defected to the Irish because John had withheld their pay, which he used for the pursuit of pleasure. John had exhibited an utter lack of responsibility and had treated the entire trip as a pleasure junket. He had thrown the land he was meant to govern into a state of anarchy, and had undone all the good work of his father.

Whilst John awaited Henry's forgiveness, his elder brother, Geoffrey, died in Paris.

A page in Latin showing King John with his dogs, from The Chronicle of England *by Peter of Langtoft, c.1300-c.1325. The charm of the illustration belies John's malevolence, callousness and greed.*

Henry, accompanied by John, went to meet with his enemy, Philip of France, to come to an arrangement for Geoffrey's lands. Henry gathered his army together in preparation for the inevitable conflict. Richard, John, and Henry's illegitimate son, (also called Geoffrey) were each given command of a section of the army. The Pope, appalled at the prospect of open warfare between the two most powerful rulers of western Europe, now intervened, and a two-year truce was signed in June 1187.

However, it was not a peace destined to last. Henry, in a bid to make a settlement with Philip, proposed that his sister, Alice, become engaged to John and that John be given the Duchy of Aquitaine. The only problem was that, for the past twenty years, Alice had been betrothed to Richard and Aquitaine therefore belonged to him. Furious with his father, Richard sought the company of Philip of France and together with some rebel barons, led campaigns into his father's lands. Henry retired to his castle in Le Mans in desperate straits. All were rising in rebellion against him and the Exchequer was empty. Now, in these desperate days, his favourite son, John, also joined Philip's side, hoping to gain more from his victorious brother than his defeated father. Shattered by this betrayal, Henry caught a fever and died on 6 July 1189. John did not attend his funeral. Richard was now King and John his unacknowledged heir. Richard welcomed John back to England and confirmed his title of Count of Mortain, giving him the county of Nottingham, and the castle of Marlborough. In addition, John was also given the counties of Dorset, Somerset, Derby, Lancaster, Cornwall and parts of Derbyshire. To further consolidate his position in England John then married an heiress, Hadwisa, who brought with her vast lands in the west and Wales.

John and Hadwisa were married at Marlborough Castle on 29 August. They were second cousins, and therefore technically not allowed to be man and wife, but John was scornful of the Church's objections and appealed to Rome.

In September, Richard was officially declared King and set about raising money for his proposed crusade. He put all that he had up for sale and, by December, having successfully secured peace with Scotland and Wales, he summoned a final council to govern England during his absence. Richard appointed the Bishop of Ely, William Longchamp, to be Chief Justicar. As a delegate of both the Pope and the King, Longchamp, who spoke no English and made no attempt to hide his contempt for the English people, now held supreme power over both Church and State. Longchamp immediately started confiscating lands and giving them to his relations and retainers. His actions aroused a storm of resentment among the people and the barons alike. John, fully aware of this, decided to use it to his own advantage. He began to set himself up as champion of the subjugated country.

John was now in a strong position. He controlled the west of England where he held absolute authority, but he wanted more and seized the castles of Nottingham and Tickhill from the barons. Meanwhile, Philip of France had returned from the Crusades, bursting with envy, and started planning mischief against Richard in his absence. He sent an envoy to John offering to help him gain possession of England and Normandy for himself. John, ever ambitious, agreed. But on the eve of his departure, John was prevented from going by his mother.

In an extraordinary volte-face, motivated by money, John then accepted an offer by Longchamp of 5,000 pounds to help him become Chief Justicar once more. The government, aware of John's lust for money, then paid John even more to stop his support of Longchamp. John may have gained a large amount of remuneration, but in one move he had lost the respect and the support of the English nobles who saw him for the duplicitous man he was.

After a largely unsuccessful Crusade, Richard was on his way home in 1193 when he was captured by Leopold, Duke of Austria and handed over to the Emperor. Despite Richard's phenomenal popularity, John now made a treacherous pact with Philip – territories were exchanged and Philip promised to help in gaining Richard's dominions. John then returned to England with a force of foreign mercenaries. He captured a couple of castles and marched on London where the barons rejected his claim. Furious, John left London.

Now England had to raise the money required for Richard's release. 70,000 marks of silver were needed and the whole country rallied together to raise a sum so vast, as to be beyond most people's comprehension. Richard sent word to John, warning him that '…you must take care of yourself, for the devil is now let loose.' Once the justicars felt safe in the knowledge that King Richard would return, they turned on John and he fled to Normandy to join Philip. But Richard himself never seems to have taken John seriously, and before returning from his year-long captivity, he reasserted John's rights to all his previous lands. This was not enough however, for the devious John. He had had a taste of the power of a king and he did not want to let go so easily, even if it meant plunging England into a civil war. He wrote to all the keepers of his castles, ordering them to fortify themselves against Richard's imminent arrival. He also offered Leopold money to keep Richard in captivity for another year.

Furious at John, the bishops now excommunicated him and the barons laid siege to his castles. When Richard returned to England in March 1194 he went straight into battle to smooth over the troubles stirred up by John, who was still cowering in Normandy with Philip. Richard charged John with betrayal and gave him forty days to answer the charges before he lost all his rights. But the manipulative John soon managed to worm himself into Richard's favour again and, one year later, he was restored to the earldoms of Mortain and Gloucester. He received a large sum of money on the understanding that he would ally himself with Richard against Philip. In return Richard designated him as his heir. Shortly afterwards Richard died of an infected arrow wound and with him went both the 'pride and the honour of the chivalry of the West.'

Although Richard had named John as his successor, hereditary succession by primogeniture was not yet law in England and John had a rival. Geoffrey's son, Arthur, John's nephew, was twelve years old and the nobles of Brittany, Anjou, Maine and Touriane saw him as the rightful heir. The most influential men in England – the Archbishop of Canterbury and William Marshall – knew that they must elect a successor with the greatest possible speed. John was still in Brittany, ironically, visiting Arthur, when he heard the news of Richard's death and immediately went to work to secure his possessions. His first act was to secure Richard's treasury at Chinon and he attached himself to Richard's household and obtained their allegiance.

John swore he would keep his promises and made a great show of his reformed conduct. He was suitably humble and submissive. Deeply superstitious, John also showed them a treasure he valued highly, a stone set in gold and hung about his neck, which he said had been given to one of his ancestors with a promise from heaven that any of his successors who wore it would never be deprived of their dominions.

Philip came out in support of Arthur, well aware that he could bend a young boy's will much more effectively than having to deal with John's fickleness and treachery. Philip sent Arthur to Paris with his son Louis and took possession of all Arthur's castles, in which he placed governors of his own choosing.

Meanwhile the strength of John's position on the Continent had improved dramatically. He had been made Duke of Normandy, Aquitaine had been brought under control by Eleanor and the capture of Le Mans had checked Arthur's supporters in Maine. He could now return to England and claim his throne.

Surprisingly John had the putative support of most of the English nobles. But before giving him their allegiance they wanted to exact a pledge from him that he would respect their customary rights. John's representatives pledged their word that John would allow them their lawful rights if they would swear allegiance and keep the peace. It was not a promise either side would keep.

John arrived in England on 25 May 1199. He was crowned two days later in Westminster Abbey by Hubert Walter, whom John appointed as his Chancellor. Once month later King John returned to Normandy. The truce with Philip was coming to an end and Arthur's claim needed to be settled once and for all. But Philip and John could not agree terms. When this became known, the French nobles, who had previously supported Richard, transferred their support to John, swearing they would not make peace with Philip without John's consent. By 1200 Philip stood in very bad grace with the Church owing to an impetuous marriage, and was more willing to come to terms with John. The treaty of Le Goulet was ratified on 21 June 1200 and a wedding was arranged between John's niece, Blanche, and Philip's son Louis.

In little more than a year, John had gained an undisputed title to all the territories of his predecessor and prospects seemed fair for a lasting peace with France. But Philip's boundless ambition, his faithlessness and duplicity, and his unceasing efforts to strengthen the French throne ensured there would never be lasting peace between the two countries.

Just as everything was looking good, John began causing discontent by alienating the loyalties of his continental vassals and a powerful group of English nobles. He had decided to divorce Hadwisa after ten years of marriage, but to keep her dowry. He then started hunting for a new wife and, after making approaches to the King of Portugal, he impetuously wed Isabella of Angoulême, (who was only twelve-years old) on 26 August 1200.

He could not have made a worse choice. Hadwisa was very popular with the English nobles and the choice of Isabella was offensive to many of the French. She had already been betrothed to the most powerful member of the House of Poitou, and the family subsequently became John's implacable enemies. Isabella would give John five children: Henry, Richard, Joan, Isabella and Eleanor.

John and his child bride arrived in England on 8 October 1200. They were crowned at Westminster Abbey and then journeyed to Scotland to talk to the Scots who were still angling for more territory. During their tour of the the north, they laid a series of crippling fines on the people, on the flimsiest of pretexts. Meanwhile the Poitou family were spoiling for a fight. They invaded Normandy, and aided and abetted by Philip, laid siege to John's castles until eventually all were captured. A furious John ordered his earls and barons to meet him at Portsmouth to go and fight. The nobles, aware that John needed them, took the opportunity to present some new demands, and they assembled at Leicester asking him to address their complaints. They wanted to return to the old system of Henry II, which would restore their absolute power in their own lands. John responded by telling them that he would take away their castles if they disobeyed him. Eventually they capitulated.

By 13 May 1201, a force was assembled. So many arrived that John sent some home, but not before taking their money; upon which he set sail for Normandy with 300 knights under the command of William Marshall and Roger de Lacy. Eventually they managed to get the French under control and John weakly let the Poitou nobles return to their lands.

Two months later war broke out again when Philip attacked Normandy, securing the border and levelling the Castle of Boutavant. He then sent Arthur to lay siege to his grandmother, Eleanor, in the castle of Mirebeau. John raced to her rescue and Arthur was captured along with 200 French knights and all the knights of Poitou. All except Arthur were sent to prison, some in Normandy, and others to Corfe Castle in England where they died of starvation. Arthur was kept at Falaise where John tried to secure his allegiance, but Arthur was an obstinate young man and was later moved to Rouen where he met a grisly death, almost certainly ordered, and maybe even perpetrated by John.

John had now been out of England for over a year and showed no signs of returning. He was completely obsessed with his young bride and could not bear to be parted from her. Even when Philip began capturing John's Norman castles he made no move, cockily saying that 'let him do so; whatever he takes I shall regain in a single day'. His English nobles were disgusted and many returned to England to tend to their estates. John was now left with only a few soldiers.

Finally John realized just how many Norman nobles had deserted him and was roused to action. But by now he had no men or money. On 6 December 1203 he returned to England, accusing his nobles of desertion and demanding one seventh of all their moveable property. Thanks to the efficiency of Henry II's Exchequer the money was all collected.

Philip had been spreading the word that John had deserted Normandy and gave him one year to re-establish sovereignty. Despite constant urging John was still loath to take up arms against Philip and, without meeting any resistance, Philip took possession of Normandy, Touraine, Anjou and Poitou. John received the news of the staggering losses with inexplicable equanimity – he was still enjoying the company of his Queen.

Finally, in April 1205, he was roused from lethargy. He summoned all the knights of England announcing that if any refused to follow him they would be deprived of their lands forever, with no possibility of regaining them. When his barons tried to dissuade him, and he accused them of plotting with Philip.

In a bitter rage John set off from England with a small company of knights intending to defeat Philip alone and single-handed. But, after three days, he turned back and took his revenge on the barons by exacting heavy fines from them.

In July the Archbishop of Canterbury, Hubert Walter, died. John was ecstatic at his death and declared that, 'now, for the first time, I am truly King of England.' Three separate deputations were then sent to the Pope. The first, by John and the monks of Canterbury, asked for confirmation of his choice of Archbishop, John Grey, Bishop of Norwich. The second deputation of younger monks, acting before Hubert's death, had chosen Reginald Grey and this was followed by a third party of the bishops who claimed to have had no say in the election. The Pope declared he would make his decision in December of the following year, hoping tempers would have cooled down by then.

Whilst awaiting the decision, John decided to head off to the Continent to redeem his lands. He was greeted with enthusiasm, Philip had not been a popular ruler.

Finally, after five months of warfare during which the chief sufferers were the general populace, Philip and John signed a truce for two years.

In December 1206, the Pope made his decision known. He declared both elections invalid and appointed Stephen Langton to the post. When the monks told Innocent III that it was impossible to elect the Archbishop without John's permission the Pope threatened to excommunicate them unless they consented. John went into an apocalyptic rage. He vented his wrath on the men who had elected Langton and accused them of treachery. He ordered his knights to go to Canterbury and expel the monks and the Prior from England, threatening that if they refused they would be burnt alive. Sixty-seven of them fled to Flanders whilst Langton remained on the Continent.

John remained adamant that he would not accept the Pope's choice and quickly made sure that all revenues from the lands of the Archbishop reverted to his Exchequer. By 1208 the Pope began to realize that John would not be moved and he placed the whole of England under an Interdict. All religious services stopped, there was no Holy Communion, no pealing of bells, and sermons were to be preached in graveyards.

John's response was swift and violent. He sent his sheriffs and officers throughout England, ordering all priests to leave immediately. He confiscated all their property and ecclesiastical revenues were diverted to the Exchequer. In addition, he had all the bishops who had agreed to Langton's election put in prison and stripped of their possessions. No justice was made available to them. Most refused to leave and faced the consequences of John's wrath.

Powerful as it was, John knew that the Interdict was not the final weapon in the Pope's arsenal. He knew that he could be excommunicated which would release all his nobles from their oath of fealty to him. He now demanded that each noble supply him with hostages and so they turned over their sons, nephews and close relatives.

By 1209 England was entering a period of renewed prosperity. Its trade was increasing and those nobles not fighting on the Continent, or in crusades, were attending to their estates. The Interdict was actually turning out to be extremely profitable for England and for John, since there was so much money coming into the Exchequer that no general taxation was needed.

By the autumn, the Pope realized it was hopeless to think that John would bow to his wishes and so he took the last step open to him – he excommunicated John. Initially this seems to have had no effect on the irreligious John, but he soon started to become increasingly paranoid, cruel and avaricious. When one of his clerics decided that he could not work for an excommunicated man, John had him arrested and put in prison. He was encased in a heavy sheet of lead, and starved to death. John then turned his attention to the Jews. From 1210 onwards John waged a campaign to extort all their money, and hundreds were imprisoned and tortured.

John now distrusted everyone except his most intimate friends. His major concerns were to increase his power and hold the barons in check, but stern repression, the taking of hostages, and land confiscation were only effective in the short term.

By 1212 plots began to hatch against John. Over the years he had violated many of the barons' wives and daughters, producing at least twelve illegitimate children, while many of their parents and relatives had been exiled and their estates confiscated. When some of the nobles learnt that the Pope had released them from their oaths of allegiance to John they wrote to Philip, inviting him to invade England.

John's behavior became increasingly erratic. When the preaching of Peter of Pontefract came to John's attention he had him thrown into prison to await the coming of his own prophecy that John would not be king in a year. Then in another extraordinary move, John wrote to the Sultan of Morocco promising to become a Muslim in exchange for help in fighting Philip. The offer was, not surprisingly, dismissed.

By the autumn of 1212, England had been under the Interdict for four years, but it had failed to curtail John's power. The Pope now decided that a worthier king should be found, and proposed Philip, urging him to conduct a holy war on John. Meanwhile, John's hold over his nobles was slipping and many of them absented themselves from his court. He heard about Philip's proposed attack and started to prepare England's defence. He commanded that all earls, barons, knights and free-serving men come to Dover. A vast army assembled at Barham Down ready to meet Philip's forces.

With the two armies poised for battle, one last attempt was made to make John submit. The Pope's envoy, Pandulf, told John of the betrayal of some of his nobles, and, despite the fact that his force was superior to the French King's, John capitulated. John was afraid to meet Philip in battle for fear that his own barons would abandon him or deliver him up as a prisoner to Philip.

On 12 May 1213, John swore to abide by the Pope's commands and agreed to let Langton assume his position as Archbishop. He also agreed to return all the confiscated monies and property. The Interdict was lifted.

In a masterstroke of deception John then surrendered his kingdom to the Pope ensuring that Philip would no longer be able to invade his lands. Philip was incensed. He had spent over 60,000 pounds on preparing an invasion force and his navy had been decimated by Count Ferrand of Flanders, a supporter of John's. John's European alliances, which he had been building up against Philip at the cost of untold treasure, was now at the height of its power. It was time for John and his European allies to launch a simultaneous attack.

At first John made good progress, but was then betrayed by the nobles of Poitou, forcing him to retreat to La Rochelle. Finally, on 27 July, the forces of the alliance clashed with Philip on the banks of the River Marcq. It is unknown which side had the greater number of soldiers, but the alliance was defeated and Philip made a triumphal march into Paris.

When the news of the crushing defeat was brought to John he knew that the years of labour and the massive expenditure had come to nothing. There was nothing left on which to rebuild his dream of beating Philip.

John returned to England and set about collecting taxes. He met with stiff opposition; the barons would still not obey John and they felt that the imposition of scutage (a tax levied in exchange for fighting at the King's side) was unfair. John was now a vanquished king with no allies and no treasure, and for the first time the barons were truly united in their opposition to his demands. By now, John was fully aware of the problems facing him and sought to win the bishops and clergy over to his side by granting them all their lands back.

On 6 January 1215, the barons presented their case to John, demanding a return, which John had already agreed to, to the Charter of 1213. John asked for more time.

In April, 2,000 knights gathered at Stamford – the list of names showed John how widespread the protest against his despotic government had become. They presented their demands to Archbishop Langton and William Marshall, but John refused to even consider them. It was tantamount to a declaration of war and led to the barons renouncing their oath of fealty and taking up arms against John with a clear conscience.

John now summoned the treacherous knights of Poitou. England was thrown into disorder and the administrative and judicial systems were paralysed. Realizing he had no way of defending himself and his castles, John pretended to submit to the barons.

On 15 June 1215, he met the barons in the meadow at Runnymede, near Windsor, where he signed the Magna Carta. It was an unprecedented experiment in forcing a

A nineteenth-century representation of the signing of the Magna Carta, June 1215. The barons' 'Great Charter' was an unprecedented attempt to force a king to keep to the law, which perhaps accounts for John's disgruntled expression. Treacherous to the last, he persuaded the Pope to annul the charter and excommunicate the barons; the latter fought back, however, and England might have fallen to the French had not John died the following year.

(© BETTMANN/CORBIS)

king to keep to the law of the land; but many of the barons – quite rightly – did not trust John. John was determined to strike back. Firstly, he incited the Pope against the barons, then he sent his few trusted advisers to raise a continental army and directed the royal castles to be ready to defend themselves.

The Pope agreed to annul the Magna Carta, and had all the barons excommunicated, as John hastened to Dover to await his mercenaries. Recruited from the dregs of society, they plundered, ravaged, and spread terror and destruction. Even in an age of cold-blooded warfare they were extreme in their violence.

But the barons who retained control of London had not been idle – their plan was to contain John's forces in Kent by blocking the roads. The defenders of Rochester Castle held out for as long as they could, and when they surrendered to John he had them all hanged. John's forces spread terrible destruction wherever they went. Instead of paying his mercenaries, John permitted them to plunder houses and churches alike.

At the end of their tether, the barons sent two men to offer the crown of England to Louis, Philip's son. News of Louis's designs on England reached the ears of the Pope and he tried to forbid such an act, but Louis completely ignored him and, by 21 May, he had landed so many troops in England that John was forced to withdraw. Louis now occupied Kent and was welcomed into London by the barons. After raiding John's treasury he set out to capture John at Corfe Castle.

Nevertheless, John was far from beaten. By October the barons were finally beginning to realize the hopelessness of the situation. Not only was John growing stronger by the day, but also Louis was proving impossible. He had taken away their lands and given them to Frenchmen and he had made it clear he despised all Englishmen.

Meanwhile, John's campaign was struck a mortal blow when his entire treasure was swallowed by the treacherous sands in the Wash.

At this point, the fate of Britain hung in the balance. If John failed, not only would he have lost the Angevin Empire, but the kingdom of England would have fallen into French hands. It would have been the Norman Conquest all over again.

Yet in a pathetic twist of fate, he contracted dysentery as a result of a surfeit of peaches and new cider and died during the night of 18 October 1216. He was forty-eight and died unmourned by most.

With John out of the way, the regency council, led by William Marshall, declared John's son as King Henry III and reissued the Magna Carta, resolving a major part of the rebels' grievances. All those barons who had been prepared to oppose John, now flocked to his son's standard, and the conflict shifted from a civil war over baronial rights, to a war of resistance against foreign invasion. Louis was defeated at Lincoln and Sandwich, by land and sea, and agreed to withdraw in September 1217.

It was the final ironic twist in the story of Henry II and his sons. By their own actions, they had won and lost an empire; and, by his death, John saved the Kingdom of England.

TORQUEMADA

THE SPANISH INQUISITOR

I hold you in the very bowels of affection for your immense labours in the exhalation of the Catholic faith.

POPE ALEXANDER VI

'In view of the suspicions arising against him from the evidence, he is condemned to be tortured for such a length of time as should be seen fit, in order that he might tell the truth. If in the torture he should die or suffer effusion of blood or mutilation, it should not be attributed to the Inquisitors, but to him for not telling the truth.'

As head of the Spanish Inquisition, Tomás de Torquemada was responsible for the imprisonment, torture and death of thousands of innocent Spaniards. Known as the 'Black Legend', he spread fear throughout the land, wielding a power and an influence rivalling the monarchy of King Ferdinand and Queen Isabella. He developed his institution with pitiless zeal and ruthless fanaticism. Clad in the austere garb of a Dominican friar, the gaunt, sunken-eyed sadist vented his hatred on Jews and heretics, forcing up to 300,000 out of Spain and destroying their lives forever.

The idea that religious dissent should be punished by force is almost as old as Christianity itself. In the year 385AD, the pious Emperor Maximus had tortured and executed the heretic Priscillian and some of his followers. In the Dark Ages the persecution of heretics seems to have fallen into disuse, but during the Middle Ages it was finally revived and elaborated on. The Catholic Church faced a crisis from the Albigensian religious movement in the South of France. The Pope therefore sent troops to eradicate the heretics, but soon realized that they had not been obliterated, only driven underground. It was decided that it required special people to be employed for the purpose and so the Papal Inquisition first came into existence. The Dominican order, a preaching order directed against heresy, was chosen for the task. They were known as the 'Hounds of the Lord'. The same period also witnessed the increase of legislation against heresy, and death by burning became the accepted way of dealing with an impenitent heretic.

By the end of the thirteenth century the Papal Inquisition had developed a system of records and officials, and its arm was notoriously long, so that the very name Inquisition started to strike terror into every heart. With complete independence, it possessed its own prisons and its activities were clothed in secrecy. The Pope sanctioned the use of torture

The Dominican friar Tomás de Torquemada, first Inquisitor-General of Spain. Known as the 'Black Legend', he was the embodiment of the cruelty, injustice and terror of the Spanish Inquisition. By the time he died – peacefully – in 1498, he had been responsible for the torture and deaths of thousands of innocent people. (© HULTON ARCHIVE)

in 1252. The Inquisitor was to be maintained by the property of the victim – and his property was taken upon arrest. No defence was permitted and the names of accusers were hidden. These were features that would also distinguish the Spanish Inquisition, though that institution developed them to a high pitch of sadistic perfection.

In the middle of the fourteenth century, more than a hundred years before the coming of the Spanish Inquisition, the Kingdom of Castille had been rent apart by a bloody civil war. The substantial Jewish community was made its scapegoats and pogroms had ensued, fanned by zealous Christian preachers. The violence had reached its zenith in 1392 with the murder of hundreds, perhaps thousands of Jews. During this time the Jews had been offered the chance to convert to Christianity. Many had accepted and became known as *conversos*. But the prevalent belief was that they still practised their faith in secret. They provoked suspicion and mistrust, and most believed, 'Jews to be more their neighbours than Christians.' Despite the prejudice around them, many Jews rose to prominence in the royal administration, civic bureaucracy and even the Church. In 1390 the Rabbi of Burgos, who had converted to Catholicism, ended his life as Bishop of Burgos, Papal Legate and tutor to a Prince of the Blood. He was not alone. In some of the major cities, Jews dominated the administration and merchant class. King Ferdinand's treasurer was a *converso*. Three of Isabella's secretaries were *conversos*, as was the official court chronicler. One of Torquemada's own uncles was a *converso*. They tended to be amongst the best-educated people in Spain, and as they rose to prominence, their success and wealth provoked envy and resentment. Their wealth was also to exacerbate the hostility of the Inquisition.

With the advance of the fifteenth century, clerical zealots and political failures began to agitate for the introduction of the Inquisitorial system to cope with the 'problem' of the *conversos*. The first minister to attempt to bring proceedings against them was the unpopular minister Alvaro de Luna. He found himself opposed by two bishops of Jewish extraction but managed to obtain, from Pope Nicholas, a series of Inquisitorial powers to discipline high ecclesiastical figures. But Luna never got the chance to use his powers – he was decapitated in 1453. Then, during the reign of King Henry IV, the agitation assumed a more menacing form. Under the influence of Alonso de Spina, the most learned anti-Semite of the fifteenth century, the Franciscans ordered the introduction of a tribunal to deal with the 'Jewish Problem', which, apparently, was growing more serious day by day. But the *conversos* had their supporters and General Fray Alonso de Oropesa mounted the pulpit in their defence. The Franciscans were silenced – for the moment, although feelings of bitterness continued. It was the nobility that revived the agitation. In 1464, in the *Concordat of Medina del Campo*, the king was forced to establish an inquiry into the conduct of the *conversos* and to punish any that had slipped back into the Jewish faith.

In 1465 Isabella came to the throne amid a blaze of civil war. She was surrounded by ecclesiastics and nobility who were constantly reminding her that steps needed to be taken against the *conversos*, on either political or spiritual grounds. Chief among them was Dominican friar, Tomás de Torquemada. Born at Valladolid in 1420, he was now at the height of his extraordinary powers. He had been the Queen's confessor when she was the Infanta and hated Jews, in spite of, or maybe because, he was of Jewish extraction. Torquemada's influence over the Queen was enormous and they shared one obsession – to stamp out heresy. As far as Torquemada was concerned the real heretics were not the Jews or Muslims, but the *conversos*, whom he suspected were not true to the Catholic faith.

It was reported that Torquemada had made Isabella take a vow that, should she reach the throne, she would devote herself heart and soul to the extirpation of heresy and the persecution of the Jews. At the time of the oath, it had been unlikely that she would attain the throne, but she had, and Torquemada rose with her.

In 1477 the civil war ended and Isabella went to Seville for a year, where she summoned a national council to discuss Church reforms. The sight of the *conversos*, many of whom were very powerful at court, stimulated Torquemada and Alonso de Hojeda, a vehement anti-Semite, to fresh efforts and condemnations. But Isabella was hesitant, after all many of her advisers and courtiers were Jewish. However, on the night of Wednesday 18 March 1478 all this was to change. A young man, in love with a young Jewess, sneaked into her house and surprised a number of *conversos* celebrating Seder. By coincidence it also happened to be Holy Week. A report that the heretics were gathered in order to blaspheme the Christian religion went round Seville like wildfire. Hojeda and Torquemada hastened to court to tell the Queen of this outrage and she finally decided to take action. A Papal Bull, (an edict of the Pope) was demanded from Pope Sixtus IV and eventually issued giving the Spanish sovereigns the right to appoint two Inquisitors to root out heresy in the Kingdom of Castille. The Spanish Inquisition was born and finally, on the 7 September 1480, a Seville tribunal was inaugurated. Miguel de Morillo and Juan de San Martin, both Dominicans, were appointed and told to get to work. An alleged conspiracy of Seville's leading *conversos* was soon unearthed and on the 6 February 1481, the first *Auto-da-fé*, (Act of faith) took place. Six men and women were burned alive. A *quemadero*, or place of burning, was constructed just outside the city walls. At the four corners, huge plaster figures of the four major prophets had been erected.

As the news spread of the establishment of the Inquisition many *conversos* fled from Seville into the surrounding countryside. The Inquisition ordered that they be returned and most demands were obeyed, such was the fear engendered by the tribunals. The Marquis of Cadiz returned over 8,000 and the Inquisition's dungeons were soon so full that everyone had to move to the great Castle of Triana, outside the city walls. Despite plague ravaging the city, the *Auto-da-fé* continued without interruption. Even the dead were not spared; their bones were exhumed and burnt. By 4 November, two hundred and ninety people had been burned and ninety-eight condemned to perpetual imprisonment.

Four months later, in February 1482, the Pope authorized the appointment of another seven Dominicans as Inquisitors. One of them, the prior of a monastery in Segovia, was to pass into history as the very embodiment of the Spanish Inquisition at its most terrifying – Tomás de Torquemada. He had previously been content with being the power behind the throne, but his fanatical devotion to his religion made Torquemada the perfect candidate for the position of Inquisitor, and with the support of the Crown, he began to hunt down the *converso* heretics. In the three years following his appointment, tribunals of the Inquisition were established in four other locations and by 1492, tribunals were operating in eight major cities. However, by that point complaints had begun pouring in from Spanish bishops and, responding to these, the Pope issued a Bull expressing his outrage that so many, 'true and faithful Christians, on the testimony of enemies, rivals, slaves have, without any legitimate proof, been

A man accused of heresy is tortured by the Inquisition, strapped to a wheel below which a fire is fanned with bellows. In the background, two monks wait with quill and paper to take down the victim's confession. Under such treatment, however, as Torquemada well knew, almost anyone would confess to almost anything, simply to end the agony. (© HULTON ARCHIVE)

thrust into secular prisons, tortured and condemned…deprived of their goods and property and handed over to the secular arm to be executed.'

Pointing out that the Inquisition was not solely to deal with the *conversos*, the Pope revoked all the powers of the Inquisition. But the decision to keep or annul Spain's Inquisitors was not the Pope's – and the Bull was seen as a flagrant challenge to the monarchy. Predictably, King Ferdinand and Queen Isabella were outraged.

Confronted by the King's defiance the Pope capitulated completely. On 17 October 1483, a new Bull was issued which established the *Consejo de la Suprema y*

General Inquisicion – to function as the Inquisition's ultimate authority. To preside over this council, *La Suprema*, the new office of Inquisitor General was created. Its first incumbent was Torquemada. All the Inquisition tribunals throughout Christian Spain were now under one centralized administration, with Torquemada at its head. Under his direction, the Inquisition rapidly took shape, and extended its activity throughout the country. It was owing to his personal zeal that verdicts of acquittal were infrequent and over three-quarters of those who perished under the Inquisition in the first 300 years of its existence, did so in the first two decades.

Torquemada became obsessed with the purity of lineage and devised the *Limpreza de Sangre*, or purity of blood document. Anyone with any Jewish blood was prohibited from holding public office or denounced as a heretic. The zenith of Torquemada's activities in Castille was reached when he took proceedings out against a prelate of high character and great learning, who happened to be of Jewish descent. One of the charges brought was that the unfortunate Bishop of Segovia had had the remains of his forebears exhumed, in order to destroy proof that they had been interred with Jewish rites. He was sent to Rome for trial and died a prisoner in the Vatican castle of St Angelo. Torquemada's accusations had been based on nothing but spite.

In the city of Ciudad alone, the Tribunal, in the two years of its existence, burnt 52 heretics and condemned 220 fugitives, as well as sentencing 183 people to perform public penance. By 1485 the Tribunal had been transferred to Toledo, where some 750 people took part in the first *Auto-da-fé*. Carrying unlit tapers and surrounded by a howling mob, which had flooded in from the surrounding countryside, the accused were compelled to march bareheaded and barefoot through the city to the door of the Cathedral. They were fined one fifth of their property and banned from public office and only allowed to wear the coarsest of clothes. In addition they were also required to go in procession on six successive Fridays, flagellating themselves with hempen cords. At the second *Auto-da-fé*, 900 penitents appeared and 750 at the third. Before the end of the year the total figures had reached 5,000. Large numbers, sometimes fifty a day, were burned and among the victims were several friars and ecclesiastical dignitaries.

Torquemada produced a handbook of instructions detailing how the secret Jews were to be identified. People were instructed to watch for *conversos* washing their hands before prayer, changing linen on the Sabbath and shopping in Jewish stores. Wholesale denunciations were encouraged by a promise of a free pardon in return for full confession, which placed thousands in the power of the dreaded Tribunal. Inquisitors had two manuals at their disposal on how to deal with heretics. The first, *The Practice of the Office of the Inquisition of Heretical Depravity*, was composed in 1324. The second was the *Inquisitors Directory* by Nicholas Eymerich. Both identified Jews as particularly dangerous for Christian society and *conversos* as the most dangerous of all. When Torqemada's train of death appeared, city gates were flung open, the resources of the city were placed at his disposal and magistrates swore him their devotion. The Inquisition would descend on a town or village at regular intervals and present themselves to the local church and civic authorities. A day would be proclaimed and everyone would be compelled to attend a special Mass to hear the Inquisition's 'Edict' read in public. On the appointed day, at the end of the sermon, the Inquisitor would raise a crucifix. Those in attendance would be required to raise their right hands, cross themselves and repeat an oath to support the Inquisition and its servants.

The edict listed various heresies, as well as Islam and Judaism, and called forward all those who might be guilty of infraction. If they confessed themselves within a stipulated period of grace – generally thirty to forty days, although being at the Inquisitor's discretion, it was often less – they might be accepted back into the Church and allowed to get away with doing penance. They would be required to renounce any guilty parties who had not come forward. Indeed, this was a crucial prerequisite for being allowed to escape with nothing more severe than a penance. For the Inquisition, 'a convert who would betray his friends was more useful than a roasted corpse.'

In Spain, as elsewhere, people would avail themselves of the Inquisition to settle old scores, to exact personal vengeance on neighbours and relatives and to eliminate business rivals. Anyone could denounce anyone else, and the burden of vindication would lie with the accused. Increasingly, people began to fear their neighbours, their business associates, in fact anyone who they may have antagonized, in addition to which they would often bear false witness against themselves, sometimes confessing *en masse*, submitting themselves to the paranoia and dread, which the Inquisition provoked.

Petty denunciations were the rule rather than the exception. In Castille during the 1480s, over 1,500 people were burnt at the stake as a result of false testimony, often unable even to determine whom their accusers were. Witnesses in investigations were kept anonymous, and their testimonies edited for any items that might betray their identities.

The Inquisition derived its energy and impetus from the very population it persecuted, its power stemming from a blatant exploitation of the weakest and most venal aspects of human nature. In theory, each case was to be examined by a conclave of theologians – the visiting Inquisitor and at least one local, but in practice many people were arrested before their cases were assessed. The Inquisition's prisons were crammed with people waiting to hear the charges against them and they might be kept for years without knowing why. In the meantime, they and their families would have been stripped of all their property, for an arrest was always accompanied by the immediate confiscation of all the accused's belongings – everything from the house down to pots and pans. Whilst in prison, the accused's property could be sold off to pay for his maintenance in captivity. When eventually released, he could find himself bankrupt or destitute. Children of prisoners are recorded as having died from starvation.

Even the most lenient of punishments, the penance, could be severe. The lightest penalty was 'discipline'. The self-confessed heretic would be obliged each Sunday to strip and appear in church carrying a rod. At a certain time in the Mass, the priest would energetically whip the victim before the entire congregation – a fitting interlude in the divine service. Punishment did not end there. On the first Sunday of every month, the penitent would be compelled to visit every house in which he had met with other heretics – and in each, would be whipped again. On feast days, he would be required to follow the procession and then be whipped again. These ordeals were inflicted for the rest of his life, unless released by the Inquisitor on a return visit. Another form of penance was the pilgrimage. Made on foot, these could often take several years, during which time a man's family might well starve. Pilgrimages could be to holy shrines or as far afield as Jerusalem.

Confessed heretics might also be compelled to wear, for the rest of their lives, a large saffron cross sewn on the breast and back of all their garments. The penitent was then exposed to constant social humiliation, ridicule and violence.

Finally penance could take the form of a fine. Such fines quickly became a source of scandal since Inquisitors often extorted large sums of money for themselves. The Inquisition was financed by money and goods obtained from their victims and bribery and corruption were rife. In 1499, the Inquisitor of Cordoba was convicted of fraud and extortion. His successor blithely followed in his footsteps. Torquemada himself, despite his vow of poverty, accumulated vast wealth.

Death afforded no release – if the penitent was not judged to have sufficiently atoned – then his bones were dug up and burnt, and his family could become liable for his penances and his debts. If the accused chose to run, his body was burnt in effigy, but if the person accused of heresy did not flee, and the charges were deemed sufficient, they were arrested and put into the hands of the Inquisitors. Since no Inquisitor cared to be wrong, every possible subterfuge was used to extract or extort a confession. One Inquisitor remarked that 'there is no need for haste, for the pains and privation of imprisonment often bring about a change of mind.' Inquisitors were licensed by the Pope to carry out torture, preferably without shedding blood and new methods of torture were invented to aid this hypocrisy. The rack, thumbscrews and other devices that caused blood to flow only 'incidentally' were favoured. Pincers and other such toys had to be white hot so that the heated metal would cauterize the wound, as the flesh was being torn open.

There was *toca*, or water torture, when water was forced down a victim's throat. There was *potro*, when the person was bound to a rack by tight cords that could be tightened further and further. Then there was *garrucha*, in which the heretic would be hung by the wrists from a pulley in the ceiling with weights fastened to his or her feet. Raising the pulley slowly, to maximise the pain, they would then be dropped a few feet abruptly, dislocating the limbs. It was certainly not unusual for a death to occur, but this was always deemed to have been accidental and not as a result of the torture.

The Inquisition realized that confessions under torture did not carry a great deal of weight – under severe pain people will say anything. The victims were therefore made to confirm the statement a couple of days later, so that the confession could be labelled 'not under duress'. Technically the Inquisition was only meant to torture once, but this was circumvented by describing the end of each session as a 'suspension'.

In administering the death sentence, clerical hypocrisy displayed itself again. Inquisitors could not themselves perform executions, which might have made them appear un-Christian. Instead they were obliged to enact the ritual whereby they handed the heretic over to the secular authorities so they could do their dirty work for them. To ensure the maximum number of spectators, executions were performed on public holidays. The condemned would be tied to a pyre of dry wood, located well above the crowd, to ensure a good view. When they were dead, the body was separated into pieces, the bones were broken and everything was thrown onto a fresh fire.

Before the marriage of Ferdinand and Isabella, Spain had been a divided country. Under their joint rule the two kingdoms of Aragon and Castille were united. Now King Ferdinand wanted to establish an Inquisition in Aragon, but he had to petition the Pope to get rid of the existing tribunals, which had been set up in the thirteenth century. Having never been keen on issuing the original Bull to Isabella for Castille in 1478, the Pope initially objected to authorising the entry of the Inquisition to Aragon. Finally however, after a great deal of double-dealing, Torquemada, the Castillian Inquisitor General, was granted the right to appoint Inquisitors in Aragon, Catalonia and Valencia. Torquemada's appointment, overriding the complete legal and constitutional separation between Castille and Aragon, created a storm, which engulfed hundreds of people, in addition to the *conversos*.

Violent opposition broke out against Ferdinand's Inquisition as the *converses* fought to be recognized as sincere Christians. *Autos-da-fé* had already taken place in Castille and Andalusia, and stories abounded of the arbitrary cruelty committed by the Inquisitors. The Aragonese and Catalonian *conversos* had little doubt concerning the fate that awaited them once Torquemada's Inquisitors arrived, which they did on 14 April 1484. However, the *conversos* of Aragon were well organized, rich and powerful and determined not to give way without resistance. It was in Saragossa, the capital of Aragon that they struck back hardest.

The Inquisitor of Saragossa was Pedro Arbues. Aware that his life was in danger, he had taken to wearing full chain mail beneath his vestments, but four prominent *conversos*, including the Master of the Royal Household and High Treasurer of the Kingdom, hired assassins and on the night of 15 September 1485, Arbues was stabbed to death whilst kneeling in prayer at the Cathedral's altar. When it was discovered who the assassins were, the whole mood of Saragossa changed, and with it that of Aragon.

Arbues was declared a saint, miracles were worked with his blood and mobs roamed the streets in search of *conversos*. One of the plotters had his hands cut off and nailed to the door of the court house, after which he was dragged to the market-place, beheaded and quartered, and the pieces of his body suspended in the streets of the city. Another committed suicide in his cell by swallowing a broken glass lamp; he too suffered the same punishment, which was inflicted on his dead body.

Hundreds of people were arrested and thrown into the dungeons of the Aljaferia, the old Moorish fortress – as many as forty to a single cell, devoid of the most basic

A contemporary illustration showing the torture and burning of Jews, accused as heretics and witches, by the Inquisition. By 1492, Torquemada had overseen the extinction of Judaism in Spain, by torturing and killing Jews as a policy, and persuading the King and Queen to order the survivors into exile.
(© BETTMANN/CORBIS)

amenities. Over 200 were burnt and a large number of Aragon's *conversos* were in the hands of the Inquisition. One murder in retaliation had turned out to be an act of mass suicide that annihilated all opposition to the Inquisition for the next hundred years.

In 1488 the Inquisition spread to Barcelona and the following year the island of Majorca came under the lash. Flight to foreign countries – especially the south of France – began to assume panic proportions. But for many there was to be no escape and Pope Innocent VIII ordered them to be handed over. Hundreds were returned, back into the waiting arms of Torquemada.

From the moment of its creation, the Spanish Inquisition had cast covetous eyes on Judaic wealth, but initially they could not get to it. The Inquisition was charged to deal with heretics i.e. Christians who had deviated from the orthodox ideals of the faith; it had no powers over different religions. So a large percentage of the population remained outside their control, but it was a situation that was not to last long.

By the end of the 1480s Torquemada had realized that the greatest threat to the purity of the Catholic Church came from practising Jews, and so the Inquisition now embarked on an anti-Semitic propaganda campaign. Extraordinary accusations would be made and repeated time after time, until they would eventually come to be accepted as valid. Managing to provoke the population, the Inquisition now petitioned the Crown to adopt the necessary measures. Initially, however, Ferdinand and Isabella demurred. They needed the Jews' money to fight to regain the city of Granada, the last stronghold of the Moors and Islam. Until the whole of Spain was reconciled to Catholicism the expulsion of the Jews would have to wait. However, with the recapture of Granada from the Moors in 1492, the religious zeal of the Spanish Inquisition was given free reign. In the flush of victory, there seemed to be no reason why practising Jews should be tolerated. The Inquisition had not been able to get its hands on them before – they were not heretics within the Church but infidels outside it, over whom no clerical tribunal had jurisdiction. It was a somewhat ridiculous situation. A *converso*, forced into baptism with a dagger at his throat would be burned alive for following the Jewish faith in secret, whilst the unconverted Jew could practise with impunity. In addition, the Inquisition reasoned, the *conversos* were corrupted by the presence of practising Jews. All Torquemada had to do was find an excuse to get rid of them.

On 14 November 1491, two weeks before the fall of Granada, five Jews and six *conversos* were sent to the stake in Avila. Accused of crucifying a Christian child and ripping the heart out, they had supposedly been performing a magical rite designed to disable the Inquisition and send all Christians, 'raving mad to their deaths'. The Inquisition made sure that every city in Spain came to hear of it, and anti-Semitic fury rose to a peak. Torquemada took the story before Ferdinand and Isabella as proof of the complicity between Jews and *conversos*.

Under appeal from Abraham Signor, a Jewish courtier who had helped arrange their marriage, Ferdinand and Isabella wavered about expelling the Jews. Signor offered them a tremendous amount of gold in exchange for the Jews being able to stay. When he heard this, Torquemada burst into the royal chambers and threw thirty pieces of silver at the King and Queen, reminding them that Judas had sold Christ for the same amount and that they were selling him out again.

On 30 March 1492, Ferdinand and Isabella, in their council chamber at the captured Alhambra in Granada, signed the decree which drove into exile 200,000 loyal Spaniards, whose ancestors had lived in the country since time immemorial. Four months later, the last Jews had departed, and the great dream of Torquemada's life had been realized. The *conversos* were now really alone. The task of the Inquisition was simplified – there was now a clean-cut division between the unconverted Jew and the converted. The former had gone into exile; the relatively simple task remained, of forcing the latter into conformity.

Six years later, Tomás de Torquemada died peacefully in his monastery in Avila in the odour of sanctity. He had been responsible for thousands of deaths and the eradication of Judaism in Spain – just as Hitler was to do throughout Europe, 450 years later. He was succeeded as Grand Inquisitor by the scholarly Diego Diez. With Isabella's death in 1504 the Inquisition lost its state support, but would remain in existence for another 300 years. Its last victim, a schoolteacher from Rusafa, was burnt alive in 1824. The Inquisition still exists today under the name '*The Congregation for the Doctrine of Faith*'. It still has the power to silence and excommunicate dissident Catholics.

PRINCE VLAD DRACULA

'THE IMPALER'

'The character [of Dracula] originates from a fifteenth-century prince of Wallachia in Romania, Vlad V, whose nickname was "the Impaler" owing to his beastly little habit of slowly impaling the Turkish invaders of his country and drinking their blood with his dinner. The name "Dracula" derives from his father, who was known as Vlad Dracul (he Devil), and Castle Dracula in the Carpathian Mountains, north of Bucharest.'
PETER CUSHING, Introduction to *Vampire Stories* (1992)

From the ancient Kingdom of Wallachia, in what is now modern Romania, a man emerged who would become renowned for devising innovative methods of torture and execution. Vlad Tepes Dracula, Prince of Wallachia, conquered and lost the throne of Wallachia three times in his life. Over his bloody, seven-year reign, the ruler of this kingdom brought terror to citizens and foreigners alike. He was a ruler whose obsession with loyalty would lead to a murderous paranoia and the death of more than 100,000 people. If Dracula ever walked the earth as a creature of flesh and blood rather than as a figure of fiction, then the person who deserved the title was Vlad Tepes. But the legend of Count Dracula is a fairy tale compared with the catalogue of terror, torture and sheer blood lust that marked the violent life of the Wallachian Prince – otherwise known as Vlad the Impaler.

A Transylvanian called Radu Negru, or Rudolph the Black, had founded Wallachia in 1290. Hungary dominated Wallachia until 1330, when it became independent. The first ruler of the country was Prince Basarab the Great (1310-52), an ancestor of Vlad the Impaler. Vlad's grandfather, Prince Mircea the Old, reigned from 1386 -1418 and it was during his reign that Wallachia was forced to pay tribute to the Turkish Ottoman Empire. The family continued to rule Wallachia, but as vassals of the Turks.

Wallachia was wracked by unrest and instability; it was threatened from the outside by the Turkish Ottoman Empire and from within by a corrupt boyar (a member of the old Russian aristocracy).

Vlad's father, Dracul, was educated in Hungary and Germany, and served as a page of King Sigismund of Hungary, who became the Holy Roman Emperor in 1410. Sigismund founded a secret order of knights called the Order of the Dragon, and Dracul was invited to join the brotherhood. This was a secret military and religious confraternity, to protect the Christian Church against heretics and organize crusades against the Turks, who had overrun most of the Balkan Peninsula. Eventually, Sigismund appointed Dracul as military governor of Transylvania, a post he held for four years until 1435. Vlad was born in the military fortress of Sighisoara in 1431. He was the second son of Vlad Dracul and Princess Cneajna of Moldavia. He had an older brother, Mircea, and a younger brother, Radu the Handsome.

From an early age, the young Vlad was already developing a taste for death. Much of his spare time was spent watching criminals being led to their execution at his father's court in the royal capital of Tirgoviste, and by the age of five, Vlad was being prepared for war. He galloped bareback, was a good shot with his bow and arrow and was initiated into the Order of the Dragon, and given the name Dracula, meaning son of Dracul.

But Vlad's father, having served as military governor for some time, decided he was not content to remain one forever. During his years in Transylvania, he gathered supporters to help him seize the Wallachian throne from its current occupant, a Danesti prince called Alexandru I. In 1437 Vlad Dracul killed Alexandru and became Prince Vlad II.

Dracul, a wily politician, sensed that the balance of power was shifting in favour of the ambitious new Sultan Mehmed II – the Turks had recently destroyed both the Serbs and Bulgars and were contemplating a final blow against the Greeks. Dracul signed an alliance with the sultan.

Despite his treachery, the Wallachians were happier to be ruled by one of their own kind than the Turks. Dracul tried to prevent some of the Turks' worst excesses, in particular their fondness for carrying off slaves, and this made the Sultan suspicious, so he tricked Dracul into a personal confrontation and, impervious to the snare, Dracul crossed the Danube with Vlad and his youngest son, Radu. Dracul was bound in iron chains and brought before the Sultan. In order to save his neck and regain his throne, Dracul swore fidelity to Mehmed II and left both Vlad and Radu as hostages.

Vlad remained a Turkish captive until 1448; Radu stayed on and became the ally of Mehmed II and, because of his weaker nature, submitted more easily to the refined indoctrination technique of his jailers.

Vlad's reaction to these dangerous years was quite the reverse. From the moment of his imprisonment in Turkey, Vlad held human nature in low esteem. Life was cheap – after all his own life was in danger, should his father prove disloyal to the Sultan – and morality was not essential in matters of state. He needed no Machiavelli to instruct him in the amorality of politics.

The Turks taught Vlad their language as well as acquainting him with the pleasures of the harem – the terms of confinement were not too strict. He also developed a reputation for trickery, cunning, insubordination and brutality, and inspired terror in his own guards. He became fascinated by impalement and its use as a deterrent in psychological warfare. He was also introduced to gunpowder and its use in cannons for warfare, and would become one of the first leaders to use gunpowder in combat.

He developed two other personality traits: he was suspicious – never again would he trust himself to the Turks or any man – and he discovered a taste for revenge. Vlad would not forgive, or forget, those who crossed him.

In December 1447, Dracul died, a victim of his own plotting. His murder was organized by John Hunyadi, the leader of the Hungarians, who had become angered by Dracul's alliance with the Turks. Dracul's eldest son, Mircea, was blinded with red-hot iron stakes and buried alive by his political enemies in Tirgoviste. Dracul's assassination took place in the marshes of Balteni, near an ancient monastery. These killings, not suprisingly, had a profound effect on Vlad, and he swore to get his revenge.

Since Dracul and Mircea were dead, and Vlad and Radu were in Turkey, Hunyadi was able to put a member of the Danesti clan, Vladislav II, on the Wallachian throne. But the Turks didn't like having a Hungarian puppet in charge of Wallachia, so in 1448 they freed Vlad, whom they believed had finally been subdued. Supported by a force of Turkish cavalry and a contingent of troops lent to him by Pasha Mustafa Hassan, Vlad made his first move towards seizing the Wallachian throne. He was seventeen years of age.

The bold coup succeeded for nearly two months, and then Hunyadi forced Vlad once more into exile and reinstated Vladislav II. Vlad, fearful of his father's assassins and equally reluctant to return to his Turkish captors, fled to Moldavia, the northernmost

Vlad Tepes Dracula, Prince of Wallachia, from a portrait of him painted when he was twenty-five. A violent warlord, he became an expert in devising new methods of torture and execution, one of which would earn him his nickname 'Vlad the Impaler'. Like many exceptionally cruel men, he was also deeply religious, embracing piety as a means of salving his conscience.
(© HULTON ARCHIVE)

Romanian principality, where his cousin and friend, Prince Stephen, was heir to the throne.

Vlad stayed in Moldavia until October 1451, then reappeared in Transylvania and threw himself on Hunyadi's mercy – he was taking a chance, but his timing was perfect. Vladislav II had recently changed sides and declared his allegiance to the Turks, and Hunyadi had begun to regret having put him on the throne and was looking around for a replacement. Vlad became the official claimant to the Wallachian throne and Hunyadi introduced his protégé to the court of the Hapsburg King in Hungary. Vlad took part in many of Hunyadi's campaigns against the Turks – he could have had no finer instruction in anti-Turkish strategy.

In 1456 Halley's Comet appeared in the sky – 'as long as half the sky with two tails, one pointing west, the other east, coloured gold and looking like an undulated flame'. In the fifteenth century, superstitious people looked upon the comet as a warning of natural catastrophes, plagues or threat of invasion. They were right. In the same year Vlad killed Vladislav II and regained the throne. Now Prince Vlad II Dracula began his infamous and bloody reign.

At twenty-five-years old, he was the very picture of a prince, dressed in a rich sable coat with gold brocade, topped off with a flamboyant red silk hat laced with pearls. His face was sallow, with large green, penetrating eyes, surrounded by deep, dark shadows – his bushy black eyebrows made his eyes appear even more threatening. Vlad boasted a fashionable moustache, which he meticulously twisted at the ends. He was not tall, but very stocky and strong. His nostrils were flared and he had a strong, aquiline nose. His appearance was cold, distant and unmistakably powerful.

Vlad's immediate priority was to consolidate his position in Wallachia. He was determined to defend his country against foreign invasion, in addition to which he wanted to break the political power of the boyars who tended to support puppet (and often weak) leaders who would protect their interests. Such a policy, Vlad decided, worked against the development of a strong nation state. Vlad was also faced with the continuous threat from rival claimants to the throne and so, once in power, he rebuilt his fortresses' security by constructing thick battlements, watchtowers and underground tunnels and, after his plans to prevent a foreign attack were completed, he turned to ensuring the loyalty of his subjects. Vlad began by employing a technique the Turks had taught him as a young man – impalement. In his hands, impalement became an art-form, the special knowledge and particular skill it took to carry out a successful impalement appealing to Vlad's meticulous nature. Vlad usually had a horse attached to each of the victim's legs, and a sharpened stake of between six and eight-foot in height and about six-inches wide, was gradually forced up vertically through the body. The end of the stake was usually oiled and care was taken that the stake was not too sharp, or else the victim might die too rapidly from shock. The stake normally started at the buttocks and was worked out through the mouth, but sometimes it was just stabbed through the victim's chest or stomach. Sometimes people were hung upside down, and babies were impaled on the stakes that killed their

The grimly imposing fourteenth-century Bran Castle, Prince Vlad's home, seen in a photograph taken in 1923. It is not difficult to see why both the man and the castle were to provide inspiration for Bram Stoker's novel Dracula, *out of which has sprung what amounts to an entire vampire industry since its first publication in 1897. (© E. O. HOPPÉ/CORBIS)*

mothers. The stake was then turned upright and planted in the ground – the longer the stake, the more important the victim. One nobleman, who wrinkled his nose as he dined with Vlad in a courtyard of cadavers, was given an extra long stake to put him above the stench of those impaled around him. The stakes were also often elaborately carved and painted, and Vlad displayed the impaled bodies on the outskirts of the city as a warning to foreigners to stay away. As it would sometimes take days for the victims to die, the pungent smell of death was always in the air.

Vlad also enjoyed experimenting with other forms of torture. He had a large pot made with boards fastened over it – people's heads were put through the holes and trapped there. Then he had the pot filled with water and a large fire made underneath. He relished the screams of agony as his victims were boiled alive.

In the year 1460, on the morning of St Bartholomew's Day, Vlad came through a forest to the village of Amlas where the residents were suspected of supporting a rival. He had all the Wallachians, of both sexes, tracked down and cut to ribbons with swords, sabres and knives – it is rumoured that over 30,000 lost their lives. The chaplain and influential people of the village were taken back to his capital and impaled. He then burnt the town out of existence.

Vlad was also determined to break the economic hold that the Saxon merchants of southern Transylvania had on trade in the country. Not only were these merchants ignoring custom duty, they were also supporting rival claimants to the throne and so, when local merchants in Brasov refused to pay Vlad's taxes, in spite of repeated warnings, Vlad led an assault on the town. He burnt an entire suburb and impaled numerous captives on Timpa Hill. Brasov has the distinction of having witnessed on its surrounding hills more stakes bearing Vlad's victims rotting in the sun, or chewed and mangled by Carpathian vultures than any other place in the principality. The scene has been immortalized on a particularly gruesome woodcut printed in Nuremberg around 1499. It depicts Vlad eating a meal, while impaled victims are dying around him. As he dines, his henchmen are hacking off limbs of other victims right next to his table. Similar woodcuts appeared throughout Europe; in fact, some of the earliest secular texts to roll off the recently invented printing press, were about Vlad the Impaler's activities. Most are tales of horror with some sort of moral for the reader. Though distortion is unquestionable, their amazing accuracy of historical, geographical and topographical detail leads scholars to accept many of them as accurate.

Tirgoviste, Wallachia's capital, was not just a seat of power, but also the nation's centre of social and cultural life. The royal palace was ostentatious and surrounded by the Byzantine-style houses of the boyars, where the upper class attempted to ape the etiquette of the imperial court of Constantinople. Suspicion reigned in the capital; anarchy was rampant; political assassination was frequent and the rapid succession of princes was the rule rather than the exception. Having perfected his preferred instrument of torture, Vlad's first major act of revenge was now aimed at the nobles of Tirgoviste, whom he held responsible for the deaths of his father and brother, Mircea. In the spring of 1457, he invited the rich landowners and their families, along with the five bishops, the abbots of the more important foreign and native monasteries, and the archbishop, to an Easter banquet at the palace.

As Vlad surveyed the wily, dishonest expressions of the boyars, he asked them how many reigns they had lived through – even the young men admitted to having been through at least seven. The princely title and all that it implied had evidently been taken lightly. Vlad began shouting furiously, blaming the instability of the Wallachian throne on their disloyalty and plotting. Then, his eyes flashing in a way that was to become characteristic, the order was given. Within minutes, his faithful attendants surrounded the hall. Some 500 boyars, their wives and attendants were immediately impaled in the vicinity of the palace and left exposed until the birds devoured their corpses. The lesson was not lost on the remaining boyars – Vlad was demanding their total submission or exile to their estates. Woe to him who chose to disobey.

Prince Vlad also seized his victims' property and passed it out to his supporters. He was creating a new nobility, loyal only to him.

He now became increasingly concerned that all his subjects work and contribute to the common welfare. He noticed that the vagrants, beggars and cripples had become extremely numerous. He issued an invitation to all the poor and sick in Wallachia to come to Tirgoviste for a great feast, claiming that no one should go hungry in his land. As the poor and crippled arrived, they were ushered into a great hall where a fabulous feast was prepared for them.

The prince's guests ate and drank late into the night, when Vlad himself made an appearance. 'What else do you desire? Do you want to be without cares, lacking nothing in this world?' asked the Prince. When they responded positively, Vlad ordered that the hall be boarded up and set on fire. None escaped the flames. Vlad justified his actions by claiming that it was necessary so that 'they represented no further burden to others.'

Vlad now instigated a strict moral code. Thieves, liars, adulterers and even children were impaled. He killed merchants who cheated their customers, and women who had affairs. A visiting merchant once left his money outside all night, thinking that it would be safe because of Vlad's draconian policies. To his surprise, some of the coins were stolen. He complained to Vlad, who promptly issued a proclamation that the money must be returned or the city would be destroyed. That night, Vlad secretly had the missing money, plus one extra coin, returned to the merchant. The next morning the merchant found the money and counted it. He told Vlad the money had been returned, and mentioned the extra coin. Vlad replied that the thief had been caught and would be impaled, adding that if the merchant hadn't mentioned the extra coin, he would have been impaled too.

Fear of Vlad's wrath ensured that crime was kept to a minimum and, as a sign of his absolute power, he had a gold cup placed in a public square. Anyone was allowed to drink from it, but no one was allowed to move it. The cup remained in the square throughout his reign.

Vlad also liked to make the punishment fit the crime. When Turkish emissaries from the Sultan refused to remove their turbans in his presence, Vlad saw this as an act of rudeness and ordered his guards to seize them, then returned the insult by nailing their hats to their heads.

Just as Vlad reacted violently to insult, he responded very well to flattery. Once a messenger was sent to Vlad from King Matthias of Hungary. It is unknown what news the messenger brought, but it angered Vlad intensely. Vlad invited the messenger to eat dinner with him personally. Before the meal, he asked him if he knew why he had invited him to dinner. The messenger, seeing two soldiers standing behind the Prince, and knowing Vlad's reputation, presumed it meant his imminent death. Thinking quickly, he replied, 'I do not know, but I know you are a wise and great ruler, and no matter what you command, even if you were to command my death, it should be done.' Vlad motioned the soldiers away and told the messenger that his answer had saved his life.

But there were two sides to Vlad's personality. One was the torturer and inquisitor, who used terror deliberately as an instrument of policy; the other was a deeply religious man who had turned to piety to ease his conscience. He took the precaution of surrounding himself with priests, abbots, bishops and confessors, whether Roman Catholic or Orthodox. He meditated within the saintly confines of monasteries, such as Tismana. He was intent on belonging to a church, receiving the sacraments, being buried as a Christian, and being identified with a religion.

Vlad felt that good works, particularly the erection of monasteries, along with rich endowments and an appropriate ritual at the moment of death, would contribute to the eradication of sin. His family had been responsible for building over forty monasteries, and Vlad built five more. Like the good medieval pietist that he was, Vlad was most concerned with the survival of the soul in the afterlife. He had particular qualms concerning those victims for whose death he was personally responsible and gave them Christian burials.

Of Vlad's romantic life virtually nothing is known. His first wife or mistress – it matters little, since all males were considered legitimate claimants to the throne – was a Transylvanian commoner, with whom he had fallen in love in 1448. The marriage was apparently unhappy. Loving Vlad could be a dangerous thing. When a mistress was caught being unfaithful, she was impaled and had her sexual organs cut out. His last wife threw herself from the battlements of Poenari Castle to avoid being captured by the Turks.

The Balkan states were torn apart by dissent – the absence of unity helped the Turkish cause and had contributed to the fall of Constantinople in 1453, three years before Vlad's second accession to the Wallachian throne.

Following the fall of Constantinople, Pope Pius II in 1458 asked Christians to take up the cross and fight the Turks. Vlad was the only one who responded immediately to the Papal plea and his courageous action was rewarded favourably – his cruel tactics may have revolted people, but they praised his willingness to fight for Christianity.

Vlad had only paid his tribute to the Turks for the first three years of his reign. He then further violated his obligation, and failed to appear before the Sultan. The Turks responded by asking for a child tribute – 500 young boys to be handed over for their armies. Turkish recruiting officers had occasionally swept down into Wallachia to obtain good, young men. Vlad resisted such incursions with a force of arms, and any Turk caught would be impaled.

Such violations of territory by both sides only further embittered Turkish-Wallachian relations. Raiding, pillaging and looting were endemic from Giugiu to the Black Sea, and the Sultan had succeeded in securing control of various fortresses and townships on the Romanian side of the Danube. To further complicate matters, Radu the Handsome, Vlad's brother, who had faithfully resided at Constantinople since 1447, was encouraged by the Turks to consider himself as a candidate to the Wallachian throne.

Sultan Mehmed II asked Vlad to meet with his representative, Isaac Pasha, but remembering how his father had been tricked, Vlad refused to go – he was also aware that, if he left the country, his enemies would seize power in his absence. There was no basis for negotiations, and so the Turks laid a plan to ambush Vlad. Knowing that he would never come to Constantinople, their orders were to capture him dead or alive. But Vlad out-foxed his opponents. He captured the Turkish envoy, and tricked the Turks into opening the gates of the city of Giurgiu and, once inside, set the city on fire. Vlad then launched a series of hostilities without actually declaring war. He kept notes on the numbers of deaths. 'I have killed men and women, old and young, who lived at Oblucitza and Novoselo. We killed 23,884 Turks and Bulgars without counting those whom we burned in homes or whose heads were not cut by our soldiers. I have broken peace with the Sultan.'

The campaign ended on the shores of the Black Sea, within sight of the powerful Turkish invasion force that had crossed the Bosphorus, on giant barges, for a full-scale invasion of Wallachia. With his flank unprotected, Vlad was compelled to abandon the offensive.

Meanwhile, throughout central and western Europe, church bells tolled from Genoa to Paris in gratitude for Vlad's endowing the crusade with a new lease of life, and taking over the leadership of the great Hunyadi. His bold offensive had given new hopes of liberation to the enslaved people of Bulgaria, Serbia and Greece. At Constantinople, there was an atmosphere of consternation, gloom and fear as some of the Turkish leaders, fearing the Impaler, contemplated flight to Asia Minor.

Mehmed decided to launch an invasion during the spring of 1462 – Vlad had given him no alternative. To defy the Sultan by avoiding an assassination plot was one thing, but to instil hopes of freedom amongst his Christian subjects was quite another. Mehmed was determined to reduce Wallachia to a Turkish province, and amassed the largest Turkish force since the invasion of Constantinople.

Vlad only had 30,900 men and so abandoned his position on the Danube and began his withdrawal northward. The idea was to draw the enemy force deep into his own territory. According to Romanian tradition, the forest and the mountains were brothers of the people that had ensured the survival of Wallachia through the ages.

As the Wallachian troops gave up their native soil, Vlad used scorched-earth tactics, creating a vast desert in the path of the invading army. His men set fire to the cities, reducing them to ghost towns, and depopulated the entire area. Boyars, peasants and townspeople all accompanied the retreating armies, unless they could find refuge in the mountains, where the wealthy sought safety. Vlad ordered the crops to be burnt, poisoned the wells, and destroyed the cattle and all other domestic animals that could not be herded away into the mountains. He ordered huge pits to be dug and covered them with timber and leaves to trap Turkish men, horses and camels. He even ordered the construction of small dams to divert the waters of small rivers to create marshes, thus impeding the progress of the Turkish cannons by miring them down.

In this parched plain, the lips of the fighters for Islam dried up. They used their shields to roast meat. The summer of 1462 was one of the hottest on record. But Vlad knew that to be really effective he would have to kill the Sultan and he started to plan.

One evening, Mehmed had retired after a heavy meal, when suddenly came the hooting of an owl, Vlad's signal to attack. Initially, the Turkish army was terrified, but they rallied and surrounded the Sultan's tent. Vlad killed several thousand Turks, wounded countless more, created havoc, chaos and terror, but he lost several hundred of his bravest warriors, and the attack failed. Sultan Mehmed survived, and the road to Tirgoviste lay open.

When the Turks finally entered the city, they found it denuded, with no cattle, men, food or drink. The gates had been left open and the city was enveloped by a thick blanket of smoke. Mehmed decided to continue his hunt for the elusive Impaler.

Just a few miles to the north, the Sultan caught sight of an even more desolate spectacle: in a narrow gorge, one mile long, he found a forest of impaled cadavers, perhaps 20,000 in all. The Sultan caught sight of the mangled, rotting remains of men, women and children – the flesh being eaten by birds that nestled in the skulls and rib cages. Mehmed found corpses of Turkish warriors caught during the previous winter, and on a higher pike were the bodies of the two assassins who had tried to ensnare Vlad before the war had begun.

Mehmed gave orders for the retreat and started eastward where the fleet was anchored, but, before leaving, he formally appointed Radu as commander-in-chief, and entrusted him with the mission of destroying Vlad and becoming King. A Turkish contingent would remain to support Radu, but the new commander was to rely principally on native support. The boyars, realizing that the Turks were stronger, now abandoned Vlad. Radu pursued his brother all the way to his fortress in Poenari.

When the Turks eventually seized the castle, Vlad was forced to escape through a secret tunnel. Now, another tragedy befell him. The servant carrying Vlad's infant son dropped him. The pursuing Turks were too close to risk turning back to look for the child, so they were forced to leave him behind. In one day, Vlad had lost both his home and his family. Vlad and his servants escaped through the forest on horseback.

Seeking help near Brasov, Vlad now went to King Matthias of Hungary, but his evil deeds had finally caught up with him. Brasov contained a large number of the German merchants that Vlad had been terrorizing for the past few years. They had got to the Hungarian court first, and told Matthias that Vlad was an ally of the Turks and that he was coming to the King as a spy. When Vlad arrived, he was immediately thrown into prison.

However, Matthias was in a difficult situation. Vlad's standing in much of Europe was very high at the time and Matthias had to come up with a reason for capturing Vlad. A series of letters were forged, which claimed that Vlad had subjugated himself entirely to the Sultan's wishes. The authors of these forgeries may well have been the same German Saxons who had written the tales of horror. It was one of the first effective demonstrations of the use of propaganda.

Matthias now had a valid pretext for giving up the campaign and breaking his alliance with Vlad, enabling him to keep the Papal subsidies for his own political ambitions. Matthias signed a secret agreement with Sultan Mehmed and recognized Radu as Prince of Wallachia. Without the formality of a trial, Vlad now had to undergo a lengthy period of imprisonment, but luck was on his side in the shape of

Iona, King Matthias's sister, whose eye Vlad had caught, and she used her influence with her brother to have Vlad freed. Subsequently, Iona and Vlad were married and, after four years, Vlad was partially pardoned, although he was required to stay within the city, where he was given a large home. With no subjects to torture, he turned to impaling rats and birds for fun.

Vlad spent the next twelve years plotting his return to the throne, and gaining the trust of his jailer, King Matthias. Vlad's marriage into the King's family re-established the status quo. Vlad was given the title of Captain, and the King prepared him for a crusade against the Turks.

The Turks had not stayed long in Wallachia. The impaled heads of several of their spies had greeted them, and Vlad had burned the city of Tirgoviste. After only a few days, the Black Plague broke out among the Turkish soldiers, and they were forced to retreat, leaving Radu behind. Vlad watched and waited, while Radu ruled Wallachia as a puppet of the Turks. Finally, in 1473, Radu was defeated. His successor was Basarab III, who was deemed totally unsuitable by the Hungarians.

In 1475, a formal treaty was signed between Hungaria, Moldavia and Vlad, and Vlad seized the throne for the third and final time. But he had many enemies, and when his allies left Wallachia, he was extremely vulnerable. His failure to bring his wife and sons with him to Wallachia suggests that he was well aware of the danger. Now the only people he could trust was a small band of 200 soldiers.

In late December 1476, near the monastery of Snagov in the Vlasia forest near Bucharest, Vlad and his force were out killing the Turks. Out of sheer joy, Vlad ascended a hill, in order to see his men massacring the Sultan's troops. Detached from his army, Vlad was struck by a lance. He defended himself formidably, killing five of his assassins, but to no avail. Finally, he was killed and his severed head was sent to Constantinople, where it was impaled on a high stake for the population to witness that the great Impaler had himself been impaled.

After Vlad's death, his wife was left with his three sons. His eldest, Mihnea, from Vlad's union with a Transylvanian noblewoman, finally succeeded to the Wallachian throne. During his brief one-year rule in 1508, he showed signs that he could be as atrocious as his infamous father. Nicknamed Mihnea the Bad, he is reputed to have cut off the noses and lips of his political enemies. He was assassinated in 1510, on the steps of a church in Sibiu.

Vlad spent more years in prison than he did on the throne, and most of his experiences seemed to reinforce one fact: life was insecure – and cheap. His father was assassinated; his brother was buried alive; other relatives were killed or tortured; his first wife killed herself; subjects conspired against him; his cousin, a sworn friend, betrayed him; Hungarians, Turks and Germans pursued him. When reviewing Vlad's life in the light of his imprisonment and the chaos of his early years, it becomes all too clear that horror begets horror.

FRANCISCO PIZARRO

CONQUEROR OF THE INCAS

'He [Atahualpa] one day told Pizarro that, if he would set him free, he would cover the floor of the apartment in which they stood with gold. Those present listened with an incredulous smile; and, as the Inca received no answer, he said with some emphasis that "he would not merely cover the floor, but would fill the room with gold as high as he could reach".'
WILLIAM H. PRESCOTT, *History of the Conquest of Peru, with a preliminary view of the Civilization of the Incas* (1847)

Francisco Pizarro, a peasant from Spain, was one of the least well-equipped conquerors in history. However, in the name of Christ, he destroyed the powerful Empire of the Incas and bestowed on Spain the richest of possessions. Pizarro also established the city of Lima in Peru thus opening the way for Spanish culture to dominate South America.

In 1493, in order to prevent a war between Spain and Portugal over discoveries in the New World, Pope Alexander VI divided the, as yet unknown, territory into two parts. Using an imaginary 'line of demarcation', the land to the east of the line, which ran north to south several hundred miles west of the Azores and Cape Verdes, now belonged to Portugal, while the land to the west was given to Spain. Almost forty years later Francisco Pizarro set out for Peru to secure the pagan Kingdom of the Incas for Charles V of Spain and the Catholic Church.

Pizarro was born circa 1476, the illegitimate son of Gonzola Pizarro and Francisca González. His father was a Captain in the Spanish military who had fought in the Neapolitan wars. There is little reliable evidence about Pizarro's early life. He is supposed to have been abandoned on the steps of the church of Santa Maria in Trujillo and, there is even a story that he was suckled by a cow. As a youth, Pizarro worked at herding pigs and had no education other than that of a hard upbringing. It is probable that he remained illiterate throughout his life.

Francisco came from Estremadura, a region in Spain that produced an extraordinarily large number of men who went off to the New World to seek their fortunes and to glorify Spain. The conquistadors' lust for gold was infinite and their religious fervour genuine. Hernán Cortéz, the conqueror of the Aztecs, had been born in a nearby town, almost ten years after Pizarro. The wide, infinite skies of Estremadura inspired them with a desire to travel and, combined with the poverty of the land and the news of fabulous discoveries on distant shores, the lure was irresistible.

In 1509, Pizarro joined the ill-fated Hojeda expedition that set off with the intention of colonizing the Panama Isthmus. It was to be a gruelling time for the inexperienced Pizarro. Left behind in charge of the new settlement of San Sebastian, Pizarro had to endure near starvation, disease and poisoned arrows from hostile natives, before the settlement had become so reduced in size that he had no choice but to flee. Using two tiny brigantine ships, Pizarro managed to cram the sixty surviving men on board. When one sank immediately he could do nothing but leave the men to their fate and sail away to Cartagena. Hojeda fared even worse. After losing his navigator, Juan de la Cosa, to poisoned arrows, Hojeda was forced to beach his ship and walk more than 400 miles through jungle and swamps to reach the newly-founded settlement of Santo Domingo. Of the 1,250 men who left Spain on the expedition, only 200 survived and Hojeda died penniless.

But luck was on Pizarro's side. Upon arrival in Cartagena, he ran into Encisco, a business associate of Hojeda's who had arrived with a relief force of 150 men. They set sail towards Uraba, but Enciso managed to lose his ship on a sandbank. Control of the expedition would have passed to Pizarro, but the emergence of the adventurer, Vasco Núñez de Balboa, denied him this opportunity.

Pizarro joined Balboa on an expedition across Panama's infested jungles, and on 29 September 1513 they waded into the waters of the Pacific. It had been the first successful crossing of the Isthmus and was an incredible achievement. On the edges of the Mar del Sur, Pizarro first heard stories of a fabulous golden land to the south and saw pictures of strange new creatures.

The news that Balboa had discovered a new ocean created a sensation in Spain, and gave new hope that a route through to the wealthy

An engraving of Francisco Pizarro, Conqueror of Peru, in full armour. He destroyed the powerful Inca Empire and immeasurably enriched Spain; like many who live by the sword, however, he was himself to die by it. (© BETTMANN/CORBIS)

Spice Islands would soon be found. But the arrival of a new Governor in Panama, Pedrarias Dávila, soon dashed Balboa's dreams of pure exploration. Pedrarias, who had been appointed Governor due to his court connections, and Balboa hated each other on sight; the small town would not be big enough to hold them both. Within a few months, Pedrarias had Balboa arrested on charges of conspiracy. Pizarro, who arrested him, had finally got his revenge for being overlooked as the leader of the Uraba expedition. Balboa was executed.

Pizarro, a true opportunist, now quickly transferred his loyalty to Pedrarias who sent him to trade with the natives along the Pacific coast. When the capital was transferred to Panama he helped Pedrarias to subjugate the warlike tribes of Veraguas, and in 1520 he accompanied Espinosa on his expedition into the territory of Cacique Urraca, situated in the present Republic of Costa Rica.

By the age of forty-five Francisco Pizarro had little to show for his numerous expeditions. His sole assets were some bad land and a collection of Indians. Accounts of the achievements of Hernán Cortéz, and the return of Pascuel de Andagoya from his expedition to the southern part of Panama, fired Pizarro with enthusiasm.

All the expeditions, prior to that of Andagoya, had been to the north up as far as Honduras. Few of the newly-arrived adventurers were sailors, and the land to the north and west offered safer prospects than the unknown perils of the great South Sea that stretched in unlimited vastness beyond the horizon. Weather conditions made the south a more difficult destination, and the Humbolt current in the Pacific Ocean ensured that the Spanish mariners were faced with calms, tropical storms and violent seas. With no sailing directions, the Spanish learnt by trial and error, and bitter experience.

In Panama, Pizarro formed a partnership with Diego de Almagro, a soldier of fortune, and Hernando de Luque, a Spanish cleric. Their plans were to form a company to conquer the lands to the south of Panama. Their project seemed so utterly unattainable that the people of Panama called them the 'company of lunatics'. But Pizarro had spent thirteen years in the Indies and he knew that the biggest prizes went to the boldest and to those who got there first. Luque, a schoolmaster and treasurer of the company's funds, provided the financial backing and with the consent of the governor they began fitting out two small boats for a voyage of discovery.

Pizarro embarked on 14 November 1524, accompanied by 112 Spaniards, a few horses, and a few Indian servants. He sailed his ship into the Bira River and then decided to continue overland. The going was treacherous, among swamps fringed with dense jungle and vast hills. Finally, Pizarro decided that travel by sea was the lesser of two evils and they returned to the ship. Once on board they were hit by calms, and the food and water began to run out. Faced with an increasingly hostile crew, Pizarro made the decision to allow those who wished to return to leave for Panama under the auspices of one of his captains, Montenegro.

It was over six weeks before Montenegro returned with provisions. In the meantime Pizarro and his men had been marooned in the swamps of Puerto de la Hambre (Port of Famine), where they had been reduced to eating shellfish and seaweed on the shore and whatever sustenance they could gain from the fetid land. But all was not lost. Pizarro had managed to make contact with the natives and listened to stories of a powerful kingdom to the south. He also had his first look at some gold ornaments and his appetite was whetted.

They headed south again, hugging the coast, determined to push their luck to the very edge of disaster, but all they found were deserted villages, a little maize and more crude gold objects. In desperation, Pizarro marched inland, but was attacked by Indians in the foothills of the Cordilleras Mountains. It was a bloody engagement and Pizarro was wounded, however the Indians were finally repulsed.

Pizarro and his crew had travelled only as far as Punta Quemada, on the coast of modern-day Columbia. Once back on board, they fled back to the Pearl Island archipelago in Panama. They finally met up with Almagro's ship at Chicama, and Pizarro discovered that Almagro had only made it a little further up the coast before being forced to return. However, the adventurers were not going to give up so easily. Almagro and Luque returned to Panama to meet with the governor. Pizarro, who hated bureaucracy, was extremely conscious of his lack of education and sent his treasurer, Nicholas de Rivera, to get money and supplies for a new expedition.

A second request to Pedrarias for permission to recruit volunteers for a new expedition was met with hostility. Their first voyage had lost money and Pedrarias was already organizing an expedition to Nicaragua. But luck was with them again and with the arrival of a new Governor, Don Pedro de los Rios, and the persuasions of Luque, the necessary funds were raised. Pizarro and Almagro were made joint leaders of the new expedition and on 10 March 1526, a contract was signed between Pizarro, Almagro and Luque. They agreed to split all conquered territory and any gold, silver and precious stones three ways, less the one-fifth required by Charles V, King of Spain.

They purchased two ships and Pizarro and Almagro directed their course to the mouth of the San Juan River. Pizarro set off with a group of soldiers to explore the mainland, capturing some Indians and collecting gold. Upon his return the two ships separated; Almagro went back to Panama to get re-enlistments and sell the gold; and the other ship, under the command of Ruiz, set sail for the south. Ruiz got as far as Punta de Pasados, half a degree south of the equator, and after making observations and collecting information, returned to Pizarro. Pizarro had ventured inland once more, but to no avail. All they had found was impenetrable rainforest and deep ravines, and had struggled back to the coast, near to starvation, to await the return of his partners. After seventy days, Ruiz returned with just the news they had been waiting for. He was full of tales of an increasingly populated, and friendly land, overflowing with riches. More importantly, he had two Peruvians on board to verify the stories.

Shortly after, Almagro returned from Panama with eighty newly arrived recruits from Spain. With full bellies and more men, the two ships sailed on to Quito, the edge of the mighty Inca Empire. Set upon by hostile natives, the adventurers had no option but to retreat. After a bitter row, Pizarro agreed to remain behind whilst Almagro returned to Panama to sell the gold they had found, and drum up more reinforcements.

Pizarro camped on the island of Gallo, a barren, flat place. Living an unhappy existence on the desolate island, it was not long before Pizarro's men became mutinous. When Almagro's ship departed they sent a note, concealed in a bale of cotton, implying that Pizarro was holding them against their will. When the note came to the governor's attention, any chance that Almagro had of maintaining the governor's support ended, and two ships were dispatched to bring Pizarro back.

When the ships reached Gallo they found the men in a state of near-starvation. Those that were left had been drenched by tropical rains, their clothes were in rags and their bodies, having been scorched by the sun, were covered in sores. Almagro and Luque had sent letters imploring Pizarro not to return nor give up all they had worked for and so Pizarro, in true conquistador fashion, decided to stay and ignore the governor's command. Drawing a line in the sand he summoned the remaining men saying, 'Gentlemen, this line represents toil, hunger, thirst, weariness, sickness and all other vicissitudes that our undertaking will involve. There lies Peru with all its riches; here, Panama and its poverty. Choose each man, what best becomes a brave Castilian. For my part I go to the South.' Then he stepped over the line – thirteen chose to remain with him, one of whom was his navigator, Ruiz.

The forlorn, abandoned men stood and watched as the two ships set sail for Panama and disappeared over the horizon. All was not lost, however, as Almago and Luque were able to persuade the governor to give them and Pizarro another chance. Reluctantly the governor agreed to back them and one ship, with no soldiers, was provided, with the stipulation that they had six months before they had to return. It had taken months to obtain consent from the governor, but Pizarro had learnt from previous experience and during this time had organized the building of rafts and relocated to the island of Gorgona, seventy-five miles up the coast. This beautiful island was stocked with fresh water and virgin forests, and by the time the governor's ship found them Pizarro and his followers were in good spirits.

Leaving Gorgona behind the ship now sailed south, crossed the equator, and arrived in the Bay of Tumbes. On the land they could see towers and temples rising above the green fields. They had arrived in the Empire of the Incas.

The following morning a fleet of rafts with Inca warriors came out to investigate the mysterious new arrivals. Pizarro invited them on board and asked his two Peruvian crew members to show them around. One of the Inca soldiers was a member of the government and he invited Pizarro to visit the city. He returned from the city with tales of a temple tapestried with plates of gold and silver, and information on the city's defences. With only a small number of men, Pizarro was unable to take what he wanted, but vowed to return later on.

For now, however, it was time to turn back, time to raise an army, to shed the cloak of discoverer, and assume the armour of conqueror. Pizarro had discovered Peru; the next thing he intended to do was to take it.

Tales of the Sun God King would be enough to set Panama ablaze with

The execution of the 'Sun God', Atahualpa, last Inca ruler of Peru, in 1533. Pizarro had captured Atahualpa by treachery, and had then received an enormous ransom in gold; nevertheless, he had the Inca put to death, having first had him convicted of a series of trumped-up charges after a farcical 'trial'. This engraving, based on a rather fanciful nineteenth-century painting, does at least capture the hypocrisy behind the conquistadors' religiosity. (© BETTMANN/CORBIS)

excitement, or so Pizarro believed. On his return, after eighteen months away, Pizarro was fêted; everyone marvelled at his achievements, but the full-scale expedition that he was proposing was deemed beyond the colony's capacity. The governor was not a conquistador so Luque proposed that they petition the Crown of Spain direct and Pizarro, full of his new-found confidence, left for Spain.

Immediately Pizarro arrived, he was jailed as punishment for an old debt, but fortunately, tales of his exploits had reached the court, and hungry for more money from the New World, Pizarro was released. He was brought to Toledo to meet with Charles V, and after securing the King's blessing Pizarro now had to deal with the Council of the Indies – a bureaucratic machine that had grown fat on the exploits of others.

Finally, on 26 July 1529, Queen Joanna The Mad agreed to Pizarro's terms. He was made Governor, Captain-General for life and granted a large salary. Luque was made Bishop of Tumbes as well as 'Protector' of all the natives in Peru, and Ruiz became Grand Pilot of the Southern Ocean with a salary to match. Almagro got virtually nothing; Pizarro had betrayed him on the premise that Almagro had not been present on the voyage of discovery.

But Pizarro's troubles were far from over. Although the crown had granted him a title they expected the expedition to be self-financing and money still had to be found. Spain might reap the rewards, but they were not prepared to take a risk financially. Elated by his success, however, Pizarro returned to his home in Trujillo to get more men. His brothers Gonzalo, Juan and Hernando joined him on the adventure. Hernando, a terribly cruel man, was to become Pizarro's right-hand man. It took a further six months to raise the money and fit out the ships. Finally they left for Panama in January 1531 and sailed to Nombre De Dios to meet with Almagro. On arrival Pizarro clashed with Almagro immediately, not helped by Hernando who was openly scornful of the old man. Eventually peace was restored, but from the start the three chief personalities were at odds.

With extraordinary arrogance and pride, the fifty-five-year-old Pizarro was now embarking on his voyage of conquest. He had three vessels, two large and one small, 180 men, 27 horses, arms, ammunition and stores. With these supplies he intended to conquer an empire that stretched 2,000 miles south from Cabo Blanco, included one of the world's greatest mountain chains and extended inland to the rainforests of the Amazon.

Initially the forces of nature halted the invaders in San Mateo Bay, 350 miles away from Tumbes. Pizarro then decided to put his men on shore and march them south. His men looted and sacked a small, undefended town. It was the height of stupidity, because for just a small immediate financial gain, Pizarro had lost not only any hope of achieving surprise, but also the goodwill of the natives. Incarcerated in their quilted cotton clothing and heavy armour, his men became victims of the tortuous heat, and many died. It was the most senseless start to a campaign that any general could have conceived.

Eventually they arrived at the island of Puna, having been joined by two more ships carrying the Royal Treasurer and administration officials. Pizarro then started a war between the Puna and the Tumbes (the Puna's mortal enemies), and the Spanish were forced to seek refuge in the forest. Evacuation became a necessity and with the arrival of more volunteers and horses, Pizarro decided to return to Tumbes on the mainland. But Tumbes was now almost a shell. Initially furious and disheartened, Pizarro ranted and raved. But his phenomenal luck had not deserted him. Unbeknown to the Spanish they had chosen the ideal time for an invasion of Peru. The Inca Empire was in the middle of a bloody civil war.

The empire had been in existence since 1250 when the first Inca, Mando Copa, had made Cuzco his capital and begun expanding his empire. By 1493, just thirty years before Pizarro's arrival, they had conquered the whole of Peru, parts of Bolivia and Equador and most of Chile – an area of about 380,000 square miles. The Inca armies contained a total of 300,000 troops.

Huayna Capac, the Sun God, had died in 1524 and faced with ill omens and a vast area to control, he decided to split the Empire between his two sons, Huascar and Atahulpa. Atahulpa was given control of the north, while Huascar was given the area centred round Cuzco. The year of Huayna Capac's death was the year that Pizarro had first landed in Tumbes. Five years after Huayna's death Atahulpa marched against his brother. In a ruthless and bloody campaign Atahulpa had laid waste to entire provinces, and in the final battle near Cuzco he captured Huascar.

Pizarro knew that now he had the chance to go for the total conquest of the vast Inca nation. With this knowledge his whole attitude changed. He set off into the interior with a small force to win over the local population and to turn his men into a disciplined fighting machine. Any Indian chiefs who opposed him were burnt and soon the whole region was pacified.

Pizarro now had 110 foot soldiers and 67 horse troops, of which only 20 were armed. Should he march now or wait for reinforcements? He pondered his dilemma, well aware that Atahulpa had in excess of 40,000 warriors at his command. Finally in September, Pizarro marched. By mid-November his tiny force was descending the Andes into Cajamarca where Atahulpa, waiting with his tented army by the hot springs, meditated on his course of action.

Atahulpa had been aware of the Spanish progress right from the start, but was unsure what to make of the visitors to his kingdom. It is highly unlikely that he felt any sense of foreboding, surrounded as he was by his vast army. He had only to speak and whatever he commanded would be done. However, he was consumed with curiosity. He had received reports of the Spanish ships, their guns and firearms and how the Spanish rode animals much larger than the Peruvian llama. So he waited with his army, letting the Spanish approach him unmolested, even giving them the stone-built security of Cajamarca for a rest camp. He was like a child mesmerized into inactivity by his curiosity.

Once in the relative safety of Cajamarca, Pizarro waited for Atahulpa to respond. Finally, he sent a delegation of twenty horsemen to arrange a meeting. It was doubtless a daunting sight for Pizarro's small band of adventurers as they rode into the heart of a great conquering army. Atahulpa greeted them wearing a collar of large emeralds; his whole cavalcade blazing with gold. The Spanish caballeros in their armour also made a deep impression and Atahulpa agreed to meet with Pizarro the following day. He set off armed to the hilt with warriors lining the route and when he was within a short distance of the town, stopped and sent a message to Pizarro saying he would arrive the next morning.

Meanwhile tensions were building in the Spanish camp and even the arrogant Pizarro would have been aware of just what they were risking and so he devised a plan. He wrote to Atahulpa implying that the Inca king lacked the necessary courage of true nobility. Atahulpa's two most trusted generals, Quizquiz and Challcuchima were fighting in Cuzco, and in his desire to demonstrate his bravery Atahulpa set off to meet Pizarro's force with only 6,000 unarmed warriors.

When he came before Pizarro, a Dominican friar named Valverde thrust a Bible into Atahulpa's hand and urged him to renounce his own divinity in favour of Jesus and acknowledge the Emperor Charles V as a king greater than himself. Atahulpa exploded with anger as he threw the Bible to the ground. Suddenly Pizarro gave the signal, and with the battle-cry, Santiago! the guns and cannon boomed out across the square as the Spanish troops poured in, their swords flashing in the afternoon sun. The steel soon turned crimson as they hacked away at the helpless wall of human bodies. The Peruvians died fighting with their bare hands in defence of Atahulpa. The attendants and some of the unarmed Incas broke down a wall and fled into the countryside, pursued by the cavalry. The butchery of those that remained trapped in the square did not stop until it was almost dark. Such was the blood lust of the Spaniards that it was only the intervention of Pizarro himself that saved the Inca king, who was imprisoned immediately.

By capturing the Sun God, Pizarro had virtually immobilized the entire Inca army. The soldiers eventually melted away into the surrounding countryside and no attempt was made to rescue Atahulpa. In the baths the Spanish found 5,000 women who they promptly defiled and gathered together everything they could find. One gold vase weighed over 100 kilograms. It was unbelievable. Pizarro suddenly found the great empire wide open and it had all been achieved by a stroke in which not a single Spaniard lost his life. Indeed, none had even been wounded, except for Pizarro himself who had received a sword cut whilst defending Atahulpa from the blood lust of his own men.

Mysteriously Atahulpa made no attempts to contact his generals, and when he saw the Spanish lust for gold, he made Pizarro an offer he couldn't refuse. He proposed that, in exchange for his freedom, one of the immense halls in Cajamarca be filled with gold, but to make sure that the terms of ransom would never be met, Pizarro insisted that another room be filled twice over with silver. Atahulpa had bought time and probably still believed that he could escape, but did not seem to doubt Pizarro's word of honour.

As several weeks passed, tension mounted in the Spanish camp, before the treasure started to trickle in. The carriers had vast distances to surmount and the treasure pile grew slowly. Irate at the time it was taking Pizarro dispatched three of his men to oversee the dismantling of the great Temple of the Sun. The men were treated like gods but behaved appallingly, even ravishing the sacred Inca Virgins of the Sun. Rumours abounded in Cajamarca of an attack and Pizarro sent his brother, Hernando and some men to investigate. By February 1533 Pizarro was joined by Almagro and reinforcements. Pizarro wanted to move on, but had to wait for the arrival of tribes who were hostile to Atahulpa.

By now the treasure amassed stood at 1,326,539 gold pesos and the rooms were still not filled. Pizarro decided that he had waited long enough and that the spoils should be divided. Hernando was dispatched to Spain to report to the Emperor and give him his share.

Meanwhile the mood of the camp was rapidly building up to the point where the men themselves would demand what Pizarro wanted most – to be rid of Atahulpa. The Inca king had now become an encumbrance. He had served his purpose. Pizarro had the gold: now he wanted power. An empire was within his grasp, but as long as the Inca king lived he provided a rallying point for resistance. His death had become a political and tactical necessity.

In order to make Atahulpa's death appear just and legal, Pizarro set up a court, with himself and Almagro as the judges, and proceeded to try the defeated warrior. Atahulpa was accused of twelve crimes including adultery, because he had many wives, and worshipping idols. Pizarro had turned Inquisitor in his new Empire.

The trial was a farce and Atahulpa was sentenced to be burnt to death. On 16 July 1533 he was carried by torchlight and placed on the stake. Some of Pizarro's generals protested, but eventually acquiesced on the grounds of expediency.

Now the Spaniards were free to march on the capital, Cuzco. Throughout the months they had stayed at Cajamarca they had been living off the accumulated wealth of the Indians, slaughtering around 150 llamas a day as though there was no end to the flocks of these animals, plundering the supplies, and demanding and receiving a steady supply of food from local chiefs. They were men without thought to the future and the curse they carried with them was the curse of their own greed. They now embarked on the destruction of the whole brilliant civilization without possessing the organization to replace it.

On 15 November 1533, one year after arriving in Cajamarca, the Spanish entered the capital. On the march the Spanish had collected a further half-a-million gold pesos of treasure. Pizarro was now joined by other Spanish troops anxious to share in the wealth of the conquered Inca empire.

He was now absolute master of Peru – and would remain so for eight years. Had he had any real administrative ability, he could have had the co-operation of the whole nation. The Peruvians were a stoic race, accustomed to passive subservience rather than active loyalty to a central Inca government. But Pizarro and his soldiers mistook passivity for cowardice, and they indulged in the worst excesses towards the population.

By 1535 the country appeared calmer and Pizarro left for the coast to found his new capital, Lima. Meanwhile, Almagro was governing Cuzco, having been made independent of Pizarro by the Emperor Charles. Unfortunately, in dividing up their areas of control, Charles had been extremely vague and both Pizarro and Almagro claimed Cuzco for their own. The city was split into factions and by the summer the Indians had finally reached breaking point. They were led by the young Inca, Manco, a son of Huayna Capac.

In a six-month siege most of the city was destroyed. Pizarro had made repeated attempts to relieve the garrison, but had failed. By now the whole country was in revolt against the senseless brutality of its foreign masters, and the Spanish only managed to hold on at the fortress of Sacahuaman. By August, the revolt had ended. Manco's supplies had run out and he was reduced to fighting a guerrilla war, moving from one fortress to another.

Pizarro attempted to meet with him but it was doomed to failure. When one of his messengers was killed, Pizarro had one of Manco's young wives captured, bound naked to a tree in front of his army, beaten half to death and then shot full of arrows. Such brutal actions would never lead to settlement between the two sides.

But Pizarro still had to deal with the conflict between Hernando and his old ally Almagro and he now dealt a fatal blow to his partner in one of the dirtiest double crosses of the conquest. Pretending that Hernando had been dispatched to Spain, Pizarro gathered his forces and defeated Almagro at the Battle of Las Salinas. Over 150 Spanish died and Almagro was captured and executed by Hernando.

Pizarro now settled down to administering his great kingdom and organized a series of expeditions to discover new lands, but while his brother Gonzalo was staggering out of the steaming forests of the Amazon, the fortunes of the Pizarro family were reaching their inevitable climax.

Discontent was rife throughout the country. More and more Spanish were flooding in every week and a band of discontented followers of Almagro's son swore revenge on Pizarro. On 26 June 1541, Pizarro was told of a plot against him, but he took little notice of it. Around midday the conspirators entered the Governor's palace and slew Pizarro, plunging their swords repeatedly into his body.

Francisco Pizarro, the peasant's son from Spain, was dead and with his death the age of the conquistadors was drawing to a close. In just over half a century a whole new world had been opened up. But the conquistadors were fighting men – the consolidation of the empire they had won was left to others. The once mighty Inca Empire was soon flooded with swarms of officials, but the new laws came too late to save the Indians.

'BLOODY' MARY I

'A CATHOLIC QUEEN IN A PROTESTANT COUNTRY'

*'The name of Mary has been covered with obloquy by reason of the unrelenting
persecution of the Protestants in her reign . . . Her temper had been soured in youth
by the harshness and injustice that insulted the honour of her mother, and the
religion to which she was sincerely attached. Her zeal for her faith hardened into
fierce bigotry, and by the persecuting spirit this feeling engendered, she unwittingly
helped forward the cause of the Reformation in England.'*
H. W. DULCKEN, *A Popular History of England* (1906)

Although the day of her death, on 17 November 1558, was declared a national
holiday and remained so for over 200 years, Bloody Mary has no monument
in England. Mary was a Roman Catholic queen in a newly Protestant country.
Guided by her divine connection to God, she believed it her mission to restore England
to the true faith. Within her four-year reign, Mary ordered the burning and torture of
over 300 Protestant heretics, and her ruthless religious policies drove thousands to flee
from England's shores, in fear of their lives.

Mary was born at Greenwich Palace on 18 February 1516, daughter of King
Henry VIII and his Queen, Catherine of Aragon. They had been married for nearly
seven years, but only one of their children – a son born in 1511 – had survived more
than a month. But Henry lived in hope. As he said after Mary's birth: 'The Queen and
I are still young. If it is a daughter this time, by the grace of God, sons will follow.'

Catherine was the daughter of Ferdinand and Isabella of Spain. She had originally
come to England to marry Henry's older brother, Arthur, who had died in 1502, a year
after their marriage. She was just thirty at the time of Mary's birth. Portraits show her
as short, with grey eyes and red hair. Henry, in contrast, was tall and athletic, with a fair
complexion and reddish-blond hair. He was six years younger than Catherine, and
appears to have been devoted to her. Their tastes matched in both intellectual pursuits
and amusements – both of them loved to dance. Henry also trusted her judgment;
when he sailed to France to wage war against the French, he appointed Catherine to
be Regent in his absence.

After her christening, the Princess Mary went to live in her own establishment.
Members of her household were identified by a special livery in blue and green. Henry
was fond of babies and made sure that she appeared at court on special occasions. He
would carry her around and proudly claim to the assembled courtiers that she never cried.

Mary was treated like the King's plaything, another ornament to be shown off like his collar of enormous diamonds. Henry called her his 'greatest pearl in all the kingdom'. She was a treasure to be protected, hoarded and, when the time came, spent to procure a lasting diplomatic advantage.

At the age of two Mary became engaged for the first time, to the Dauphin of France. Rivalry between England and France was as strong as ever, and Henry now saw a chance to use his daughter as a political tool. The treaty contained the codicil that if Henry were to die without an heir, then Mary would succeed him. No woman had ever been crowned Queen of England in her own right, but there was still the hope that Henry and Catherine would have a son.

Throughout her childhood Mary was taught not how to rule England, but how to make the transition from daughter to wife, her education being intended to provide her with an intellectual chastity belt. From the age of three Mary only saw her parents at Easter and Christmas, and during the long months in-between she rode in her litter from palace to palace. For a young child it was an empty, lonely existence consisting mainly of prayers, priests and study; it was not a world of indulgent parents or nurses.

In August 1525, Mary, the newly created Princess of Wales, was sent to Ludlow Castle. She was now at the centre of her own imposing court and it brought about a transformation in the way that she saw herself. Her life became geared to her office and she was often called away from her studies to receive the reverential attention of local landowners, awed by the majesty of the occasion.

Mary had come to Ludlow a sheltered girl of nine; she left it a seasoned royal personality of eleven. She saw herself as special, set apart by her lineage, and from now on she expected to be treated as the revered heir to the throne of England. When she

Mary I, Queen of England, holding a rose, the emblem of the Tudor dynasty of which she was a member. A Roman Catholic queen in what had become a Protestant country, she pursued religious policies that resulted in the execution of hundreds of Protestants, and drove thousands more into exile. After she died, the anniversary of her death was kept as a national holiday in England for more than 200 years.

(© ARCHIVO ICONOGRAFICO, S.A./CORBIS)

returned to her father's court in 1527, however, her whole life was about to be turned upside down – her father had fallen in love.

Anne Boleyn was the daughter of Sir Thomas Boleyn and Elizabeth Howard, a daughter of the Duke of Norfolk. She had been brought up in the French court and, as a result, had a chic that marked her out in the English court. Dark, with sparkling black eyes and a long, swan-like neck, she was a complete contrast to Catherine. And she had ambition. Unlike every other woman Henry had courted, she refused to succumb to his wooing. She would be his wife or nothing.

Henry was totally infatuated, although he had doubts about arranging a second marriage, as it would require a special dispensation from the Pope before it could go ahead. He had been married to Catherine for over eighteen years and she had been pregnant at least seven times, but all they had produced was one living daughter. Based on the Old Testament text from Leviticus, 'if a man shall take his brother's wife, it is an unclean thing ... They shall remain childless,' Henry became certain that God was punishing him for the sin of marrying his brother's widow.

Henry eventually decided that he must divorce Catherine, even if this meant that his only legitimate child, Mary, was thereby made a bastard. He had to set matters right between God and himself – and open the way to marry Anne. But the people were on Catherine's side: they cheered her and booed Anne. Henry banned Catherine from appearing in public on pain of being denied access to Mary.

In June 1529, Henry forced Catherine to appear before the Legatine Court set up to investigate their marriage. She defended herself as best she could, but it was hopeless. Everyone knew what the king wanted. Henry kept up a pretence of visiting Catherine and receiving her at court until July 1531. Then, in a particularly brutal move, he transferred the court from Windsor to Woodstock without warning, leaving Catherine and Mary behind. That was the last time the king saw his first wife. She was moved from house to house, always further from London and the court. Mary was permitted to visit her mother at Enfield in January 1532, but they did not meet again although Catherine wrote to Mary regularly.

Anne Boleyn was triumphant. Henry moved her into the Queen's apartments and showered gifts and favours on her. In return, Anne allowed him to make love to her. By Christmas 1532, she was sure she was pregnant. Desperate for a legitimate heir, Henry married Anne in a private ceremony in January 1533. On 23 May, later that year, the Archbishop of Canterbury, Thomas Cranmer, officially pronounced Henry's marriage to Catherine as having been null and void.

On 7 September 1533, Anne gave birth to a daughter, Elizabeth. Within days of her half-sister's birth, Henry stripped Mary of all her titles. Thereafter, instead of being addressed as the Princess of Wales, she was to be known simply as, 'The Lady Mary'. But Mary had no intention of accepting this mildly – she wrote a letter to the King stating that while she was an obedient daughter, she was legitimate and to deny it was to offend God.

Mary had inherited pride and obstinacy from both of her parents. Henry was furious and Mary was given a half-hour's notice to pack up her things and move to Hatfield to join Princess Elizabeth's household as one of her maids of honour. Mary refused to pay homage to Elizabeth. Instead she acknowledged her as her 'sister', just as she had acknowledged Henry Fitzroy as her 'brother'. Fitzroy was Henry's illegitimate son by Elizabeth Blount.

Advised by the Spanish Ambassador, she maintained her claim to legitimacy and the title of princess for many months in the face of severe persecution. Anne Boleyn incited her aunt, Lady Shelton, who was in charge of the household, to do everything in her power to break Mary's spirit. When Mary maintained her rights, her jewels, her servants and finally even her clothes were taken from her. When Henry or other dignitaries came to visit Elizabeth, Mary was locked in her room in which the windows had been nailed shut. Once when Henry came to visit, Mary managed to escape from her guards and reach a roof terrace to watch him leave. As he noticed her there, kneeling in supplication, he bowed his head and touched his hat to her before riding away.

For Mary the tortuous years of the royal divorce were a time of shocks, disillusionment and anguish. Until the age of eleven Mary had been a romantic little girl, encouraged to dream of marriage to a prince or emperor. She mistook flirtation for the deep bonds of love and had no idea of the compromises and heartbreak involved in a marriage of state. Now, without abandoning her romantic notions, Mary added another, darker dimension to her understanding of how men and women treated one another. She watched her beloved father turn against her adored mother, injuring her and causing her great distress. She watched her mother respond by treading a tortuous emotional path that ultimately resolved itself in voluntary self-destruction. She taught herself to maintain a serene exterior at all times, and turn inward her feelings of hatred and lust for revenge. At times it seemed that Mary's Catholic faith was all that sustained her.

Henry's court became a wasps' nest of enemies, petty jealousies and backbiting, and at its centre was Anne, whom Mary saw as a shameless, petulant woman who was scheming, ambitious and dangerous. Mary, once an adored jewel, was now only the daughter of a cast-off queen. She looked to Catherine as an example, but in modelling herself on her mother Mary was adopting the behaviour of a desperately troubled woman. The marks would remain with Mary all her life.

In 1534, realizing that he would never receive an annulment from the Pope, Henry VIII made plans to appoint himself head of the English Church. Following a series of Acts the Pope's authority in England was destroyed and the autonomy of the clergy dissolved. Henry portrayed himself as Moses, delivering his people from bondage, a selfless ruler carrying out his sacred duty. What had begun as a dispute with the Pope over his divorce from Catherine had ended with the total schism of the Church of England from Rome.

Mary was told in late 1534 that she must take the Oath of Supremacy, otherwise she would be sent to the Tower. A few days later she fell ill. Mary had been ill before, but this was the most serious attack to date and it lasted six months. Many suspected an attempt on her life as Anne had issued many threats against both Catherine and Mary, while the king had spoken openly of the danger that the two women posed to the realm.

By the following spring she seemed to be in greater danger than ever. Four monks had been tried and convicted of treason. Their punishment was to be hung, disembowelled while still alive, and then beheaded. The brutality of their treatment was significant, even in an age of barbaric execution. The monks, and the hundreds that followed, were guilty of refusing to sign Henry's Oath of Supremacy. These executions increased Mary's desperate desire to escape. A prisoner under the control of pitiless and hostile enemies, her health was collapsing under the ongoing strain. To make things worse, her father had recently described her as his worst enemy. But escape was an impossible dream.

Towards the end of 1535 Catherine became ill again. She died on 7 January 1536 without being allowed to write a last letter to her daughter. Lady Shelton broke the news to Mary four days later, 'most unceremoniously [and] without the least preparation'. Mary's first thought was to ask to see her mother's doctors. She wanted to know whether Catherine's death had been caused by poison. It seems likely that her suspicions were confirmed. Henry, on the other hand, rejoiced and celebrated. When he first heard the news it is recorded that he shouted, 'God be praised, now we are free of all suspicion of war!'

However, things were about to improve for Mary. In April 1536, Anne Boleyn was arrested and tried for adultery. On 19 May, she was beheaded on Tower Green. Now it was Elizabeth who was declared illegitimate, but Mary was still not out of danger. Copying a couple of letters drafted for her by Thomas Cromwell, she had submitted a general plea for forgiveness to the king in the most humiliating terms. But Henry was not satisfied. He sent the Duke of Norfolk, the Earl of Sussex and the Bishop of Chester to see Mary. They had orders to force her to renounce her stand for papal supremacy and for the legality of her mother's marriage. But Mary was steadfast. In the face of the most terrible legal and physical threats, she remained resolute.

Henry was absolutely furious. He believed that Mary, backed by a conspiracy, was working against his plans to reorganize the succession. His new queen, Jane Seymour, was pregnant and he wanted her baby to inherit the kingdom. Despite Jane's intercessions, he decided that Mary would be tried for treason, but the royal justices temporized, refusing to indict her until she had been given one last chance.

Mary was fully aware that her life was in mortal danger if she did not sign the document, known as 'Lady Mary's Submission'. She was only persuaded to submit by the arguments of the Spanish Ambassador. He pointed out that if Mary was executed, any chance of her succeeding to the throne and restoring Catholicism would die with her. Rending her conscience, Mary finally signed the submission on 15 June 1537. Shortly afterwards she wrote to the Pope denying that she saw her father as the Head of the Church and expressing her loyalty to the Catholic faith.

Henry was delighted that she had finally accepted his terms. Within a few weeks, father and daughter had had a private meeting in a country house. Queen Jane was also present. Henry gave her a draft for a thousand crowns for 'small pleasures' and allowed her to build up a new household at Hunsdon. Many of her mother's servants came to serve her there. Her jewels were returned and she received gifts from the courtiers, who were always well aware of whose star was rising and whose falling.

Mary had grown to adulthood surrounded by personalities, circumstances and extremes of emotions exaggerated to the point of caricature. She was predisposed to see life in monumental proportions. She came to think in terms of absolutes, of overriding forces intervening to shatter, rescue or sustain her. If her life were to be significant, it too would have to be defined with reference to a purpose beyond the ordinary. Outwardly, she was all conformity to her father's will, but inwardly she maintained her adherence to the Pope and to her mother. It was a dangerous game to play and Mary was well aware that one false move could revive the charges of treason. In the autumn of 1536, Mary was recalled to court. The years of Anne had not lessened Mary's popularity with the people of England. Vast crowds gathered at the palace awaiting her return and Henry once more became aware what a potent political symbol his daughter had become.

Within eleven days of Anne Boleyn's execution, Henry had married his third wife, Jane Seymour. She and Mary got along well, and she did much to smooth Mary's path back to court and her father's good graces. When Jane gave birth to Henry's longed-for son, Edward, on 12 October 1537, Mary was made godmother. Twelve days later, Mary was the chief mourner at Jane's funeral.

In the interval between 1537 and 1540, Mary watched appalled as Henry brutally suppressed her beloved faith through murder and intimidation. Abbeys, monasteries and nunneries had, through the centuries, become very wealthy and Henry, by appropriating their property and wealth, transferred it all back to the crown. Then he gave much of the land away to leading nobles. For Mary, the Protestant Reformation represented all that was wrong with her father's country; it was against all her teachings.

Henry continued to use Mary as a pawn in his power broking. She was proposed variously as a bride to the Dauphin of France, Dom Luis of Portugal, her cousin the Emperor Charles V, Charles Duke of Orleans and the Duke of Cleves. Unfortunately for Mary, who longed for the romantic ideal of marriage and children, she never married during her father's lifetime. This was partly due to the fact that Henry could never decide on a dowry and partly to his fear that any foreign prince who married Mary might try to force a claim to the crown. 'While my father lives,' said Mary, 'I shall be only the Lady Mary, the most unhappy lady in Christendom.'

In 1544, Henry restored both Mary and Elizabeth to the succession. His sixth wife, Catherine Parr, whom he had married in July 1543, was widely believed to be unable to have children. Mary's long submission to her father's wishes had restored her to his lasting favour, while Edward was only seven years old.

By Christmas 1546, the King was gravely ill and knew he was dying. Mary was at his side and he told her he was unhappy that he had not succeeded in arranging a

'Bloody' Mary with her husband, Philip, son of the Holy Roman Emperor and later King of Spain, whom she had married in 1554, aged thirty-eight. The match did little to increase 'Bloody' Mary's popularity with her English subjects, not least because Philip, too, was a Catholic. Nominally the pair ruled as joint sovereigns (as this contemporary decoration from a plea roll from the Court of King's Bench dated 1558 tactfully implies), but in practice Mary held the reins of power. (PUBLIC RECORD OFFICE KB27/1185[2])

marriage for her as he had wished. Henry VIII died on 28 January 1547, leaving his nine-year-old son as King. The young Edward VI was a supporter of the Protestant faith, and the advisers that now gathered around him shared his beliefs. Most of them had profited directly from the redistribution of the monastic lands and self-interest provided a powerful incentive.

Soon new reforms of the church in England and Wales were instituted. Henry's church had been essentially the Catholic Church without the Pope. Edward's church moved rapidly towards genuine Protestantism. The Bible was made much more widely available and Cranmer started work on a new communion service, designed to replace the mass. Out in the countryside, zealots smashed images of the saints, replaced altars with communion tables, and whitewashed the insides of the churches to obliterate the frescos that had adorned them until that point. In all of this, Mary was a serious embarrassment to the government. She was the heir apparent, until Edward married and had children, and was known to be staunchly Catholic. Despite her best endeavours not to become involved, she was inevitably the focus of any plot against the reforms.

In 1549, the Act of Uniformity prohibited the use in church of anything except the Book of Common Prayer, Cranmer's masterpiece. The result was a whole series of uprisings across the south of England. The rebels demanded the return of the

Mass, the sacraments, and the restoration of two abbeys in every county. There were financial reasons for the rebellions as well – enclosures had meant that many small farmers had lost their land, agricultural rents had been raised, and there were resulting food shortages – but the main thrust was against the religious reforms. The rebellions were put down brutally, and many of the ringleaders were hanged. At the same time, Mary was fighting a private battle to retain her chaplains and her mass. Eventually Mary gained her point when the King's Privy Council backed down, but she was well aware of the ongoing danger.

It was during this period of unrest that Mary seems to have come to identify herself personally with the fate of the Catholic faith in England. More and more, she presented herself as the upholder of the old religion, attending up to four Masses a day where previously she had heard only one. Wherever she travelled within the kingdom, she took her chaplains and made sure that she was seen to be practising as a Roman Catholic. This tactic was very popular and added to the Council's problems in dealing with her.

In October 1549, Edward gained a new Protector, the power-hungry John Dudley, Duke of Northumberland, who had overthrown the Duke of Somerset in the aftermath of the uprisings. He proved to be as avid a reformer as Somerset and even more corrupt. Dudley quickly gained great influence over Edward and used him to attack Mary and her religious practices. Dudley was also promoting Elizabeth, who was happy to conform to the new reforms, by receiving her at court regularly and giving her royal escorts of 100 horsemen. In March 1551, Charles V threatened to declare war on England if Mary was denied the Mass. At this, the Council capitulated for a time.

They resumed their attack on Mary later in the year and managed to prevent her from continuing to hear Mass publicly. However, Mary ensured that one of her priests survived the Council's purge. By now, Edward's health was causing serious concern and it seemed likely that he would not reach adulthood. In early 1553, Edward had a 'tough, strong, straining cough' and it seems that he was suffering from advanced tuberculosis. By May, he was feverish all the time, covered in ulcers and coughing up blood.

Dudley began to panic at the thought of Mary's succession. He persuaded the king to write out the 'Device for the Succession' personally, which disinherited Mary and Elizabeth, and put in their place Jane Grey, the granddaughter of Henry VIII's younger sister, Mary. On 21 May, Jane was married to Dudley's son Guildford, thereby securing, as he hoped, Dudley's hold on the kingdom. Edward died at Greenwich on 6 July 1553 – he was only fifteen. Both Mary and Elizabeth were summoned to his deathbed, but both were wise enough to stay away.

After Edward's death, Mary retreated at first to Kenninghall in Norfolk. From there she wrote to the Council, demanding that they proclaim her queen. Meanwhile, Dudley and the rest of the Council in London suppressed the news of his death while they took control of the Tower of London and gathered weapons and men. On 10 July, Jane was brought to the Tower and formally proclaimed queen of England. There was little enthusiasm for the announcement.

On 12 July, Dudley led a force of 3,000 men out of London towards East Anglia. Mary's followers were gathering at Framlingham, Suffolk, including many members of the nobility and their forces and, 'innumerable companies of the common people'. Dudley began to lose supporters to her, and the final blow came when part of the fleet moored off Great Yarmouth mutinied and went over to Mary's side. This gave the incentive to the rest of the Council to declare Mary Queen of England on the afternoon of 19 July.

Henry Machryn described how this was received: 'As not a soul imagined the possibility of such a thing, when the proclamation was first cried the people started off, running in all directions and crying out, "The Lady Mary is proclaimed Queen!"' There was a terrific explosion of joy at the news. People emptied their purses to throw coins to the crowds; bonfires were lit throughout the city; and rejoicing went on through the night with dancing, singing and feasting. When Mary heard the news in Framlingham, she set up a crucifix in her chapel and ordered her household to sing the *Te Deum*. She was thirty-seven years old and still unmarried.

Of the conspirators who tried to place Jane on the throne, only a few were initially executed, including the Duke of Northumberland. Lady Jane and her husband, Guildford, were found guilty of treason, but Mary refused to execute them. Guildford's brothers, the other three sons of John Dudley, were kept in the Tower, but not killed. The Duke of Suffolk, Jane Grey's father, was released.

Mary faced a monumental task. The idea of a woman ruling was against what was considered to be the natural order. Women were thought of as inherently weak, sinful and requiring male guidance at all times. This was particularly the case in England where, as Carolly Erickson notes, 'Through the sheer force of his size, his magnetism and his power to dominate others, Mary's father had reshaped the office of king.' All of Mary's education, upbringing and cultural heritage predisposed her to submit her judgment and status to men's authority. She was an intelligent, well-read woman, but naturally inclined to defer to men at every turn. This conflict between upbringing and status was to dominate the rest of her life.

Mary started her reign in a spirit of tolerance. She told the imperial ambassador that she 'wished to force no one to go to Mass … [but she] meant to see those who wished to go should be free to do so'. In this spirit, she held two separate funeral services for Edward: a Protestant one in Westminster Abbey and a requiem Mass in the Tower. In August she announced that everyone could continue to worship as they chose until a new Parliament could legislate for an 'orderly change'. However, there were many clashes between militants on both sides.

She was hampered by her Council, who indulged in bickering and infighting. The survivors of Edward's Council, led by William Paget, were at odds with the new members, led by the conservative Bishop of Winchester, Stephen Gardiner. Many of them lacked experience of government, and practically all had an eye to the main chance. Mary called her first parliament soon after her coronation, which took place with great celebrations on 1 October 1553. By that time, Emperor Charles V had already offered his son, Philip of Spain, as Mary's husband, and Mary had agreed to marry him.

This did not please the ordinary people, who disliked all foreigners on principle, and the Spanish in particular. The common perception was that they were proud, stole whenever possible, and were lecherous in the extreme. Members of Parliament made representations to Mary about this, but she was furious at their presumption – this had never happened before, even when the ruler was a minor. She was determined to go ahead with the marriage, not least because she had fallen in love with Philip's portrait. Suitably chastened, Parliament turned its attention to repealing the Protestant laws. The first to be abolished was Henry VIII's act condemning his marriage to Catherine of Aragon. The Book of Common Prayer was banned, but Mary could not make them admit that the Pope, and not she, was the Supreme Head of the church in England.

Mary's relationship with her heir apparent, Elizabeth, was distant. She did her best to treat Elizabeth fairly, but could only regard her as a bastard. She was well aware that Elizabeth, despite her protestations, was opposed to Roman Catholicism, and that Protestants were waiting for Mary to die whereupon Elizabeth, 'would remedy all in time'. Seventeen years younger and blessed with immense charm, she would have been a serious rival to Mary at any time.

Elizabeth was in as dangerous a position as Mary had been during Edward VI's reign. One English nobleman, Edward Courtenay, Earl of Devonshire, was a descendant of Henry VII's queen, Elizabeth of York, and had a distant claim to the throne. He was proposed as a husband to both Mary and Elizabeth, despite being vain, impulsive and completely lacking in any royal presence. Every plot against Mary included a provision for Elizabeth and Courtenay's marriage. Courtenay was involved in a plot in January 1554, which was sparked off by the prospect of the Spanish marriage, but betrayed the whole when questioned. None the less, the uprising in Kent, led by Sir Thomas Wyatt, went ahead.

Wyatt decided to march on to London. He camped out around Blackheath and Greenwich on 30 January 1554. He demanded custody of the Tower with the Queen in it and the removal of her counsellors whom he would replace with his own. The loyalty of the city seemed to be in doubt and it was Mary herself who resolved the crisis. Instead of seeking her own safety in flight, she made a public speech at the Guildhall in which she exhorted the men of London to '…stand fast against the rebels, both our enemies and yours, and fear them not, for I assure you I fear them nothing at all!' In response to her urging, Londoners rushed to defend London Bridge. Although Wyatt and his troops managed to cross the Thames and enter London on 7 February, the city did not rise. Eventually he and his troops surrendered when they discovered all exits from the city blocked by Mary's troops.

Mary realized the mistake she had made before in her lenient treatment of

Northumberland's rebels, and vowed not to make it again. In all, roughly 100 rebels were hung, although the Queen pardoned 400 others. Lady Jane Grey and her husband were put to death, as they provided a focal point for heretics and Mary's enemies. Elizabeth had been summoned to London for questioning and was eventually imprisoned in the Tower as well.

Philip landed at Southampton on 17 July 1554 and met Mary for the first time a few days later. She was thirty-eight, thin and careworn – very different from the Spanish notion of beauty. She, on the other hand, thought he greatly resembled his portrait and was delighted. They were married in Winchester Cathedral on 25 July. By September, Mary's doctors were telling her she was probably pregnant. Unfortunately this was not the case, although it was not discovered until after the due date of birth in April. Mary hung on, hoping against hope, until August, but eventually she accepted there would be no baby. Following Charles V's abdication, Philip was needed to rule over Flanders. He left Mary in Greenwich on 29 August 1555, and sailed to Flanders a few days later. They were not to meet again for over eighteen months.

Philip had a difficult time in England. He spoke no English when he arrived and the English people were very hostile to his retinue. Although he had the title of king, and was named first in legal documents, he had no real power in England. Mary only complied with Philip's wishes when they agreed with her own. He certainly did not love Mary, and doubtless he felt lonely and isolated. The summer of 1555 was a particularly bad one, with many crop failures, so there was much unrest in the country, especially in London. The burning of heretics added to the conflict.

Mary had always intended to restore Papal supremacy in England. Soon after becoming queen, she started negotiations with the Pope, who sent Cardinal Reginald Pole, an English nobleman, to England as his Legate. He landed in England on 20 November 1554. On 30 November, he received Parliament's request to be reunited with Rome and granted the Papal absolution. By Christmas, Parliament had reinstated the Heresy Act at Mary's bidding and the burnings began the next month.

It seems probable that committed Protestants were a minority in England and Wales at this time. Most of the people would have accepted whichever religion the monarch and Parliament decreed should be followed. The Protestants, however, had actively campaigned against the return of Catholicism since the start of Mary's reign. They took every opportunity to ridicule the ceremonies. Priests were attacked and processions disrupted. Mary had allowed many of the most ardent Protestants to leave for the continent where they had started a long-distance propaganda campaign against everything that Mary and her government were doing.

The first burnings for heresy took place in February 1555. Over that year, Nicholas Ridley, Bishop of London; Hugh Latimer, Bishop of Worcester; John Philpot, Archdeacon of Westminster; John Hooper, Bishop of Gloucester; and some seventy-five others were all burnt at the stake on Mary's order. Gross incompetence on the part of the executioners often made the deaths much more cruel than was intended. Sometimes the gunpowder strapped to the heretic's waist failed to explode;

at others the green wood, intended to produce suffocation smoke, failed to burn properly and the execution was greatly prolonged. 'Bloody Mary' was beginning to gain her reputation.

Many of those sent to the stake were ordinary, and ignorant, villagers. They had little or no grasp of the intricate religious arguments involved. One who did was the ex-Archbishop of Canterbury, Thomas Cranmer, who was burned in March 1556. Despite having recanted, he was still condemned to death. At the stake, he threw his recantation into the flames and proclaimed himself a true Protestant. By his death, Cranmer and many others were regarded as martyrs for the Protestant cause. Much resentment was stirred up against the Queen, Cardinal Pole and her government. Another conspiracy, centring on an invasion of English political exiles, was discovered early in 1556. Mary was convinced that some members of her Council were involved and felt even more isolated. Throughout the spring and summer of 1556, there was a serious drought in England and that increased tension within the country.

Mary had little support from Philip in Flanders. His letters usually included a demand that she prepare for his coronation. Mary, dealing with a restive Parliament that was even more distrustful of foreigners, eventually told him bluntly that there was very little chance of this ever happening. She also heard that he was spending lavishly with money he had borrowed and that his adventures with women were becoming notorious. None the less, she continued to act the dutiful wife, although she complained to his father about his neglect of her.

Mary also wrote to the former emperor about her campaign against the heretics. She was becoming aware that she was losing support among Catholics, as well among Protestants, who thought that the people who were being burned as heretics did not deserve such a dreadful punishment. Her one desire was to re-establish the Catholic Church in England, but her chosen method seemed to be causing more harm than good. But if she did not persecute wrong beliefs, how were people to be convinced of the one true religion? It was a dilemma she was never to solve.

When Philip finally returned in March 1557, he brought war with him. The new Pope, a Neapolitan named Paul IV, hated Hapsburg power and was allied with the French. Philip's army was about to besiege Rome, but Philip's monetary reserves were low and he needed financial support urgently. He turned to his neglected wife, who forced people to loan her 150,000 ducats. She sent this to him within a few weeks, along with promises of naval support. Once he had returned to England, she set to work to persuade the Council to agree to declare war on France. War was duly announced on 7 June 1557. By 6 July, Philip was on his way back to France. He had an army of 20,000, plus field guns and artillery, and was looking forward to the coming campaign. He was not to see Mary again.

Philip's army won a major battle at St Quentin, and took a number of other towns in northern France. Meanwhile, in Italy, his army came to terms with the Pope. Calm was restored for a while, but Henri II of France had spotted an opportunity. England's one remaining foothold in France – the city of Calais and its surrounding territories –

had been an annoyance to the French kings for over a century. In early January 1558, the French mounted a surprise attack on the city, whose defences had been run down, probably due to lack of money. On 7 January the city fell. Mary was by turns devastated and furious at its loss. The English blamed its loss on the money and men that Mary was still sending to support Philip.

There was a major financial crisis in February 1558. Bad harvests, epidemics and wildly fluctuating prices had compounded the problems caused by heavy expenditure at court and the costs of supporting Philip and his wars. Taxes were very high and all the Council could do was to argue. Mary had other worries. She had believed that she was pregnant again, but had not told Philip until December in case they were disappointed once again. Now she decided to move to Greenwich to prepare for the birth there, but again the baby never came.

In March, Mary made her will at Philip's urging, but did not name Elizabeth as her heir. She was sick for much of the year, suffering from depression and 'intermittent fever'. Meanwhile, Elizabeth was making preparations in case she had to fight for the throne. Ambassadors and courtiers made tactful approaches to her as Mary's life slowly drained away.

On 6 November the Council visited Mary in her bedchamber and urged her to name Elizabeth as heir. She agreed and sent two Council members to Hatfield to announce the news to Elizabeth. She also sent her 'rich and precious jewels' and asked Elizabeth to promise to uphold the Catholic religion, take care of her servants and pay her debts.

By 14 November, Mary was fading in and out of consciousness. She had told her most intimate servants of a secret sorrow oppressing her. They thought it was Philip's absence, but she answered, 'Not only that, but when I am dead and opened, you will find Calais lying in my heart.' Before dawn on 17 November, Mary ordered Mass to be celebrated in her room. By the end of the service her ladies thought she was asleep, but she in fact had died peacefully. Her betrothal ring was taken from her finger and carried to Hatfield by members of the Council to prove to Elizabeth that Mary was dead. Later that same day, after hearing the celebrations as London welcomed the accession of Elizabeth, Cardinal Pole died. The two architects of the Catholic restoration were dead and Elizabeth had a free hand to choose which path England should follow.

IVAN IV, 'THE TERRIBLE'

TSAR OF ALL THE RUSSIAS

*All the Russian sovereigns are autocrats and no one can find fault with them,
the monarch can exercise his will over the slaves whom God has given
him...If you do not obey the sovereign when he commits an injustice, not
only do you become guilty of felony but you damn your soul, for God himself
orders you to obey your prince blindly.*

IVAN IV, letter to Prince Andrew Kurbskii

Even before Ivan's birth the Patriarch of Jerusalem had predicted that his father, Vasily III, would have 'an evil son'. Just after his birth in the middle of a violent thunderstorm another prophecy foretold that, 'a tsar is born among you: two teeth has he. With one he will devour us; but with the other – you'. By the time of his death, fifty-four years later, Ivan IV well deserved his name of *Grozny* or Terrible. He had ordered and participated in the ruthless extermination of thousands of people; devoted associates and sworn enemies alike perished amid hideous tortures. Villages, towns and an entire city perished. Ivan's tumultuous rages knew no bounds and he even killed his adored son in a fit of rage. The first Tsar of all the Russias, he had absolute power over millions of lives. A masterly manipulator, he lacked any compassion for his subjects, whom he tortured, robbed or raped purely for his own amusement.

Ivan was just three years old when the great bell of the Kremlin tolled for the death of his father. The Russian court was plunged into violence as Elena Glinskaya, his Catholic mother, fought to hold on to power, imprisoning and killing those who stood in her way, irrespective of her late husband's wishes. The regents, named by his father on his deathbed, were jealous and greedy for power. Intrigues and plots ruled the day. Outwardly Ivan was treated well, but only when he was in the public eye. The regents tortured and killed people in front of the young impressionable Ivan, and nobles, sobbing in terror and fleeing from imminent death at the hands of a court rival, would wake him up at night.

In this forbidding climate of spying, poisoning and violence, Ivan came to view life as might a predatory animal, eager to pursue his prey and enjoy its suffering. He took his frustration out on defenceless creatures such as dogs and cats when, after piercing their eyes and dropping them from the high towers of the Kremlin, he would run down the stairs to watch them die a slow death. It was more than an amusement; it was an apprenticeship.

Ignored by his mother the seven-year-old became isolated and paranoid. His beloved nurse, Agrafena Obolensky, was sent to a convent by regent Prince Vasily Shuisky – Ivan and his younger brother, Yuri the idiot, were little more than beggars in the Kremlin. Armed men roamed the palace, frequently bursting into the Grand Prince's room, shoving him aside, overturning furniture and taking whatever they pleased.

In 1538 Ivan watched as his mother died in agony; poisoned with mercury by the boyars, members of the landed nobility who ranked just below the princes. The boyars also had one of Ivan's few loyal confidants, Fydor Mishurin, skinned alive and left on public view in a Moscow square. For the rest of his childhood Ivan lived amid terror and brutality as rival families fought for power and his hatred grew with each vile act performed. It was to have a devastating effect on his sanity, and on his attitude towards the nation as a whole.

At the age of thirteen Ivan graduated from torturing animals to killing people. Just after Christmas, Ivan invited the boyars to a banquet and they watched in amazement as Ivan stood up and loudly accused them of taking advantage of his youth to further themselves. He declared that he held everyone responsible, but would be satisfied with the blood of their leader, Prince Andrew Shuisky. Stunned, the boyars listened without objection, dumbfounded by this act of authority. Instantly, Ivan's guards moved forward to seize the prince. He was thrown into an enclosure with a pack of starved hunting dogs and savaged to

Ivan IV, Tsar of All the Russias, from a later painting by Victor Michailovitch Vasnetsov. Brutal, manipulative and wholly without compassion, he was also given to catastrophic fits of rage that helped to earn him the sobriquet 'the Terrible'; under his rule thousands of people were exterminated, often after the most hideous torture.
(© BETTMANN/CORBIS)

death. With Shuisky dead, the boyars conceded that their rule had ended, and that Ivan had complete power. The Glinsky family now reigned supreme.

Ivan was by now a very disturbed young man as well as a voracious drinker. He roamed the Moscow streets with a gang of thugs, drinking, stealing from people and raping women. He often disposed of victims by having them hanged, strangled, buried alive or thrown to the bears. But Ivan never lost the notion of his exceptional dignity. When he became drunk, when he fornicated, it was God who was getting drunk and fornicating, through him. He believed that God was saving him for a special purpose. Ironically he became increasingly devout, believing that the church would support his views and that he was God's representative on earth, but even his way of worshipping was violent. As he knelt in front of the altar he would throw himself down before religious icons, banging his head so hard against the floor that he developed a callus. It was a habit that was to remain with him throughout his life.

By the age of sixteen Ivan had become a volatile young man, but one ready to assume the role for which he had been born. The Russian people, ground down by the boyars, tried in vain to attract the attention of their young sovereign, but Ivan, drunk with arrogance, violence and piety, refused to be troubled by external events. One day, while out hunting near Novgorod, he was approached by fifty councillors with a petition complaining of the oppressive measures that afflicted them. Ivan refused to listen and, illogically believing an attempt had been made on his life, he had the perpetrators decapitated without being able to defend themselves. One of the victims had been his childhood friend, Fydor Vorontzov, who had just been released from prison. Ivan now believed that his justice was infallible and his power sacred.

Tall and thin, hawk-nosed, his face lengthened by a reddish brown beard, and with bright blue piercing eyes, Ivan stood before all the boyars and court in the vast throne room and announced his own succession, and in a significant break with tradition he demanded his own title – Tsar of all the Russias. At a stroke Ivan had distanced himself from the princes and boyars in Moscow and placed himself above all other European heads of state. He even had a hastily prepared genealogy made up to prove that he was the direct descendent of the Roman Emperor Augustus.

Not long after this Ivan chose his first wife, Anastasia Romanovna, in the traditional ceremony of *smotriny*, when all the young, virginal princesses and daughters of noblemen were presented to him. Although Ivan had initially wanted to make a marriage alliance with a European court, the union was a happy one, for Ivan and for Russia. His new Tsarina was to keep some of Ivan's cruelty under control. He called her his 'little heifer' – finally Ivan had someone to love. They married in February 1547 and were to have thirteen years of happy marriage. The silent, strong Anastasia bore him six children, two of whom survived infancy.

Within months of both his marriage and accession, however, Ivan had a new problem to face. Moscow, a city largely constructed from wood, was slowly being consumed by fire. Thousands died and were made homeless, but to Ivan, steeped in his own importance, the disaster could mean only one thing: God had singled him out for personal punishment. His horrified suspicion was confirmed by a visit from a priest called Sylvester, who told him that the fires were God's punishment for his sins, and Sylvester urged Ivan to purify his soul. Having always thought that he and God were friends, Ivan decided on a huge act of public penance and in a cynical move that was to become a pattern of his reign, he also made use of the opportunity to strengthen his regal position.

Up until now it had been the Glinsksys that had maintained control over Russia. Loaded with honours and riches, they oppressed the people, extorted money and ruthlessly meted out punishment to those who dared to complain. They were hated by the common people and viewed by most of the boyars as symbols of tyranny, dishonesty and vice. In a packed Red Square, Ivan, draped in gold and spangled with jewels, prostrated himself before his people apologizing for the behaviour of the boyars and promising to act as the people's protector, urging them to be united by love. He claimed that his soul had been seized by terror and his spirit subdued when pity entered his heart. The Glinsksy family fled for their lives.

Shortly after this speech, Ivan began reforming the government. He created a new type of council, the *Izbrannaya Rada* or Chosen Council, composed of members of the nobility and clergy who were known for their wisdom, sober judgement and devotion. The assembly was dominated by two men; the Metropolitan of Moscow, Macarius, the most cultivated man in Russia; and Sylvester, the mystical preacher who dared to speak to the Tsar as a simple penitent. Ivan then embarked on a massive overhauling of the State, the Church and the Army, creating an elite force called the *Streltsi*. He demanded that all territories under his control should adhere to the same laws, and condemned corruption. Ivan was obsessed with the idea of unifying his country and taking judicial, administrative and fiscal powers away from the local nobility.

Ivan also imperiously demanded that Russia start trading directly with England, and he created trading links with Sweden and Holland. Domestic success was coupled with significant military victories on Russia's southern and eastern borders, but Ivan had three causes for concern: the Swedes, the Poles and the Tartars. Using the *Streltsi*, who were equipped in European style, and given wages and uniforms, he first captured the city of Kazan, stronghold of the Tartars, and by 1554 his victories had added nearly one million square kilometres to the realm. It was during the campaign against the Tartars that Ivan first became known under the title Grozny, although initially it was given to reflect his qualities as a mighty ruler, rather than his role as an instigator of terror.

But Ivan's penchant for sadism and revenge was never far from the surface. In March 1553 he fell dangerously ill and subsequently demanded that the boyars swear allegiance to his one-year-old son, Dimitri. Initially they refused, fearing that if the Tsar died, it would mean anarchy and a return to the rule of the regents. Furious at their disloyalty, all Ivan's old hatreds resurfaced, but bound by an oath he had made to God to forgive the schemers if he should recover, Ivan coldly bided his time. Ironically, just after Ivan's recovery, the royal couple was visiting a monastery to give thanks to God for his revival, when a nurse dropped Dimitri into the river and the

Despite his many failings, Ivan IV did much for Russian commerce, and also for the country's culture. The Cathedral of St Basil the Blessed in Red Square, Moscow, was constructed between 1555 and 1560 on Ivan's orders, in honour of St Vasily (of which the English form is Basil), the father of the Eastern Orthodox Church. Nevertheless, it is said that Ivan, on seeing the finished building, ordered the architect to be blinded, so that he would never be able to design anything more beautiful. (© ARCHIVO ICONOGRAFICO, S.A./CORBIS)

baby drowned. Nine months later Anastasia gave birth to another son, Ivan.

For thirteen years, thanks to the advice of his wife, alongside Sylvester, and Alexei Adashev, (the Chamberlain) Ivan had governed the country with relative wisdom. Even foreign observers had acknowledged he was an outstanding sovereign. However, on 7 August 1560, Ivan's beloved Anastasia died after a lingering, painful illness. The people of Moscow wept for their charitable Tsarina, their lamentations drowning out the priests' chanting. Ivan walked, bare-headed behind the coffin, supported by his brother and afterwards haunted the empty rooms his wife had left behind, ranting and screaming in desperation. Once more isolated and trying to comprehend the reasons for this punishment, Ivan became convinced that Anastasia had been poisoned and suddenly all his old cruelty resurfaced. His moods swung from violent fits of temper to feelings of remorse, whilst blasphemy and superstition succeeded his more pious moments. The God that had taken away Anastasia was cruel and irrational – from now on he would behave the same way. Like God, he was now exempt from all moral laws, and since God had offended him, he had the right to offend God.

Ivan raged against the boyars as he banged his head on the floor, in full view of the court, and began to smash up the furniture. His suspicion then descended into paranoia and he had whole families obliterated. From every side informers flocked into the Kremlin, eagerly pandering to Ivan. To oblige their Tsar, judges no longer required any genuine evidence, and many of the nobility, who had fought loyally in the Tsar's wars, were tortured and strangled alongside their children. He had Sylvester exiled to a monastery, where he died in obscurity and Adashev imprisoned where he died two months later in mysterious circumstances.

Henceforth, Ivan's married life would be unstable, underlining his egocentricity, insecurity and manic temperament. In 1561, he married a Circassian beauty, Maria Temriukovna, but he soon tired of her. She died in 1569 and he married Martha Sobakin, a merchant's daughter, but she died two weeks later. Ivan's fourth wife was Anna Koltovskaya, whom he sent to a convent in 1575. He married a fifth time to Anna Wassilchikura, who was soon replaced by Wassilissa Melentiewna. She foolishly took a lover, who was impaled under her window before she, too, was dispatched to a convent. After his seventh wedding day, Ivan discovered that his new bride, Maria Dolgurukaya, was not a virgin. He had her drowned the next day. His last wife, Maria Nagaya, whom he married in 1581, outlived him.

The prisons and monasteries of Russia now overflowed with Ivan's victims. The harder he struck, the more he wanted to strike, and the blood that was shed, far from quenching his thirst, whetted his appetite for fresh excesses. To replace the boyars who were guilty of having displeased him, Ivan chose men of the petty nobility with narrow minds and supple backs, men who never contradicted him and who encouraged him in his debauchery. Over the next year Ivan was to lose his brother Yuri, his youngest son Vasily and Metropolitan Macarius. Ivan's last links with the past had gone – there was no one left who had been a witness to his childhood or whom he felt he could trust.

Shortly before Christmas in 1564, Ivan suddenly packed his belongings and treasures and secretly left Moscow for Aleksandrovskaia Sloboda with his family, announcing his intention to abdicate. It was an absurd notion, because, for sixteenth-century Russians, he was not just considered the Head of State, but the State itself. However, it was a brilliant stroke of manipulation. Ivan wrote two letters, the first listed the disorders, betrayals and crimes of the nobility and generals, accusing them of looting the treasury and mistreating the peasants. The second letter, addressed to the foreign and Russian merchants and all the Christian people of Moscow, told how he loved them as much as he hated the boyars and churchmen. The letters were broadcast and Russia was thrown into confusion, the populace pleaded for his return and a delegation of senior clergy and nobility was sent to the Tsar to beg him to reconsider. His gamble had paid off, and after a month Ivan returned victoriously to Moscow, but not before he had demanded, and received, absolute power to punish anyone he considered disloyal, and the ability to dispose of their estates. Henceforth he would be the sole interpreter and executor of the will of God, with authority above and beyond the Church. The reign of terror was about to begin.

On 2 February 1565, Ivan re-entered Moscow. According to witnesses, the thirty-four-year-old Tsar had the appearance of an old man. His face was grey and wrinkled, his eyes were dull, his hair scant, his lips thin and clenched and his forehead deeply furrowed. As his eyes wandered over the crowd they had a demented look. Within a month of his return Ivan had divided Russia in half. The *Zemshchina*, which would be under Ivan's power, would keep its Duma, or parliament of boyars and functionaries; and the *Oprichnina*, the richest part, would be the Tsar's private domain, which he would administer as he pleased. On 4 February, the very day the *Oprichnina* was established, the executions began.

To help him instigate his absolute rule of evil, Ivan created the *Oprichniki*, Russia's first Secret Police. The mere sight of the *Oprichniki* instilled fear. They rode through the streets of Moscow and into the countryside dressed in black, riding black horses, carrying brooms and dogs' heads as symbols of their mission to sweep away treachery and then gnaw it to death. Ivan was establishing a new nobility consisting of paid servants. Among the *Oprichniki* all that counted was devotion to the central cause, satisfying Ivan's desires. Many were vicious criminals without any remorse. They were above the law and to insult them was a crime punishable by death. They could impose fines, torture, rape, pillage and burn without any fear of reprisal.

The boyars now realized that by confiscating their villages, peasants and property, Ivan meant to break their power permanently. It is estimated that as many as 10,000 members of the nobility died at the hands of the *Oprichniki*, and 12,000 families were forcibly relocated and their lands seized.

The more Ivan oppressed the country, the more he felt he was hated; the more he felt hated, the more determined he was to discover who was plotting against his life. Anxiety prevented him from sleeping and he saw evil omens everywhere. Moscow no longer seemed safe, and so it was that Ivan moved back to Aleksandrovskaia Sloboda, to a palace surrounded by moats and ramparts. The interior of the sinister palace reflected the four different aspects of Ivan's personality. Some of the rooms were superbly decorated; others were crammed with precious books and parchments; still others resembled monastic cells, whilst lastly, rooms underground were divided into a series of dungeons.

Ivan also created Russia's first secret police, the Oprichniki, a brutal, if fanatically loyal, force devoted to carrying out their master's bidding. This engraving shows the people of Kasan submitting to Ivan – at the point of the sword. Even to insult the Oprichniki, let alone resist them, was punishable by death. (© BETTMANN/CORBIS)

Delirious with fervent piety, Ivan handpicked the most aggressive 300 *Oprichniki* and installed them in the palace, which he transformed into a monastery. The men, he announced, would be his monks, and he would be their abbot. Each brother wore a black cassock over his gold-embroidered coat trimmed with fur. Ivan sincerely believed he had created a new monastic order.

Following a rigid timetable including a four-hour service followed by lunch and a short nap, Ivan and his men would visit the dungeons for an afternoon's torture and executions. They regularly performed sacrilegious masses that were followed by extended orgies of rape and torture. Frequently, Ivan would act as master of ceremonies, in which, with sharp and hissing hot pincers, ribs were torn out of men's chests. Drunken licentiousness was alternated with passionate acts of repentance. After throwing himself down before the altar with such vehemence that his forehead would be bloody and covered with bruises, Ivan would rise and read sermons on the Christian virtues to his drunken retainers, whilst during gargantuan eating sessions, which would follow the sermons, entertainments would be laid on to amuse Ivan. Maliuta-Skuratov, one of the cruelest and most debauched of the brotherhood, would force naked peasant girls, with hair flying and breasts swaying, to chase after hens while the *Oprichniki* shot arrows at the terrified victims. After a short sleep Ivan would return to the church to pray. Lifting up his soul he would hear God whispering in his ear the names of new victims to sacrifice. It was on his knees, between prayers, that he would give his bloodiest orders.

By the age of thirty-four, Ivan had become a figure of fear. His anger was made more deadly by a long wooden staff whose steel pointed end he used to maim or kill with. He used to lash out at people who offended him. Prince Boris Telupa was, 'drawn upon a long sharp-made stake, which entered the lower part of his body and came out of his neck; upon which he survived for 15 hours, talking to his mother who had been brought to behold the sight. After her son's death she was given to 100 gunners, who defiled her to death, and the Tsar's hungry hounds then devoured her flesh and bones.' No one was immune to Ivan's evil – his treasurer, Nikita Funikov, was boiled to death in a cauldron. In fact Ivan's delusions were so extreme that in 1567 he applied to Elizabeth I for political asylum whilst at the same time offering himself as her suitor.

Around the Tsar there was nothing but weakness and cowardice. He was being advised by men like Bomelius, a Dutch adventurer, who claimed to be a doctor of magical sciences and who further fanned the flames of Ivan's paranoia by reminding him how many enemies he still had.

As his stranglehold tightened, few were prepared to challenge Ivan's rule. In 1568, when Metropolitan Philip, the head of the Russian Orthodox Church, begged for mercy on behalf of men unjustly accused of rebellion, Ivan did not initially dare to attack him directly. Instead he contented himself with having a few clergy arrested and tortured, but a few months later, when Philip ill-advisedly reprimanded Ivan for allowing an *Oprichnik* to wear a skullcap whilst celebrating mass, Ivan's patience snapped and he had him arrested. Whilst in prison, Philip failed to bless the Novgorod expedition, the result of the trip being the massacre of up to 60,000 citizens of the city, and he was strangled by Ivan's faithful henchman, Maliuta-Skuratov.

Driven even further by the desire to demonstrate his omnipotence, Ivan could no longer be satisfied with punishing individuals; he had to punish whole towns. For a long time he had been irritated by the presumption of Novgorod, a town that had only recently been united to the crown. Initially content with taking over 650 hostages back to Moscow, a forged letter containing the signatures of all the notables of the city, written by a criminal with a grievance against the city, gave Ivan the excuse he needed. In December 1569, Ivan left Moscow at the head of an army of his *Oprichniki*. He was accompanied by his son, Ivan, who shared his father's taste for crude pleasures and blood. On his way to Novgorod, Ivan amused himself by ordering the massacre of the inhabitants of Klim, followed by five days praying in a monastery whilst the *Oprichniki* went from house to house, torturing whomever they pleased.

Then, on 8 January 1570, Ivan entered the terrified, deserted city. First he sacked and looted the cathedral and the next day he set about the task of bringing justice to Novgorod. A German mercenary wrote that, '…the Czar mounted a horse and brandished his spear and charged in and ran people through while his son watched the entertainment.' Every day for five weeks a thousand citizens were brought into the main square where they were systematically tortured and slaughtered. The *Oprichniki* variously flogged their victims, broke their limbs, cut out their tongues, slit their nostrils, castrated them and roasted them over slow fires. Then they were flung into the icy waters of the River Volkhov, whole families at a time. Those who rose to the surface were dispatched with boat hooks, lances and axes by the *Oprichniki* in boats. By the end there were so many bodies clogging the Volkhov, that it overflowed its banks. Finally, on 12 February, Ivan had one survivor from each street brought to him. Expecting death, they saw that Ivan wore a kindly expression. He had emerged from the bloodbath refreshed and rejuvenated. He told them to go home in peace. The decimation of Novgorod was over, but the city would never recover.

Later the same year, the terror reached a fever pitch in Moscow as Ivan instigated mass trials. Ivan watched from his balcony as workmen set up seventeen gallows, an enormous cauldron of water suspended over a vast pile of wood, a frying pan as big as a man, and ropes stretched taut to saw bodies in two by friction. Over 300 people were hanged, boiled or hacked to death in front of St Basil's Cathedral in Red Square, which had been built in celebration of Ivan's military victories.

But Ivan's policies were now coming home to roost and the Tartars invaded Moscow. On the morning of 24 May 1571, the Tartars set fire to houses on the outskirts of Moscow and a high wind spread the blaze. The citizens tried to find safety in the Kremlin, but the gates had been barricaded and many were crushed to death by the onslaught of more terrified Muscovites. In less than three hours, Moscow was reduced to a smoking ruin – only the Kremlin – surrounded by its high walls remained intact. The Tsar fled to Aleksandrovskaia Sloboda. In 1572 the Tartars returned again to Moscow, but fortunately for Ivan, Prince Vorotynsky, with a massively outnumbered force, managed to win a resounding victory. Russia was safe from the Tartars and although he had nothing whatever to do with the victory, Ivan took all the credit, returning to Moscow triumphant. Six-years later, Ivan personally tortured Vorotynsky to death – he had become a national hero – something Ivan could not tolerate.

The strength of Ivan's army now gave him security and deciding that the *Oprichniki* were a blot on his image abroad, he dissolved them. This led to even more chaos as the chain of command broke down. Ivan's policy of dividing Russia into two had had a disastrous effect on its defensive capabilities and its society had been thrown into mass confusion with the peasants suffering under the yoke of serfdom and the nobility fearing for their lives. The *Oprichniki* and Ivan had led the country to catastrophe by ravaging almost all the land under its control. Great stretches of countryside remained uncultivated and famine and plague arrived in Russia.

By 1578 Ivan was in great physical pain. He had developed large saline deposits on his backbone and the slightest movement would cause him agony. He could not wear himself out with fasting and prayer and the physical exhaustion made it impossible for him to kneel or bow down.

Ivan's rages, now fuelled by physical torment, extracted a terrible price. On 9 November 1582, he assaulted his daughter-in-law because he did not like the dress she was wearing, causing her to miscarry. Ivan, the son and heir, quarrelled with his father and in the heat of the argument Ivan struck his son on the head with his wooden staff. He died a few days later. Fydor, the new heir, was a dwarf with a huge head and nose, who was both incompetent and childless. Ivan's power, limited by nothing and no one, would have to pass into the hands of a nobody.

Knocking his head against his son's coffin and making animal noises, Ivan was consumed with guilt and fear and demented by paranoia; he now became addicted to the ingestion of mercury, which he kept bubbling in a cauldron in his rooms. Fearing God's wrath, Ivan stopped all executions, repented for what he had done, and asked God to forgive him. One year later he gathered his sons together and warned them to be merciful rulers and think before casting people into disgrace. He asked for special lists to be made for prayers for those wrongly killed and sent money for their souls to be prayed for.

Wreathed in fat, Ivan's debauchery had left its mark although he had long looked older than his years with long white hair dangling from a baldpate onto his shoulders and in his last years he had to be carried on a litter. His body swelled, his skin peeled and, 'he began to swell grievously in his cods, with which he had most horribly offended above fifty years, boasting of a thousand virgins deflowered and thousands of children of his begetting destroyed.'

Just before his death the Tsar summoned sixty soothsayers who told fortunes by the stars and they told him he would die on 18 March 1584. That day, Ivan went through his will, just in case, but he felt well, despite the gloomy predictions. He sent his adviser Belsky to warn the soothsayers that they would either be burnt or buried alive for their obvious lying. But the soothsayers were adamant. 'The day will end only when the sun goes down' was their reply. Having taken a bath, the Tsar settled down to play chess and dropped dead. An Englishman, who happened to be present, Jerome Gorsay, wrote that the Tsar was 'asphyxiated'. Other contemporaries, agreeing that his death was violent, suggested that he was poisoned, but it is unlikely that we will ever know what really happened. An analysis of his skeleton found no traces of violence, but then he was so weakened by illness that he could easily have been smothered.

Ivan left behind a joyless Russia. The chaos in which the administration was in, the bitter resentment of the boyars who had survived his purges, the foreign enemies whose hatred that Ivan's campaigns of pillage, torture and desolation had sharpened – all compounded to leave the country weak and divided. Countless acres of cultivated land had been abandoned by farmers during the terror of the *Oprichniki*, and forests had begun reclaiming the land.

During his reign of darkness hardly a family of noble birth was left whole, and some had been completely eliminated. Through his campaign of terror Ivan, Tsar of all the Russias, had created a system in which people who learned to hold their tongue, who not only never allowed themselves to speak their mind, but also did not even try to have an opinion, survived. He had laid the foundation for the top-heavy, unpredictable, often tyrannical autocracy of Tsarism – foundations that would eventually lead to its demise.

ELIZABETH, COUNTESS BATHORY

'COUNTESS DRACULA'

'You are like a wild animal. You are in the last months of your life, you do not deserve to breathe the air on earth, nor see the light of the Lord, you shall disappear from this world and never reappear in it again. The shadows will envelop you and you will find time to repent your bestial life.'

THE PROSECUTOR

Against the backdrop of mighty European monarchies like those of Elizabeth I, Ivan the Terrible and Louis XIII, one country remained mired in ancient superstition. Transylvania was the dark mystery of Europe, and at its heart was an evil woman, the Blood Countess. She was a sadist who perpetrated incredible cruelties upon her servants and peasant girls, murdering over 650 of them during her reign of terror. Cachtice Castle, a massive mountaintop fortress, was the site of her blood orgies and became known to the peasants as the 'Castle of Vampires'.

Elizabeth Bathory was born in 1560 and raised on the family estate of Esced in Transylvania. The Bathory family was rich and one of the most powerful Protestant families in the whole of the country. Her father George was a minister, who married his cousin, Anna. The illustrious family tree contained a number of war heroes as well as a cardinal and a future king of Poland. But Elizabeth also had some stranger relatives, perhaps the result of the constant intermarriage among the few Hungarian noble families. One of Elizabeth's uncles was reputedly addicted to rituals of Satanic worship, her aunt Klara was a well-known bi-sexual who enjoyed torturing her servants, and Elizabeth's brother, Stephan, was a drunk and a lecher. Many members of Elizabeth's family showed signs of epilepsy, madness, and other psychological disturbances. As a child, Elizabeth was prone to frequent fits in which she would be overcome with rage and uncontrollable behaviour.

Shortly after her birth the Ottoman Empire began to sink into a slow decline. The Turks hold over Transylvania had been weakened by a succession of Sultans for whom the harem held more attraction than the battlefield. News of some of the strange goings-on at the Ottoman court would have undoubtedly reached the ears of the young Elizabeth.

Around the age of six she witnessed an event which was to leave a lasting impression. A band of gypsies were invited to her home to provide entertainment at the court. During their stay, one of their number was accused of selling his children to the Turks. He was found guilty and sentenced to death. His long, plaintive cries, echoing throughout the castle ensured Elizabeth's rapt attention and at dawn she escaped from her governess and ran outside the castle to witness the punishment. There she saw a horse held fast to the ground. Soldiers slit open its belly, then grabbed the condemned man and shoved him inside, until only his head stuck out of the dying animal. Meanwhile, another soldier, armed with a long needle and coarse thread, sewed up the culprit in the belly of the horse.

Elizabeth was exceptionally intelligent, becoming fluent in Hungarian, Latin and German, at a time when even the ruling Prince of Transylvania was barely literate. She also learned at an early age that one could deal ruthlessly with disobedient peasants. At an age when most children learn to control their aggressive tendencies towards others, Elizabeth was under no such constraints. In 1571, when she was eleven, one of her cousins became the ruling Prince of Transylvania. Two years later, when the peasants rose in rebellion, he ordered that the noses and ears be cut off the fifty-four suspects under the shadow of the gallows.

Later that year, Elizabeth became engaged to Ferenc Nadasdy, the 'Black Hero of Hungary', who was a cruel and ruthless warrior. He was born in 1555, of noble birth, but not of as wealthy a lineage as the Bathorys. He had attended school in Vienna, but was not a good student although he was a fine athlete and popular amongst his peers.

Elizabeth was developing fast. She liked to dress in men's clothes and play men's games. Unfortunately, she became pregnant by a local peasant. When she gave birth, her bastard daughter was given away to a peasant with the assurance that she would never reappear during Elizabeth's lifetime.

At the age of fifteen, she married the twenty-one-year old Nadasdy, on 8 May 1575, at Varanno Castle. It was a spectacular wedding to which even the Holy Roman Emperor Maximillian was invited. He did not attend because of the distances involved in getting to Varanno, but he sent a delegation and an expensive wedding present.

Ferenc was a soldier who spent much of his time away from home fighting the Turks. He was one of five sharp-sabred heroes known as the, 'Unholy Quintet' who inspired fear in the enemy. Elizabeth was left in charge of Castle Sarvar, the Nadasdy family estate, in Hungary. Already a renowned beauty, she had also acquired the reputation for cruelty to her servants. She relished her power and ran the estate like a torture chamber. She had innumerable lovers, both men and women, and anyone found trespassing on her land could not expect to leave.

For the first ten years of their marriage, Elizabeth had no children because she and Ferenc were rarely together. Then around 1585 she bore a daughter, Anna, and over the following nine years gave birth to two more girls, Ursula and Katherina, and in 1598 bore her first and only son, Paul. Judging from letters written to her relatives, Elizabeth was a protective mother.

To kill some time, besides admiring her own beauty, she began to visit her lesbian aunt, Countess Karla Bathory, and to participate in orgies. Elizabeth then realized where her true passions lay: the inflicting of pain on large-bosomed young girls. Not only was Elizabeth becoming infatuated with her specialized carnal pleasure; she was also developing an interest in the occult. She met Dorothea Szantes, a black magic witch who encouraged Elizabeth's sadistic tendencies. Dorothea and Elizabeth's servant, Thorko, instructed Elizabeth in the ways of witchcraft. Later, she wrote to her husband to tell him of her discoveries. 'Thorko has taught me a lovely new technique, you catch a black hen and beat it to death with a white cane. Keep the blood and smear a little of it on your enemy. If you get no chance to smear it on his body, obtain one of his garments and smear that.'

Elizabeth's husband was, by all accounts, a vicious man, whose principal hobby was the torture of servants, although he did not torture them to death, as his wife did. Now he began to teach his cruel and promiscuous wife the subtle art of inflicting pain. Elizabeth took to her education with monstrous zeal. One of Ferenc's favourites was the honey torture, which involved stripping a girl naked, smearing honey over her, and leaving her tied up next to the estate's beehives.

Between them, the murderous lovers devised some ingenious methods of torture. When they suspected a servant of 'faking' illness they would have pieces of paper, soaked in oil, put between the toes and set on fire – very few servants in the Bathory household pleaded illness again.

A servant's escape was intolerable to Elizabeth and the punishment was nearly always death, although the method of execution varied. When a twelve-year-old girl named Pola somehow managed to escape from the castle, she was brought back, clad only in a long white robe. The Countess advanced on the young girl and forced her into a large cylindrical cage, too narrow to sit in, yet too small to stand in. Once the girl was inside, the cage was suddenly hauled

Elizabeth Bathory, the 'Blood Countess' of Transylvania, said to have been one of the most beautiful women in Europe, but also a murderess and sadist whose nationality and antecedents, quite apart from her terrifying cruelty, made it inevitable that she should be linked to the legends of the vampire Dracula. From a copy of an original portrait, since lost, from 1585.

(© 1997-2001 BY DENNIS BÁTHORY-KITSZ; WEBLINK: HTTP://BATHORY.ORG)

up by a pulley and dozens of short spikes jutted into the cage. The girl tried to avoid being caught on the spikes, but Ficzko, Elizabeth's dwarf, manoeuvred the ropes so that the cage shifted from side to side. Pola's flesh was torn to pieces.

In the dead of winter the Countess would have young women stripped naked and taken into the courtyard below her window. Water was then poured over the victim until she froze like an ice statue. Elizabeth would sit and gaze at her beautiful human sculptures for hours.

Records surviving to this day indicate the cruel and sadistic nature of the Countess. She would beat, torture and kill her servants with alarming enthusiasm. High birth bestowed complete authority during this period; serfs and peasants were barely considered human. A peasant could sometimes leave the service of his lord, but in practice this rarely happened, since the lord could accuse the peasant of a crime and have him convicted by the courts. It was perfect territory for a countess in love with torture.

Elizabeth was known to stick pins beneath the fingernails of the household staff as punishment for breaking her rules. If the girls did not complete their sewing by the time that Elizabeth was due to dress for dinner, they would be taken away for torturing. One day she put her fingers in a seamstress's mouth and pulled it until the girl's mouth split at the corners. Elizabeth would always make sure that she could see her victims' faces as they writhed in agony. She also chastised suspected thieves by heating a coin, then forcing the culprit to hold it until it seared a mark into the palm. If a servant failed to press the Countess's garments adequately, a hot iron would be held to her face, scarring her for life. Girls in their teens were routinely forced to strip naked in the presence of male serfs, to humiliate them. Terror, pain and death were an exciting pastime for Elizabeth Bathory.

Near the close of 1603, Ferenc suddenly became very ill, and died on the morning of 4 January 1604 – apparently by poison. Rather than curtailing Elizabeth's cruelties, Ferenc's death was just the beginning.

Only four weeks later, Elizabeth decided that she had mourned long enough and moved to the Nadasdy mansion in Vienna. She began making appearances at court, much to the horror of Rudolf, the Holy Roman Emperor, who found her brazen. But most of her time Elizabeth lived at Castle Cachtice, a forbidding fortress high above the River Vah. The castle contained a vast labyrinth of caves that would later bear witness to the worst of her atrocities.

But routine torture was not the limit of Elizabeth's excesses. In 1604 an enigmatic figure, Anna Darvulia came into the Countess's life. This, 'wild beast in human form' taught Elizabeth many new techniques of torture and became one of the most active sadists in her entourage. Darvulia made it her business to know everything about everyone in Elizabeth's service. She insisted on taking only girls, 'who have not yet tasted the pleasures of love', and most importantly, only peasant girls.

Countess Bathory was a woman of exceptional beauty. Her long raven hair was contrasted with her milky complexion. Her amber eyes were almost cat-like, her figure was voluptuous. But Elizabeth's beauty was beginning to show the ravages of time.

Firstly she tried to conceal the decline through cosmetics and the most expensive of clothes. But these would not conceal the ever-spreading wrinkles. Then a minor household incident inspired the Countess to pursue her love of death with a renewed vigour.

One fateful day a servant girl was attending to Elizabeth's hair and either pulled it or remarked that something was wrong with her mistress's headdress. The infuriated Countess slapped the girl so hard that blood spurted from her nose. The blood splashed against Elizabeth's face and where it had touched her skin, the Countess observed in a mirror, that a miracle had seemingly occurred. To her eyes, the skin had lost its lines of age. Elizabeth as to became exhilarated in the knowledge that she could regain her lost youth. Her witch, Darvulia instructed the credulous Elizabeth as to how she might again be young. The Countess believed the ancient credo that the taking of another's blood could result in the assimilation of that person's physical or spiritual qualities.

Following this discovery, she took the girl to her torture chamber and slitting her wrists, emptied her body of blood. Elizabeth then recruited her old nurse, Iloona Joo, her faithful servant Fizcko and Darvula and Dorothea to kidnap and kill more young girls on the pretext of hiring them as servants.

On some days Elizabeth had stark-naked girls laid flat on the floor of her bedroom and tortured them so much that one could scoop up the blood by the bucketful afterwards. Then the Countess had her servants bring up cinders in order to cover the pools of blood. When one young servant girl died too quickly, Elizabeth recorded that, 'she was too small'.

Even when Elizabeth was ill the tortures continued. 'She could not move from her bed and could not find the strength to torture her miscreant servant girls so she demanded that one of her female servants be brought before her. Dorothea Szentes, a burly, strong peasant woman, dragged one to her bedside and held her there. Elizabeth rose up from her pillow, and like a bulldog, opened her mouth and bit the girl first on the cheek, then she went for the girl's shoulders where she ripped out a piece of flesh with her teeth. Still not sated, Elizabeth proceeded to bite the girl's breasts.'

Over a period of ten years well over 600 young girls disappeared throughout the land. Once they were inside the castle, they would be pierced, tortured, killed and drained – all for the purpose of ensuring Countess Bathory's eternal youth. But with every kill the Countess was becoming more and more careless.

Elizabeth was renowned for throwing parts of her victims from her carriage window. Bodies piled up around her estate, and she was heard to boast of her new methods of torture in polite society. Disposing of the bodies was developing into a major logistical problem. At one point there were five bodies left under a bed in Castle Cachtice awaiting disposal, while the Countess went off on a trip. In order to throw off local suspicion, Elizabeth ordered that food should still be brought in for the five girls, so that the other servants would think they were still alive. To eradicate any possible identification of the mutilated bodies, a cover of lime had been strewn over them, then one after another the corpses were dragged out at night for burial. But Katerina Beneczky, who had been put in charge of disposing of the bodies, was too weak to haul the bodies out for herself. The decaying flesh began to stink up the whole house. Finally it got so bad that no one could bear to be inside. Elizabeth was forced to look outside the castle and was able to convince two peasants to help. The stinking lumps of flesh were thrown into a garden bed behind the castle where the potatoes and rhubarb were grown.

Bizarrely Elizabeth went out of her way to ensure that the dead girls were given proper Christian burials, at least initially. She enlisted the aid of the local Lutheran pastor, Andreas Berthoni, but when he was presented with two girls whose veins had been split open and drained of blood, he refused to perform his duties, because too many were coming to him who had died in, 'unknown and mysterious circumstances'. Day after day, month after month, year after year, Elizabeth continued to relish the blood of young girls, believing that it would help her gain 'inner beauty'. Darvulia had always stressed the importance of using only peasant girls, who had no recourse, but Darvulia was becoming increasingly incapacitated by blindness and epilepsy, and Elizabeth started to lose all sense of aristocratic decorum.

When Darvulia died, Elizabeth found herself ageing even more. Then another sorceress named Erzsi Majorova told her that the virginal victims must be of noble birth and so she began collecting some girls from the surrounding local nobility. But it was not so easy to get aristocratic girls. The entire system worked against it. The ladies, usually from the lower gentry, would have to be convinced that a living experience alongside the highly-placed and richly-connected Countess would bring with it incalculable rewards.

After word had spread about the strange goings-on, few well-bred girls would take the bait. So Elizabeth's assistants would procure peasant girls, have them washed

Cachtice Castle, the seat of Elizabeth Bathory, from a nineteenth-century engraving. When she was eventually convicted of the most revolting crimes against some 650 young girls, she was sentenced to be imprisoned for life within one of the towers of her own castle, where she was walled up in a cell within only a single tiny opening through which food was passed to her. There she died in 1614 – according to local legend, from having been starved of virgin blood. The ruins of the castle, including the remains of the tower in which she was imprisoned, still stand today.
(© 2001 BY DENNIS BÁTHORY-KITSZ;
WEBLINK: HTTP://BATHORY.ORG)

down and scoured. They were then coiffured stylishly and dressed in fine flowing garments. The girls would be ushered into a large dining hall where they took their seats in accordance with strict instructions. All were expected to speak in a low voice and await the main event, the coming of the Countess. Eyes turned anxiously towards the doorway. Finally, Elizabeth, often dressed in a luxuriant red robe embellished with lavish pearls, made her grand entry. Then the blood would begin to flow.

By now, the sheer number of murders Elizabeth had committed was beginning to tally against her. Sometimes a mother of one of the victims would inquire about what had happened to her daughter. One such woman was Anna Gonczy, who had heard from some of Elizabeth's servants that her daughter had died whilst in service to the Countess. She asked to see the dead body of her child. Elizabeth's servants, of course, refused to show her the body, because it had the telltale signs of torture on it. The woman persisted until threatened by Elizabeth's officials. Only later would Anna realise the full horror of her daughter's last moments.

The power of Elizabeth's connections made her virtually unassailable. When a new pastor, the Reverend Janos Ponikenusz, investigated the subterranean passages between the church and castle, he found nine boxes containing the mutilated remains of the recently murdered girls. No one had even bothered to nail the boxes shut. He reported the discovery to his superior, the very Reverend Elias Lanyi – calling the Countess Bathory, 'the worst killer under the sun'. His report never reached its destination – the Countess's henchmen intercepted it.

In the summer of 1610 Elizabeth Bathory became gravely ill. She decided to visit Piestany, a health resort. Before she left, she ordered that all the female servants should go on an eight-day fast. Dorothea Szentes was charged with making sure that the girls adhered. They were told not to drink or eat anything. At night they were bathed in cold water and obliged to stand naked in the fortress courtyard to ensure that no violation of the rules could take place. But Dorothea did her job too well. When Elizabeth was ready to leave for Piestany, there was no servant well enough to accompany her. An aristocratic girl from the town of Domolk was chosen. She was never to return from the trip and was dumped from the carriage on the busy road.

In the winter of 1610 Elizabeth evidently still felt that her social position made her virtually untouchable before the law. She had her servants throw four dead girls from the castle ramparts in full view of the Catholic villagers. When she was denounced by local Christian ministers she paid no attention. After all, what did peasants matter? For a long time she was able to weather the controversy. She was a pious lady – she observed religious rituals, even getting seminary students to sing the requisite dirges and funeral psalms over the dead girls' graves.

The life of a Transylvanian peasant was a hard one. They were in general, treated very harshly; they were recruited by force and bodily punishment was very much the norm. They were considered chattels and had no real rights. Elizabeth's servants realized that any direct resistance to her tyrannical rule would be futile, but they were able to engage in some subterfuge. Realizing that Elizabeth's cruelties abated somewhat when she had visitors, they did all they could to lengthen the guests' stays: they released their horses go and hid wagon wheels.

Despite her great wealth and extensive properties, which she had inherited largely through her own family, Elizabeth was always complaining about a lack of money. It had been common practice among the Hungarian nobles to finance their knights, usually out of their own pockets. The crown very rarely had the cash and Ferenc had lent a large amount of money (17,408 gulden) to King Matthias. After her husband's death, Elizabeth had been trying to ensure that the Hungarian King honoured his debts to her husband. She needed the money for her rather expensive pastime. As rumours spread about the Countess's practices only the brave, foolhardy or desperately poor could be lured into her service. Her cohorts would often have to go to distant villages and offer increasingly high prices to recruit the girls. Murder is, after all, an expensive business.

Elizabeth resorted to selling two of her family castles; the crown purchased the first, Theben Castle, an important frontier fort and the second, Beckov, was pawned for 2,000 gulden. By this time the rest of her family were fully aware of Elizabeth's tendencies. Her cousin, Count Thurzo, Palantine Prince of Transylvania, gathered the rest of the clan together and arranged for Elizabeth to leave Cachtice Castle, sojourn in Varanno and there be spirited off to a convent where she, 'would end her days.' Several days before his plans could be put into action however, Count Thurzo learnt that Impre Megyert had registered a formal complaint against Elizabeth before the Hungarian Parliament. The Parliament was to listen to the testimonies and accusations against the Countess for three days. Times were changing and not in Elizabeth's favour. The lawlessness and extraordinary power of the nobles was coming to an end as the Holy Roman Emperor, the Archduke Matthias II, was determined to restore order.

The Archduke started an investigation of his own into Elizabeth Bathory. Gabor Bathory, a cousin of Elizabeth's, wanted to dispose of King Matthias II and expand Transylvania and absorb some of the Empire's lands into his own. As a member of the Bathory clan, Elizabeth got caught in the political crossfire and suffered the consequences. Her family, fearing they would lose their property rights if she was found guilty of crimes warranting the confiscation of their estates, became active accomplices in her capture and subsequent trial.

From the end of March 1610 to the beginning of July, the testimonies of thirty-four witnesses were recorded – some of whom were nobles. It was in Matthias's interests to destroy Elizabeth. If she were to be found guilty, her property would be confiscated, and, most important of all, her claims to the debt which the crown owed her would be void.

Finally, Reverend Ponikenusz managed to get his report to Count Thurzo. The title Palantine allowed Thurzo to act with the full authority of the king in his absence, but he was in a very delicate position. As the widow of one of the leading lords of the realm, Elizabeth could not be arrested without a special act of Parliament.

Under pressure from the Hungarian Catholic nobles, Parliament was summoned to Bratislava, Hungary's temporary capital after Budapest had fallen to the Turks. The nobles listened to the complaints and testimonies. They were particularly indignant that Elizabeth had indulged in her barbaric acts on girls of noble birth, not only peasant girls. But Count Thurzo was in a quandary. In the midst of his attempts to find some face-saving device and preserve Elizabeth's properties from confiscation by the king, an emissary from King Matthias arrived – asking Thurzo to go to Castle Cachtice, find out the facts, and punish the guilty – by royal command.

Thurzo wanted to handle things to the Bathory family's advantage and so he planned his visit to Elizabeth's castle to coincide with the Christmas holiday, when the Hungarian Parliament was not in session.

By December 1610, Elizabeth was aware that the net was closing in and she took steps against her plotters. She had long been an advocate of poisoning and sorcery. She had Majorova mix up a batch of potion. After Elizabeth had taken a bath in the potion, it was made into a special seed cake. Her plan was to serve the cake to the King and Count Thurzo who were expected at Castle Cachtice. But something went wrong and when she instructed some of her retainers to eat the cake, all they got were stomach upsets. She did not try it again.

Elizabeth's last victim, Doricza, was a buxom, powerfully built girl from Croatia. Accused of stealing a pear, the girl was ordered to appear in the laundry room. Once she arrived the usual, 'home justice' began. The girl was first made to undress, then had her hands tied behind her back. Elizabeth then beat her with a club – but Doricza refused to die – so someone else had to take over the job. When she was refreshed Elizabeth resumed the beatings, pausing only to change her blood-stained shirt for another. But Doricza hung on. Finally she was stabbed with a pair of scissors – a twisted lump of flesh was practically all that remained.

On the night of 30 December, the castle was raided. The group moved rapidly through the main courtyard, then Count Thurzo stumbled over something in the dark – it was the body of a young girl – a body that had been cut and torn to shreds. Once inside the building he descended down 150 feet to be confronted by an iron-spiked door. Inside the air was damp and fetid, but through the haze he noticed a fifty-year-old woman crouched over a stool. When she turned to him in a state of frenzy, Thurzo realised it was Elizabeth. 'You shall pay for this intrusion' she shouted. 'Not so, my lady' he responded 'this is not one of your servants, but the Palatine Prince of Hungary who has come to bring justice to these accursed walls.' Meanwhile, the Count's companions crowded into the room to survey the carnage. Elizabeth's cohorts were rounded up and Elizabeth was dispatched to her room. Inside, the castle the authorities found the body of one dead girl in the main room, drained of blood, a bowl of blood in another, and girls imprisoned in the dungeons, pierced with holes, but still alive. Under the castle they found over fifty corpses.

The trial began on 2 January 1611. It became a huge, public event and the packed gallery was shocked to hear detailed accounts of the Blood Countess's gruesome tortures and the pleasure she received from it all. Count Thurzo had already secretly arranged that Elizabeth would not be brought to trial. The Countess was tried purely on a criminal basis, while her cohorts in terror were charged with vampirism, witchcraft and practising pagan rituals. The testimonies of her four accomplices were taken and their sentences pronounced. The testimonies of the four placed the body count at between thirty and sixty, but a fifth witness revealed the missing piece of the puzzle.

This witness was called 'Zusanna' and she revealed the single most shocking piece of evidence in the trial; a list and register in the countess's chest of drawers, which put the number of girls killed at six-hundred-and-fifty. The list was in the Countess's own handwriting. Elizabeth and her cohorts had kept full details of their crimes!

Local woman Erzsi Majorova was sentenced to death for taking the bodies from the Countess and disposing of them for a fee. Iloona Joo and Dorothea Szentes were sentenced to have all their fingers, which they had used as instruments in so many butcherings, torn out by the public executioner with a pair of red-hot pincers; and after that their bodies were thrown alive onto a fire. Elizabeth's dwarf, Ficzko was decapitated and afterwards drained of blood and then burnt.

Although Elizabeth repeatedly denied her guilt and petitioned to appear before the court many times, her pleas were ignored. Thanks to a letter-writing campaign led by her powerful family and the machinations of Count Thurzo she was sentenced with the words: 'You are like a wild animal. You are in the last months of your life, you do not deserve to breathe the air on earth, nor to see the light of the lord, you shall disappear from this world and shall never reappear in it again. The shadows will envelop you and you will find time to repent your bestial life.' Elizabeth was condemned to life imprisonment in her own castle.

Stonemasons were instructed to wall Elizabeth into her cell. She was to live in a single walled-up room, with only a small opening for food to be passed through. Four gibbets were built at the corners of the castle to demonstrate to the peasants that 'justice' had been done.

On 31 July 1614, Countess Elizabeth Bathory dictated her last will and testament to two priests. She left everything to her children. One month later, four years after her imprisonment, a curious guard approached her cell to try and get a look at the infamous Countess. Even at the age of fifty-four, she was said to be one of the most beautiful women in all of Europe. The guard looked in through the door slot, but there was no movement. Then he saw a figure on the bed lying face down. The Blood Countess was dead. Legend has it she was starved of virgin blood.

Her body was intended to be buried in the church in the local town, but the local inhabitants found it, not surprisingly, abhorrent that she would be placed on hallowed ground and so her body was moved to the town of Ecsed, the original Bathory seat and the place of her childhood.

RASPUTIN

THE 'MAD MONK' WHO BROUGHT DOWN A DYNASTY

Understanding Rasputin is the key to understanding both the soul and the brutality of the Russia that came after him. He was a precursor of the millions of peasants who, with religious consciousness in their souls, would nevertheless tear down churches and who, with a dream of the reign of Love and Justice, would murder, rape and flood the country with blood, in the end destroying themselves.

EDVARD RADZINSKY

In December 1916, the bloated, castrated body of a man was dragged from the freezing waters of the River Neva in St Petersburg. As news of his identity leaked out, headlines in Russian newspapers screamed, '**GRIGORI RASPUTIN HAS CEASED TO EXIST!**' People from all walks of life, both rich and poor, celebrated the death of the 'mad monk' who had risen from the lowest rung of society to become perhaps the most hated man in Russia. Implicated in murder, corruption, extortion and debauchery, Rasputin was instrumental in wiping out the 300-year-old Romanov dynasty and changing the history of Russia forever. Against a backdrop of the First World War and the rumblings of a burgeoning revolution, this semi-literate Siberian mystic had come to exercise a malign, almost hypnotic power over the last Tsar and Tsarina of Russia, Nicholas II and his consort, Alexandra.

Variously regarded as a saint, a sinner and a devil by those who knew him, Grigori Yefinovitch Novykh was born in 1869 into a peasant family in the village of Pokrovskoe, deep in the vast, little-populated wastelands of Siberia. Uneducated – he never went to school – the young Grigori was virtually illiterate. He was, however, rowdy and lascivious, a drinker, a brawler and a thief, and thereby acquired the name 'Rasputin', from the Russian word *rasputnik*, meaning libertine or debauched person.

Yet his life was to change forever when, after a visit to a monastery in the Urals he, 'perceived the Divine Grace' as he himself described this epiphany. There, he became fascinated with the Russian Orthodox faith, and at the same time discovered his ability to calm people in distress and to predict the future. He gave up drinking, smoking and eating meat, and began to test himself with severe fasting. His conversion to a 'Man of God' was sealed once he discovered the *Khlysty*, an extreme quasi-Christian sect. Relatively little is known about this heretical cult, although it seems to have combined elements from older, orgiastic pagan practices with a crude form of

Christianity. The *Khlysts* believed that only by actively sinning could one eventually reach a state of purification and be truly purged. Stress was laid on penitence, but also on ecstatic communal rites and dancing, often culminating in wild sex orgies involving the entire group.

Whether driven, as a result of his new faith, by religious fervour or by more basic human urges, as a young man Rasputin plotted the corruption of women from nearby villages, and even had a cabin built in a remote spot to ensure the secluded seduction of hundreds of impressionable girls. Even so, his adherence to the *Khlysts'* hybrid of mysticism and eroticism did not entirely strip him of familial instincts. He married a local girl named Proskovia, who bore him two daughters, Maria and Varvara, and a son, Dimitri. He was not destined to play the doting father for long, however.

Rasputin now styled himself a *starets* or holy man. Reverence for *startsy* was an age-old tradition in Russia, deeply ingrained in the collective consciousness. Established over centuries on the vast spaces of the Ukraine, the Urals and Siberia, this near-worship of the holy men formed one of the cornerstones of a Russian's faith. Yet a *starets* was not a priest or monk but, as Dostoevsky wrote in *The Brothers Karamazov*, 'someone who takes your soul, your will and makes them his. When you select your *starets*, you surrender your will and give it to him in utter submission, in complete self-renunciation.' Rasputin was to embrace this belief wholeheartedly, helped by the credulousness of many faithful Russians in their dealings with holy men.

He sought to capture the minds and souls of simple-minded believers, high and low, rich and poor, in order to bend them to his will. Preaching a doctrine of salvation through sin, he emphasized to his flock, which was largely composed of women, that sins of the flesh were especially efficacious for achieving God's forgiveness, and thus salvation. Fixing them with his hypnotic eyes – and all contemporary sources agree about the extraordinary penetrating quality of his gaze – he urged them to yield unresistingly to temptation, offering himself as both the means of temptation and the vehicle for their lapse into sin.

Playing upon the general reverence for a *starets* and upon his mystical powers of suggestion and hypnosis, Rasputin travelled through Russia preaching and fornicating. To his immense willpower, great physical presence and strength, natural wit and peasant's cunning was added an almost miraculous intuition. All these features merged in a man whose vigour and magnetism were to make a strong impact upon the weak, and especially upon those whose lives were hedged around with hesitations and doubts.

As the twentieth century dawned, rumours of the remarkable *starets* began to filter beyond the borders of Siberia. In 1903 Rasputin arrived in St Petersburg. Now in his early thirties, he presented an imposing, if shaggy, figure, clad in a sable coat thrown over peasant blouse, trousers and boots. His untrimmed and filthy hair and beard, laced with bits of food, gave off, it is said, a potent odour reminiscent of a goat. None the less, he joined the St Petersburg Theological Academy, where he came to the attention of Father Ioann of Kronstadt, a figure of immense moral authority in Russia at that time.

The starets *(holy man) Grigori Rasputin, a photograph published after his murder in 1916. Scheming, malevolent, treacherous and priapic, he nevertheless exercised an almost hypnotic control over those who met him, and especially women. The influence he exerted over the Russian royal family, and especially the Tsarina, sealed their fate; in killing Rasputin in order to preserve the old regime, his murderers had in reality struck that regime's last blow. (© THE ILLUSTRATED LONDON NEWS PICTURE AGENCY)*

The influential priest gave his blessing to Rasputin, calling him a 'God seeker'.

It was not God that he sought, however. Not long after his arrival in St Petersburg, Rasputin began to gather around him a group of noblewomen who, having heard about the strangely charismatic *starets*, sought his company and, through his crude lovemaking, his blessings. Largely uneducated, except in social graces, often rather empty-headed, or simply bored with their privileged, over-protected lives, many of these women found it titillating to be ravished by this malodorous peasant. Rasputin ate with his hands, tore at his food with blackened teeth, used the foulest language in their presence, gave them graphic descriptions of the horses mating on his father's farm in Siberia, and took them quickly and brutally, with the vaguely muttered assurance that, 'Now, Mother, everything is in order.'

The city to which Rasputin came – the capital of the Russian Empire since the days of Peter I 'the Great' – was at the beginning of its Silver Age, an era marked by shocking scandal, extreme debauchery, a kind of frenzied searching for meaning and experience, and deep, passionate belief. The artists and intellectuals of the time had embarked upon a voyage not only of intellectual and artistic discovery, but also of unrestrained sexual exploration, which led them, and their aristocratic patrons, to

Tsar Nicholas II, with three of his daughters, in Bolshevik captivity following his abdication in 1917. On 18 July the following year, the Tsar and all his family were brutally murdered in Ekaterinburg, fulfilling a prediction that Rasputin had made in a letter.
(© THE ILLUSTRATED LONDON NEWS PICTURE AGENCY)

experiments with pederasty, lesbianism and every variety of sadomasochism. Suicide, murder, opium and alcohol – all formed an integral part of life in the upper echelons of St Petersburg society.

Tsar Nicholas and his German-born wife, the former Princess Alix of Hesse and by Rhine, styled in the Russian form Alexandra but known to her intimates as Alix, created for themselves a very different world. Refusing to live at the Winter Palace in the capital, where the Romanov dynasty had resided since the building's completion in 1762, Alix had created a home for them at the Alexander Palace in Tsarskoe Selo, half an hour's train ride from St Petersburg. She attempted to confine her children and Nicholas in a sort of everlasting cosy tea party, and thereby created a world for them as unhealthy as it was unreal, a world peopled by fawning mediocrities, saccharine and false emotions, and little contact with the realities of their increasingly turbulent country. Strange and questionable characters came and went, basking in the Tsarina's favour but in reality doing no more than preying upon her strong but guileless faith in charlatan healers and spurious holy men.

Initially, the Tsarina had turned to faith healers and other dubious practitioners because of her intense desire for a son. She had given birth to four daughters, the Grand Duchesses Tatiana, Olga, Militsa and Anastasia, but there was still no male heir to the Romanov dynasty. In desperation she turned to a Doctor Philippe, a man who, although not without a following in St Petersburg society, had been convicted on three occasions in his native France of practising medicine without a licence. Philippe claimed to be able to see into the future, to change the course of events and to communicate beyond the grave. Eventually he was forced to leave Russia after a series of false predictions, but even then the royal couple were sorry to see him go, although he promised that, 'Someday you will have another friend like me who will speak to you of God.'

On 30 July 1904 Alix finally gave birth to a son, whom they named Alexei. By September, however, the royal couple were concerned by, 'the constant bleeding from his navel' and when the Tsarevich was found to be suffering from haemophilia, a disease which is transmitted through the maternal line, Alix believed that the fault lay with her. Medical experts from all over Europe had little comfort to offer. Nicholas and Alix turned to Dr Zhimsarian Badmaev, a Tibetan herbalist, as well as to outright fakers and itinerant 'holy men', sincere or otherwise. But modern science, Tibetan herbs and the ravings of the supposedly godly could not cure the boy. The Tsarina retreated deeper into her cocoon of anxiety and misplaced guilt.

Rasputin was already nearing middle age when he came to the attention of Nicholas and Alix. He had a group of oddly assorted sponsors in St Petersburg – the Bishop Feofan (who would eventually denounce him as immoral), certain Montenegrin princesses who were close to the imperial family, and a highly influential intimate of the Tsarina named Anna Vyrubova, a plump woman without looks, birth or culture, but who had an astonishing capacity for backstage intrigue and manipulation. She herself had been brought out of a coma by Rasputin following a riding accident, and revered him as a saint.

When the Grand Duchesses Militsa and Anastasia, who had discovered Dr Philippe years before, began to sing Rasputin's praises, backed by Anna Vryubova, the *starets* was summoned to the royal presence. The date was 1 November 1905, and Tsar Nicholas recorded the meeting in his diary: 'Had tea with Militsa and Stana [Tatiana]. Met a man of God, from Tobolsk province.' It was to be the start of a fateful association, for no single figure, except perhaps Lenin, would influence the lives of Nicholas and Alix and their children so directly, or so catastrophically.

For a couple of years meetings between Rasputin and the royal family were rare. In the meantime, however, his fame in St Petersburg grew. Even the Prime Minister, Peter Stolypin, who had no time at all for mysticism and was to become one of the holy man's most bitter opponents, invited Rasputin to pray at the bedside of his sick daughter.

Rasputin cut an exotic figure in the fashionable salons of Russian society. In the frenetic world of St Petersburg, he attracted women to him as honey attracts bees. He had an inner power that they found difficult to resist. Then there were his eyes . . . According to Maurice Paléologue, France's Ambassador to Russia at the time, 'The whole expression of his face was concentrated in the eyes – light-blue with a curious sparkle, depth, and fascination. His gaze was at once penetrating and caressing, naïve and cunning, direct and yet remote. When he was excited, it seemed as if his pupils became magnetic.'

As his fame spread, a trail of rumours drawn from his Siberian background began to gain credence. The aura of disturbing stories about incredible erotic adventures and orgies fanned the lustful imaginations of the aristocracy and petty bourgeoisie alike. Rasputin recounted some of these stories himself – as his fame and influence grew, the unbridled *muzhik* (Russian peasant) would revel in the ostentatious divulging of confidences.

Despite the stench of scandal that went with him everywhere, the royal family continued to meet with Rasputin – though only in private. In a small stone house in Tsarskoe Selo belonging to the devoted Anna Vyrubova, Nicholas and Alix would come to listen, enraptured by the holy man's words. He brought comfort with his soothing conversations, and with his predictions that all tumults and upheavals would soon be over.

At the end of 1907, the young Tsarevich, Alexei, started bleeding, and for the first time Rasputin was summoned to his bedside. Amazingly, his presence immediately calmed the boy, and his internal bleeding slowed and eventually stopped. The Tsarevich's illness had fatally chained the Tsar's family to the notorious *starets* forever. For Alix, Rasputin was a true believer, a man with a prayer on his lips, oblivious of his own self, caring for the destinies of common people and pleading for the miserable. To her, he filled the role of her teacher and confessor. Convinced he was God's messenger, she adopted him as the royal family's mascot. His advocacy for them before the throne of God promised them hope for the future. But as Rasputin drew closer and closer to the royal family, the gentry and officials became increasingly horrified. Educated, refined society began to grumble. After a time, the rows and scandal surrounding the Tsarina's holy man attracted the attention of the Dowager Empress, the widow of the Tsar's father, Nicholas I. As a young woman she had been told a prophecy which foresaw that: 'Your son will reign, will be climbing the mountain to attain wealth and great honour. Only he will never reach the top, stricken by a muzhik's hand.' But Nicholas and Alix had already formed their own, unshakeable opinion of Rasputin and refused to heed the Dowager's order that, 'the fiend incarnate be banished from St Petersburg.'

Rasputin's rise to power within the imperial court had begun as Russia was attempting to establish a constitutional monarchy. In the wake of the country's humiliation in the disastrous Russo-Japanese War of 1904-5, public pressure had forced the Tsar and his advisers to establish, in 1905, a parliament, the Duma, the first in Russia's history. A year later Nicholas had appointed a new Prime Minister, Peter Stolypin. Many believed that Stolypin was Russia's last hope of attaining intelligent and enlightened government. Russia prospered under his guidance, but to the Tsarina he was an arch-enemy. She hated him because he dared to vilify her beloved Rasputin. Stolypin repeatedly told the Tsar that he needed to distance himself and his family from this untrustworthy man. At one point, he even brought to the Tsar documented proof of Rasputin's evil affairs. Nicholas, however, ignored him, not wanting to take away from Alix the one man she believed could save her son's life. Thwarted, Stolypin therefore decided to take action himself. He ordered the *starets* to leave the capital, thus further outraging the Tsarina, and in due course Rasputin left St Petersburg, beginning a journey to Jerusalem and the Holy Land.

His banishment from the capital was to be short-lived, however. On the evening of 1 September 1911, during a royal performance of Rimski-Korsakov's *Tale of the Tsar Saltan* at the Kiev Opera House, Stolypin was shot at point-blank range by a revolutionary, Bogrov. Mysteriously, the assassin was executed before a full inquiry could be made; worse still, Nicholas had lost the last truly able statesman to serve him. In October 1912, while the Tsar and his family were at their hunting lodge in Spala, Alexei fell and struck the side of a bathtub. Bruised and bleeding, he was in terrible pain, and a notice announcing his death was drawn up. Desperate, the Tsarina telegraphed Rasputin. 'God has seen your tears,' he wired back, 'Do not grieve. The Little One will not die.' Hours later, Alexei's temperature fell and the bleeding stopped. To Nicholas and Alix it was a miracle sent directly from God, and Rasputin's future as a holy man in whom the Tsarina placed absolute confidence was assured. He had regained full favour within the imperial family. When he was away Alix liked to imagine she was kneeling before him, hearing his voice and feeling the touch of his hands. Her daughters wrote letters to him, assuring him of their ardent love.

With his position in the palace secure, and with the assurance of the Tsarina's protection, Rasputin became increasingly powerful and untouchable. The Tsarevich's illness was a closely guarded secret, but the complete ignorance of the Russian people about Alexei's disease – and, hence, the reasons for the Tsarina's confidence in Rasputin – created a threatening situation. All sorts of fantastic tales about vast debauches at Tsarskoe Selo, in which the women of the royal family and their followers gave themselves to Rasputin in a wild and unrestrained frenzy of lust, began to circulate from mouth to mouth, from salon to salon.

The censors did their best to hide this embarrassing upstart. They daubed ink over newspaper columns that carried stories about or referring to him. The black blotches came to be known as 'caviar', but readers knew whom the caviar were protecting, and they invented stories of their own. A society hostess, irritated that her guests talked of nothing else, put up a printed sign in her dining room: 'We do not discuss Rasputin here.' But people did discuss him; indeed, nothing would stop them. The talk centred on his position at the very pinnacle of society. 'Dark powers behind the throne,' 'The power of Rasputin!' 'Infamous stories about the Empress,' the British Ambassador's daughter, Meriel Buchanan, noted in her diary. 'The filthy gossip about the Tsar's family has now become the property of the street', wrote an agent of the *Okhrana*, the Tsar's brutal and corrupt Secret Police.

Crude cartoons were passed around portraying Rasputin emerging from the naked Tsarina's nipples to tower over Russia, his wild eyes staring from a black cloud of hair and beard. Gambling dens used playing cards in which his head replaced the Tsar's on the king of spades. A caricature in the form of an icon showed him with a vodka bottle in one hand and the naked Tsar cradled like the Christ child in the other, while the flames of Hell licked at his boots and nubile women, naked apart from angels' wings and black silk stockings, flew about his head. A photograph of Rasputin with a collection of society women was reproduced by the thousand. Mikhail Rodzianko, a leading politician, declared that he was horrified to find that he recognized many of these worshippers from high society, and added that he had received a huge mass of letters from mothers whose daughters had been disgraced by the impudent profligate.

On 29 June 1914, in the village of Pokroskoye, a peasant woman, Khonia Guseva, a former devotee, attempted to kill Rasputin by stabbing him in the stomach. The wound was a slight one, however, and he returned to St Petersburg and was dining with the Tsar by the 22 July, anxious to consolidate his position and to show that he had recovered. His grip on Nicholas and Alix was tightening.

In 1914 Russia went to war with Germany and a wave of patriotic fervour broke over the country. Nicholas was cheered wherever he went, and flags, icons and portraits of the Tsar sold out. In the capital, the German Embassy was destroyed by the fervent mob. Peasants were mobilized by the hundreds of thousands all over Russia – many of them would never return, victims of the corruption and mismanagement in the government perpetrated by men appointed under Rasputin's guidance.

Over the next two years the government went through four Prime Ministers and six Ministers of the Interior, many of whom had been happy to pay large sums to Rasputin for their position. Prince Vladimir Volkonskii suggested that a sign should be put up reading 'Piccadilly – the show changes every Saturday.' As a consequence of Rasputin's and Alix's meddling in state affairs, and Nicholas's acquiescence, Russia's

Rasputin surrounded by courtiers of the Tsar and Tsarina. His influence over even the Russian aristocracy was profound, if often sinister; nor did he make any concessions to their tastes and manners, affecting peasant dress (as in this photograph taken around 1911) and manners, and often with filthy hands, face, hair and clothing. (© BETTMANN/CORBIS)

government was deprived of every reasonably able statesman. By the autumn of 1916, the behaviour of the Tsarina and her holy man had left Russia with a motley assortment of rogues, incompetents, nonentities and madmen at the heart of government. Rasputin arranged for the appointment of placemen to key government posts, often selected for the most trivial of reasons; Alix supported his decisions, overriding all objections, and the Tsar confirmed them. Alexei Khvostov was appointed on the basis of his fine bass voice. Rasputin's minion Boris Stürmer became Prime Minister in the autumn of 1916. Stürmer, a 'shallow and dishonest creature who emits an intolerable odour of falseness', excited disgust. He maddened the United States Ambassador, David Francis, by gazing at himself in a mirror with enraptured admiration during appointments, twirling the waxed ends of his moustache.

The second most powerful position of state, that of Minister of the Interior, was gifted by Rasputin to Alexander Protopopov, who strutted around in high boots and an operatic uniform he had designed himself. He suffered from syphilis, was prone to hallucinations, and was considered insane; in his talks with the Tsarina he would repeat warnings and messages he had received from the spirit world.

Meanwhile, letters to the Tsar from highly placed officials overflowed with unwise or corrupt advice. Embroidered by the hand of the Tsarina, Rasputin's influence was spreading all the way to the front line, with devastating consequences. By replacing the

War Minister with Vladimir Sukomlinov, a money-grabbing incompetent, but nevertheless a close friend, Rasputin signed the death warrants of thousands of Russian soldiers. A chronic shortage of weapons and supplies developed almost immediately. By early 1915, two out of three Russian soldiers were being sent to the front line without rifles, ammunition or boots. With no wire for field telephones, communication increasingly had to be by radio, but since there was also a shortage of code books, many radio messages were picked up and easily deciphered by German intelligence. As the casualties – from disease and privation as well as from enemy action – rose and trenches began to choke with bodies, people at home started to demand answers. When Rasputin refused to replace his puppet, the carnage grew worse.

Russia had been heavily engaged on the Eastern Front since the outbreak of war, and her armies had suffered terrible casualties in a series of actions against German and Austro-Hungarian forces. While thousands of Russian soldiers were drowning in their own blood, Rasputin's refusal to relieve his friend Sukomlinov of duty resulted in a groundswell of accusations that the German-born Tsarina and her chief adviser were colluding with the enemy.

By mid-1915 the Russian army was on the brink of collapse. As a result, Nicholas, on the advice of Rasputin and Alix, decided to assume the position of Commander-in-Chief of the Russian armies in the field. It proved a fateful decision. For the majority of Russians in those days, the Tsar was a semi-mystical, almost god-like figure – powerful, all-seeing, almost impossibly remote, and certainly far beyond the judgement of the masses. Nicholas ruled 130 million people who lived over more than 8.75 million square miles and the prevailing belief was that he was a divinely appointed monarch and subject to no man. Now his deeply flawed character, stubbornness and inability to make effective decisions became all too obvious – he lost his god-like status in the eyes of many ordinary Russians yet despite 5 million dead, and the loss of Warsaw and his Polish territories, the Tsar remained confident that the army was loyal.

Totally isolated from reality, Nicholas had stationed himself in the provincial town of Mogilev far away from the front. He had taken over a hotel and took daily walks by the river with his English setters. In the evening he watched movies. His favourite was a twenty-two reel detective serial called, *The Secrets of New York*. Meanwhile Rasputin's hold on the Tsarina was growing increasingly vice-like and, in the absence of the Tsar (who may have gone just to get away from the two of them), Alix became virtually the sole ruler of the Empire, with 'the Friend', as she called Rasputin, immediately behind her in the role of *éminence grise*.

The troops no longer thought of themselves as Russian soldiers, '…they were just men who were going to die.' They told each other that the government had been paid a billion roubles by Berlin to ensure that as few of them as possible survived the war. But their most special hatred was reserved for the German-born Tsarina; they thought she was in league with the enemy, that she talked to Germany on a radio concealed under the eaves of her palace, that she passed secrets to her sister, Princess Irene of

Prussia and that to accept a decoration from her meant certain death. When Nicholas attended medal ceremonies to award the Cross of St George, they laughed and called it the 'Grigori Cross'.

The Tsarina meanwhile rarely left the Alexander Palace in Tsarskoe Selo. She lay for much of the time on a chaise-longue in her boudoir, a terrier at her feet. To her, Russia was the countryside and Rasputin, the honest peasant in blouse and boots, simple and holy, her Friend, was its personification. Mail that she received from the 'real Russia' was forged by the secret police on the orders of Protopopov, Rasputin's friend. Genuine letters told a different story.

The mood on the streets of St Petersburg now became increasingly nasty. The *Okhrana* said that it was no longer possible to prosecute all who insulted the Tsar and Tsarina because the numbers were too great for the courts to cope. A letter sent by the London *Times'* representative warned that the Romanov dynasty was in danger – banners calling for their dismissal were found everywhere.

Meanwhile Rasputin, when not with Alix, was carrying on life as normal in his apartment at 64 Gorokhovaia Street, a nondescript block where he shared his stairway with a masseuse and a seamstress. The whole of Rasputin's flat bore the stamp of bourgeois well-being and prosperity yet, located near the railway station, in a modest part of town, it enabled Rasputin to preserve his image as a man of the people. Into this apartment streamed an endless number of women – all seeking favours from Rasputin. In return he received money, wine, sweets or sexual favours. He was constantly under surveillance by the *Okhrana* who noted down who spent the night and what bribes they bought whilst his personal life was gossiped about among the police agents and their friends. Worse than that, the rumours about his private life were that he was committing gross acts of public indecency. At the Iar restaurant, an infamous drinking den in Moscow, Rasputin exposed himself to a number of women and made obscene remarks. When supper was over, a drunk Rasputin talked of the Tsarina as his 'old girl' boasting that he could do anything he liked with her. Eventually he had to be dragged away by the police, swearing eternal vengeance. Russia seemed to have fallen into the hands of a debauchee so dissolute as to defy all polite description.

Still the royal couple refused to hear the truth about Rasputin. In September 1916 when General Dzhunovskii showed Nicholas details of his behaviour at the Iar restaurant he was sent into retirement. Purishkevich, one of the leaders of the Duma, asked all the ministers to throw themselves at the Tsar's feet and beg him to get rid of Rasputin.

On December 8 the Union of Towns, an important municipal body, went into secret session. The resolution it passed read, 'the government, now become an instrument of the dark forces, is driving Russia to her ruin and is shattering the imperial throne.' Dark forces was simple code for Grigorii Rasputin. The widely distributed pamphlet was addressed to, 'Father Grigorii, new saint of the devil, reviler of Christ's teachings, ruiner of Russian land, defiler of wives and maidens.' It urged Rasputin to rejoice at the Tsar's dulled mind, the Tsarina's delectation, at their daughters' seduction and at the propagation of dark forces – 'Rejoice', the pamphlet said, 'Rejoice, foul receptacle of Satan!' Slowly they were becoming aware that nothing would break the royal couple's dependence upon Rasputin – he would have to die and very soon a new ally joined Purishkevich's cause. Prince Feliks Yusupov, a transvestite and a member of one of the most illustrious families in Russia, who carried, 'God in one eye and the devil in another'. Together they recruited Grand Duke Dmitrii Pavlovich, who had been touted as a possible husband for the Tsar's daughter, Olga, and for almost a month the three conspirators laid their plans. They used the Princess Irina Yusupova, easily one of St Petersburg's most beautiful women, as bait to lure Rasputin into a trap. Although she was not in St Petersburg at the time, Prince Felix told Rasputin that Princess Irina was coming back for a secret assignation with him. As Rasputin licked his lips at the prospect of seducing the most beautiful woman in society, Yusupov was preparing a special chamber in which to murder him.

On the ground floor of the Yusupov Palace on the River Moika, he ordered workmen to refurbish a suite of rooms with costly Persian carpets, antique art objects and elegant furniture. There was a white bearskin rug in one corner and in the midst of this cosy arrangement Yusupov had his servants place, 'the table where Rasputin was to take his last cup of tea.'

By the night of 16 December all was ready. Cakes filled with chocolate and rose cream were lovingly prepared and laced, by a physician, with potassium cyanide. More poison was added to the glasses into which the Madeira and Marsala, Rasputin's favourite drinks would be poured.

Sometime before midnight Yusupov set out into the snow to collect Rasputin. When Rasputin arrived he was told that the Princess Irina was still entertaining guests upstairs but would arrive shortly and, as the sounds of Yankee Doodle (played on a phonograph by the other conspirators to simulate the princess's party) drifted down from an upstairs room, Rasputin descended the staircase to await his fate.

Prince Yusupov now served Rasputin the poisoned drinks and cakes, but to his utter horror Rasputin continued to eat and drink and asked for some gypsy songs to be played. The poison was not working and some time later, having spoken with his accomplices upstairs, Yusupov fetched a revolver and shot Rasputin. He aimed at the heart and Rasputin went down onto the bearskin rug like a broken marionette. Just as the conspirators were rejoicing however, Rasputin struggled to his feet, lurched his way up to the main floor and fell out of a side door into a courtyard. The assassins were frantic – twice they fired – and missed. By then Rasputin was almost at the gate to the street – Purishkevich, biting his left wristbone until it bled, to ensure total concentration, raised his pistol and fired twice and Rasputin fell – hit in the back and the head.

But despite the two bullets, Rasputin's life was not yet extinguished and so the conspirators tied his hands over his head and eventually dumped his body under the ice of the River Neva. An autopsy carried out shortly afterwards showed that the poison and the bullets had not killed Rasputin – the cold, icy river had claimed that privilege – his lungs were filled with water.

Within a few hours of the murder it was well known in the government and diplomatic community who the perpetrators were and they were hailed as heroes and saviours of Russia. The streets of St Petersburg resounded with exclamations of joy, and the bridge from which Rasputin's body was dumped became a popular place to take a walk, people lingering for hours at the railings, not quite believing that Grigori Rasputin, scourge of the people, was finally dead.

As Alexandra vowed eternal vengeance, Nicholas was powerless to punish the perpetrators; their star was too high in the public firmament. Instead Yusupov was banished to his estates, Dimitrii to the Persian Front and Purishkevich, the originator of the conspiracy, escaped totally unscathed and with his prestige massively enhanced.

Faithful to the end, the Tsarina buried Rasputin at Tsarskoe Selo. The Tsar recorded in his diary, 'at 9 o'clock we drove with all the family and turned into a field where we witnessed a gloomy picture; the coffin with the body of never-to-be-forgotten Grigori, murdered by the bigots in Yusupov's house. The weather was grey with 12 degrees of frost.' However Rasputin's body would not remain to rest in peace for long; on 22 March 1917, a group of revolutionary soldiers disinterred the coffin and burned the remains. The ashes were scattered to the winds.

In a letter written shortly before his death Rasputin had predicted his demise. He wrote that if common assassins killed him, then the Tsar had nothing to fear, but if he were slain by the aristocracy then none of the Tsar's family would remain alive for more than two years, but would be killed by the Russian people.

There were seventy-four days between Rasputin's death and the Tsar's abdication, and on 18 July 1918 the prediction came true when the Tsar's entire family was assassinated in a basement of an isolated farmhouse. Rasputin's death had come too late to change the course of events. His dreadful name had become too thoroughly a symbol of disaster. In raising their hands to preserve the old regime, Rasputin's assassins, had, in reality, struck its final blow.

JOSEF STALIN

A TWENTIETH-CENTURY TYRANT

A single death is a tragedy, a million deaths is a statistic.

The mark of Stalin's evil was that he turned morality on its head: what was bad became good, what was good, bad. This was a man who lost sight of the fact that human dignity and well-being lay at the heart of all progress.

MIKHAIL GORBACHOV

In March 1953, the people of the Soviet Union were devastated by the news that the country's Head of State was dead. At the funeral of the man known as Uncle Joe Stalin, people wept openly. To the Russians, Stalin was a saviour, the great leader who had plucked them and the country from the jaws of Hitler's Nazis and kept the Americans at bay. As they filed past his coffin few cared to recall that Stalin had another, darker reputation, as the murderer of millions of his own people, more than the Tsars had accounted for over four centuries. A ruthless bureaucrat Stalin turned a popular revolution, based on ideals of freedom and equality into a totalitarian dictatorship maintained by terror.

Born Iosif Vissarionovich Dzhugashvili, on 21 December 1879, in the Caucasian town of Gori, Georgia, he was the only one of four children to survive infancy. His father, Vissarion Dzhugashvili, was an unsuccessful cobbler and drunk, who beat his son and wife heavily. When Stalin was eleven, his father was killed in a brawl, and it was left to his mother, Katerina, to keep the family together. She took in washing and sewing, hired herself out for housework, and nursed young Joseph through smallpox, which left him facially disfigured; and septicaemia, which left his left arm slightly crippled. An illiterate peasant girl, Yekaterina was deeply religious, puritanical, ambitious, and intent on securing for her son a training for the priesthood, one of the few careers in which the non-Russian Georgian poor might rise to higher station. He was enrolled in the local Orthodox parochial school in Gori in 1888.

Highly gifted, Stalin won a free scholarship in 1894 to the Orthodox theological seminary in Tiflis, to begin his training as a priest. But he preferred revolutionary literature to the Bible and in his fourth year joined *Mesame Dasi*, a secret socialist group espousing the ideas of Georgian autonomy and independence. Expelled from the seminary in May 1899, just as he was about to graduate, Stalin first tried tutoring and then clerical work at the Tiflis Observatory.

Calling himself Koba or 'Indomitable', the young Josef joined the Social Democratic Party of Georgia in 1901 and plunged full-time into revolutionary work. He organized assassinations, strikes, demonstrations and bank robberies to swell the Bolshevik coffers. By 1902, the *Okhrana*, the Tsarist Secret Police had published a picture of Josef Dzugashvili – one of the most successful revolutionary operatives in southern Russia.

In June 1904 Stalin married Yekaterina Svanidze, a simple, devout peasant girl; however, she died of typhus on 10 April 1907, leaving a son, Yakov. Yakov would later try and kill himself; a failure for which his father would mock him. Yakov would die in a Nazi concentration camp in 1943 after Stalin had refused to trade for his life.

Stalin's own life between the turn of the century and 1917 was no less miserable. He spent a lot of time on the run from the Tsarist authorities, as well as in Tsarist prisons, or in exile in the frozen wastes of Siberia. However in March 1917, the work of Stalin and other revolutionaries in Russia and abroad paid off. Demoralized by three years of slaughter fighting the Germans in the First World War, and disaffected

Lenin, the Soviet Union's first leader, sits with the man who will succeed him, the Georgian Iosif Vissarionovich Dzhugashvili, better known by the name he adopted, Stalin – 'man of steel'. The photograph is in fact a fake, combining two separate images to make Stalin appear to be Lenin's favoured son, and thereby strengthening his case when the question of succession arose after Lenin's death in 1924.
(© THE ILLUSTRATED LONDON NEWS PICTURE AGENCY)

by years of poverty and repression at home, the Russian people rose up against the Tsar, Nicholas II. The Russian Revolution had begun.

When he heard that the Tsar had abdicated, Stalin rushed from his Siberian prison to the capital, Petrograd, known today as St Petersburg. The city was in turmoil, filled with joyous workers, mutineer soldiers and sailors and returning exiles. A provisional government under the leadership of Alexander Kerensky had taken control – to the fury of Lenin, the newly returned leader of the Bolshevik Party. However, the provisional government's refusal to withdraw from the war with Germany played into the hands of Lenin and the Bolsheviks. Aligning themselves with troops reluctant to go to the battlefront, Lenin encouraged an armed coup led by Trotsky, the head of the Petrograd Soviet in October 1917.

From October of that year Stalin would make himself central to the activities of the new government and adopted a new name – Stalin – 'Man of Steel'. In later years, Stalin would portray himself as central to the October Revolution, but in fact he was a mere functionary, barely mentioned in memoirs and simply remembered as a 'grey blur'. Stalin would also portray himself as Lenin's closest ally and the person directly responsible for directing the Revolution. He even had a faked photograph of himself and Lenin hanging on the wall of his dacha at Kuntsevo. During Stalin's attempts to create an important history for himself in retrospect, he first subjected the real heroes of the revolution to silence, and then had them written out of the history books. By 1937 he had disposed of thirty-seven of them in a more brutal fashion. Only those who spouted the new version of events remained. The fewer real veterans there were, the more Stalin's role became inflated.

From the moment the Soviet Union came into being it was in a continual state of crisis. Withdrawal from the War in 1918 was followed by a bitter civil war between the Revolutionary Bolshevik government and the White Army, Tsarist sympathizers supported by forces from western Europe.

During the Civil War of 1918-21 Stalin took on a huge number of mundane jobs that nobody else wanted. He was the Commissar for Nationalities, the Commissar for Rabkrin, a member of the Revolutionary Military Council, the Politburo and the Orgburo and Chairman of the Secretariat – with the result that he gained a reputation as a poor orator, a plodding theorist and a prickly character. All the Party leaders made the same mistake of underestimating Stalin's potential power, and his ambition to use it, which he gained from his many posts. Lenin was as guilty as the rest.

As Chairman of the Secretariat and the only Politburo member in the Orgburo, he promoted his friends and dismissed opponents. During 1922 alone, more than 10,000 provincial officials were appointed, mostly on Stalin's personal recommendation. They came from humble backgrounds with little formal education.

In 1919, Stalin ran the Workers' and Peasants' Inspectorate, which gave him the power to investigate every official in the country. By 1922 there were very few Party leaders, or members of the Politburo, whom Stalin did not have under surveillance and he would use these often incriminating findings for blackmail to get what he wanted. With cold, ruthless efficiency Stalin began his climb to control the Party. In April 1992 Lenin agreed to make Stalin General Secretary. It was to prove a crucial appointment for it was a position that placed Stalin perfectly for the next crisis within the new state: who would succeed Lenin as Party Leader.

Lenin first showed signs of illness in 1921, for the past four years he had been working sixteen hours a day without a break. In May 1922 he suffered a stroke and pleaded with Stalin to give him poison. But Stalin refused: Lenin was more useful to him alive.

In the next seven months Lenin became increasingly close to Stalin's greatest rival, Trotsky, and wary of Stalin. So when, in December, Lenin suffered another stroke, Stalin took charge. He obtained from the Central Committee an order giving him the power to keep Lenin in isolation from people and news. His secretaries were secretly reporting to Stalin, who could no longer mask his contempt for the dying man.

In the last year of his life Lenin had realized what a bad leader Stalin would be, calling him disloyal, rude, arrogant and capricious. He intended to make his feelings clear at the next Congress, but suffered another stroke that made it impossible for him to talk. However, he wrote a secret letter to be read out. Realizing how fatal this would be to his ambitions, Stalin delayed the Congress and suppressed the letter. Such are the quirks of fate; if Lenin's final stroke had not left him paralysed, Stalin's name today would only occupy footnotes in Russian history books.

The USSR's heroic revolutionary age was over, and from 1921-28 the regime plunged into the more mundane task of running the country from day to day. The Civil War of 1918-21 had had a traumatic effect on the new regime. It led to comprehensive nationalization of the economy and, politically, to the establishment of virtual one-Party rule, harsh repression of opponents of the regime, abolition of freedom of expression and association, and the growth of centralized Party bureaucracy that dominated the formal organs of government. The egalitarian, socialist aims of the Revolution were being replaced with rules more suited to the oppressive regime that was forming.

Stalin rose to power because he embodied, perhaps more than any of his old colleagues, this new spirit. Office politics, patient calculation, and compromise were all required to operate a growing bureaucratic regime. Stalin, with his restless, emotional, vain, cynical, and often vindictive temperament, and lack of physical appeal, had internalised so profoundly the role of administrator that he projected everywhere in public (in imitation of Lenin) a humble air, simple dress, personal asceticism, calmness, efficiency, and fatherliness – qualities that appealed to his colleagues, to the public, and, perhaps most important of all, to the new generation of Party functionaries of humble origin flooding the Party in the 1920s.

Stalin's masterstroke was that he always portrayed himself as one who implemented the will of the majority. His colleagues did not fear the power of the

Party machine over which Stalin presided, but rather the attempt on anyone's part to assert the kind of personal authority Lenin had exercised. Stalin exploited this miscalculation superbly, playing carefully on the mutual rivalries and suspicions of his colleagues and helping them to oust one another, while quietly staffing local and central Party organs with his own followers.

By 1927, Stalin was in complete control of the Party and all real opposition was eradicated with Trotsky's deportation from the Soviet Union two years later. Supporters like Kamanev and Zinoviev were expelled from the Party although Stalin would wait almost ten years until he had them shot for treason and would only turn his attention to Trotsky much later. For now Stalin had a much bigger target in his sights.

He introduced his first Five Year Plan for massive and accelerated industrialization of the Soviet Union, convincing the country that they had to be strong to resist enemies, both real and imagined, who were massing to destroy their Socialist paradise. Believing that the Soviet Union was 100 years behind the West, and had to catch up as quickly as possible, he began to change agriculture and industry. This could only be achieved, he believed, by creating a, 'command economy' and forcing farmers and industry to modernize. Stalin began to force all peasants to join collective farms. They had to pool their machinery and livestock on large farms, which were then controlled by the State. Forced to hand over their produce to the government, they were either paid wages or had to feed themselves on what was left over. The ensuing result was a devastating famine. Peasants burnt their crops and killed their animals, rather than hand them over. Minority groups, like the Kazakh nomads, who knew nothing of cereal cropping, were ordered to cultivate wheat on pain of execution. Nearly two million died as a result and their whole way of life was obliterated.

The State's unreasonable demands for grain, forcibly extracted, meant that the peasants starved. Those who refused to join the collectives had their houses, tools and belongings confiscated. In all, some nine million men, women and children were evicted, cast into starvation, oblivion and death. In the south, the Ukraine was particularly badly hit by a famine affecting nearly thirty million people – some even resorted to cannibalism.

The programme was partly financed by savage taxes on richer peasants, the Kulaks, who had been permitted by Lenin to sell surplus food to ease shortages. Soon the Kulaks lost not only the right to sell, but also their land and livestock. Then Stalin announced the elimination of the Kulaks. Millions were ordered to join the vast state-run collectives. Millions more were herded into towns to become forced labour in the new state-owned factories. Others disappeared into the growing network of corrective labour camps. More than twenty-five million were forcibly evicted and more than three million killed. What began as an economic policy turned into a scene of despair, bloodshed and terror. Between 1932-34, five million people starved to death and agricultural production fell by 15%.

The blood even seeped into Stalin's own home. On 24 March 1919, Stalin had married his second wife, Nadezhda Alliluyeva, the sixteen-year-old daughter of an old

Georgian revolutionary friend, Serge Alliluyev. She bore him two children: Vasili (1919) and Svetlana (1925). At one time Nadezhda had helped Stalin, telling him secrets learned from her job as a confidential code clerk in Lenin's private office however, in 1932, at a party in Stalin's headquarters, he insulted her in front of others. Nadezhda left the room and shot herself in the head. The official explanation was that she had died of appendicitis. Stalin did not even attend her funeral and her death removed one of the few remaining checks on his absolute authority as well as depriving his soul of the last vestige of human warmth. His son, Vasili, died an alcoholic. But as ever, the greatest victims were the Russian people.

Each factory or business was taken over by the State and given a target that it had to meet every year, over five years. The targets were worked out by *Gosplan* in Moscow. This organization consisted of half-a-million workers who did nothing but set targets for every factory and works only to then check how much was actually produced. This put immense pressure on workers and managers, but punishment for failing to meet the targets was severe. Managers of factories could be executed. Workers were forced to work longer hours and were not allowed to change their jobs. Being away from work became a crime. Many factories faked production figures, or disregarded the quality of goods produced. So long as the numbers were right, nothing else mattered. It was estimated that half of all tractors made in the 1930s broke down.

In private, Stalin was identifying himself with the great despots of history. He was fascinated by Genghis Khan, whose belief that, 'the deaths of the vanquished are necessary for the tranquillity of the victors', he concurred with. He had also taken a shine to Augustus, the first Roman Emperor, who had disguised the autocratic nature of his rule by refusing the title of King, just as Stalin was permitting himself at most the unofficial title of Leader. Those who objected to Stalin's methods ended up in the slave labour camps, the Gulags. Deliberately situated in the harshest areas of Russia, prisoners were turned into slave labourers and worked to death. Huge industrial schemes like the Knieper Dam and the Bellmore Canal became a living hell for hundreds of thousands who died during their construction. By 1933 nearly a million Soviet citizens languished in forced labour camps. Further millions were in prisons, deportation camps or compulsory resettlement areas. No one was safe from being branded as an enemy and if Stalin found many enemies outside the Communist Party, he found as many inside.

At the seventeenth Party Congress in February 1934, 300 older Party members voted against Stalin as Party Leader and in favour of Kirov. Stalin was infuriated and his revenge was swift. In December, Kirov was assassinated – almost certainly on Stalin's orders – and then he enlarged the powers of the NKVD, the Secret Police, who began rounding up Stalin's opponents. Evidence was fabricated and the leading Bolsheviks were given 'Show Trials', where they were forced to confess to ridiculous crimes which they could not possibly have committed. Confessions were extracted under torture. Of the 1,200 delegates at that fateful Congress, over 1,100 were arrested, executed or died in the Gulag labour camps; of the one hundred and thirty nine Central Committee members, ninety eight were shot. Not only were his opponents exterminated, they were quite literally made to disappear. From their headquarters in Lubyanka prison, the NKVD, under Stalin's orders, spread fear through the entire country.

The Great Terror of 1937-38, following quickly after the violent campaigns of collectivisation and industrialization, left no one in doubt about the consequences of even covert disobedience. It was not a thunderclap in a cloudless sky, but a worsening of a storm already raging. Victims were tried by *troiki*, consisting of the local NKVD Chief, Party Secretary and Procurator. Trials were derisory and brief and sentences carried no right of appeal. As the terror intensified pretty well anybody who held a political, administrative or managerial post lived in fear.

Between one, and one-and-a-half million people were killed by firing squad, physical maltreatment or massive overwork in those two years alone. Vans and lorries marked 'Meat' or 'Vegetables' would carry the victims out to a quiet wood, where shooting grounds and long, deep pits had been secretly prepared. Trains, full of victims, would pass through towns at night to avoid public scrutiny. The terror was chaotic and confusing – thousands went to their death not knowing what they had done and shouting their loyalty to Stalin – their Man of Steel.

The Soviet Union in the 30s will be remembered above all for its bloody purges of all areas of society: political and private. From 1934-38 at least 7,000,000 people disappeared. These included the Bolshevik leaders whom Stalin had forced out from 1925 to 1927, poets, scientists, managers of industries who did not meet their targets for production and millions of ordinary Soviet citizens. It would not have taken place but for Stalin's personality and ideas. He directed the state's machinery against, 'anti-Soviet elements' and, 'enemies of the people'. He used his victims as scapegoats for the country's pain; and in order to sustain his industrialization plans, he needed to keep his mines, timber forests and construction sites constantly supplied with slave labour.

Next Stalin turned to the army. Stalin wanted to ensure that only his own policies were being promoted and by the time the military purge was over, nearly 40,000 officers had been arrested, almost 15,000 shot and the rest sent to the camps to die. Practically the entire High Command of the armed forces was obliterated.

Even exile abroad would provide no haven. Stalin's political *bête noire*, Trotsky, was tracked down to Mexico in August 1940 where NKVD agents murdered him with an ice pick. Stalin wanted to wipe out all opponents, but more so all those long-serving Party members who knew that his glorious past was a fiction and he was not Lenin's true successor. Stalin claimed that he alone had been responsible for the successes in the Civil War.

No unit of social life – including the family – would be free from Stalin's control. Denunciation became the order of the day. Young girls were rewarded for betraying their fathers to the authorities, even when his crime was as lowly as having stolen two potatoes from a collective farm. Even harmless old peasant women muttering their dissatisfaction about housing standards would be dispatched to the Gulags. Casual jokes against Stalin

Stalin cradling his daughter, Svetlana, in a photograph taken in 1937 at the Russian leader's country house in the suburbs of Moscow. By that date, Stalin was already responsible for the deaths of millions of Russians, making the friendly 'Uncle Joe' image of this photograph a hollow mockery. (© BETTMANN/CORBIS)

or the state were treated as treason. Every citizen was a target and it didn't matter whether the charges were real or not, so great was the paranoia and persecution.

By 1939 the whole fabric of Russian society was under threat and Stalin began to realize that if the Soviet State fell apart, his career would be over. However, although Stalin's terror eased up in 1939, there was to be little respite in the slaughter. Despite a treaty of non-aggression that had been signed between Stalin and Hitler in 1939, on 22 June 1941, Germany invaded Russia. The effect was devastating and Stalin was almost completely unprepared, due for the most part to his unwillingness to listen to reports that Hitler wanted to conquer Russia. Weakened by the purges in the 30s, the Red Army had no effective leadership and its armies were annihilated by the better-armed and better-led Nazis. Long-silent church bells rang out in occupied towns as people celebrated their freedom whilst disillusioned Russian troops surrendered in droves. In less than six months, the invading army of just over three million had captured nearly four million of the Red Army. Behind the lines, rumour, confusion and panic began to spread.

But Hitler threw away his chance to capitalize on Russian misery, and refused to allow 800,000 Russian volunteers to fight for Germany. Freed towns were soon appalled at the cruelty of the invading forces. The Nazis were besieging Leningrad and were less than a mile from the Kremlin in Moscow. Stalin appealed over the radio to, 'his friends' the Russian people to help him throw off the yoke of Nazism, and with the onslaught of the icy clutches of winter, the tide began to turn. However, even as the Russian people laid down their lives for the Motherland, Stalin found ways of terrorizing them. During the Battle for Stalingrad, the most savage conflict of a merciless war, Stalin formed units of the NKVD who were ordered, on pain of death, to advance behind the Russian troops. If any soldiers tried to retreat they were to be shot. Soldiers were forbidden to surrender and their families, if they did, would lose their state allowances. Tens of thousands of deserters lost their lives in this way.

By 1945 the position had changed and the Red Army pushed west destroying Hitler's armies and arrived at the gates of Berlin in May. But Stalin's repression followed them. Alarmed that his troops would become contaminated by the ideas of the American and British troops in Germany, he arrested those who had even embraced their fellow victors, sending them to labour camps for re-education. This was Stalin's reward for the sacrifice of twenty million dead. More than three million Russians had

The 'Big Three' war leaders, Churchill, Roosevelt and Stalin, posing for official photographs at the Yalta Conference in February 1945. The meeting aimed to resolve the disarmament and partition of Germany, now facing imminent defeat; Stalin, however, had another agenda that would see much of Eastern Europe fall under Soviet influence. (© THE ILLUSTRATED LONDON NEWS PICTURE AGENCY)

escaped to the West by 1945, by 1948 almost all had been forcibly repatriated. When they got back to the USSR thousands were marched straight off the boats and trains into makeshift execution yards. At ports on the Crimea, Soviet air force planes flew low to try and drown out the sound of gunfire. Those who escaped the quayside massacres were bundled into a closed train for a lingering death in the Gulags.

For the rest of the world the consequences of Stalin's victory would be forty years of Cold War, as, in Churchill's words, an, 'iron curtain' descended on Europe, driving it between democratic western Europe and the Communist east. Russia's isolation in the grip of a dictator was complete.

The Soviet victory in the Second World War came at a terrible price. It has been estimated that deaths stood at twenty six million, over 800,000 had died in the siege of Leningrad alone while 622,000 had died in the labour camps. One in eight of the pre-war population was dead.

Ironically, the more severe Stalin became, the more he was revered by the people. A combination of propaganda and the ever-present threat of persecution turned him into a demigod and his rule depended upon the presence of enthusiastic support in society. As Stalin fully developed the cult of personality, kindergarten children learned nursery rhymes extolling their great leader. The idea was that the Russian people owed everything to the Party, to the State, and to the Leader. The people had to continually thank Stalin for all the theoretical gifts and presents, the social services, the jobs and lives. Slogans like, 'Thank You Comrade Stalin for a happy childhood' were widespread. One of the most iconic images of Stalin was, 'Friend of the Little Children'. Taken in the Kremlin in 1936, Stalin was pictured holding six-year-old Gelya Marikova. Ironically a year later, Gelya's father, Ardan, was executed on Stalin's orders, accused of spying for Japan. Soon after, Gelya's mother was shot as the wife of an enemy of the people. Authorities erected loudspeakers in public streets so that announcements could be broadcast. The Cult of Stalin served a definite political purpose. It provided a focus of loyalty and patriotic feeling. The Tsar-like image of Stalin was useful in affirming that the State had a strong, determined leader. The only art that Stalin would permit was Socialist Realism, which he said, 'aided the process of ideological transformation in the spirit of socialism' and he made sure there were plenty of vast pictures of himself all over Russia.

By 1956, 706 million copies of Stalin's works had been published. In 1949 at a parade in Red Square, to celebrate his seventieth birthday, an image of his face was projected into the sky above the Kremlin. The perfect Stalin was everywhere while the real Stalin hid himself from view.

The end of the war marked a turning point in Stalin's psychology; he was deified by his people but became increasingly paranoid and insecure. No one was left to threaten him and yet he saw enemies everywhere. So paranoid was he in fact, that he employed fifteen personal food tasters. His tea had to come from specially sealed packs, which were used just once. When a woman who always prepared his tea was spotted taking leaves from a pack with a broken seal, she was thrown into Lubyanka prison. Tunnels were dug to link his office with other government buildings. When forced to appear above ground, he used only an armour-plated car with bullet-proof windows three-inches thick.

As Stalin's paranoia grew, so did his wrath. The persecution of Party operatives and citizens alike continued. Even his own relatives died. In Leningrad, sensing the over-confidence of the Communist Party there, Stalin executed 2,000 Party workers. Central Soviet leadership was like a gang, and Stalin as its leader relied upon its fellow members to organize the State's institutions. Competence and obedience were pre-requisites. The penalty for disagreement was, 'seven grams of lead' in the head. Even his most trusted and long-serving ministers were not exempt. The wife of Stalin's private secretary was shot and he was dispensed with. The Head of State's wife spent seven years in a prison camp to guarantee her husband's behaviour, and Molotov's wife was sent to the Gulags. A year before her arrest in 1949, Stalin had told Molotov that he should divorce her on the grounds that she was Jewish. Stalin thought that the Jews were a, 'dangerous alien element who were loyal to Israel' rather than to him. When his daughter, Svetlana, fell in love with a Jew, Stalin had him labelled a British Agent and dispatched to an Arctic labour camp. Recent research suggests that Stalin had, in fact, like Hitler, devised his own Final Solution.

Having been brought to the brink of extinction by the Nazis, the Jews were to be Stalin's next target; in fact the years 1948-53 were to be black ones for Soviet Jewry. Jewish theatres and journals were closed and Jewish intellectuals arrested. The medical profession was another vehicle for his paranoia. In what has become known as the 'Doctors Plot', Stalin persecuted Jewish physicians, arresting them on charges of poisoning people with drugs and killing them on the operating table. Ironically, it was Stalin's persecution of the Jewish doctors and the atmosphere of fear that surrounded him, which contributed to his death.

As he lay dying from a stroke in the bedroom of his dacha outside Moscow on March 2 1953, his staff were too frightened to disobey his orders and enter his room. Early intervention could have saved his life, but he lay there for almost twelve hours until a guard entered. His personal physician, Professor Vinogradov was in chains in Lubyanka prison, being beaten on Stalin's orders. The doctors who were called were unfamiliar with his medical history. He was beyond salvation and died on 5 March.

Through a succession of bulletins, the Soviet people had been made aware that Stalin was gravely ill. At four in the morning of 6 March 1953, it was announced, 'The heart of the comrade-in-arms and continuer of genius of Lenin's cause, of the wise leader and teacher of the Communist Party and the Soviet Union, has ceased to beat.'

Stalin's body was washed by a nurse and then carried via a white car to the Kremlin mortuary. There, an autopsy was performed. After the autopsy was completed, Stalin's body was given to the embalmers to prepare it for the three days it would lay in state. Thousands of people lined up in the snow to see it. The crowds were so dense and chaotic outside that some people were trampled underfoot, others rammed against traffic lights, and some others choked to death. From under the glass, the chemically treated body could still terminate innocent lives.

The exact death toll during Stalin's years in power is still being accounted for, estimates run into ten's of millions, but it is a measure of the fear he invoked and the propaganda sleight-of-hand he performed, that his funeral was the scene of the most extraordinary grief. Stalin had taken Russia from the wooden plough to the nuclear age in thirty years. He had caught up with the advanced countries that had spent centuries making the transition. But in the process, the lives of more than twenty million Soviet citizens had been sacrificed. Another fourteen million languished in the Gulag camps at the time of his death.

ADOLF HITLER

FATHER OF THE FINAL SOLUTION

'I am responsible for the fate of the German people, I am the supreme Justice...and everyone must know that for all future time that if he raises his hand to strike the state, then certain death is his lot.'

ADOLF HITLER

At the end of the Second World War, Germany lay in ruins. The Führer, Adolf Hitler, lay dead in a Berlin bunker, killed by his own hand. The monstrous dictator who manipulated the minds of the masses had promised his people a brave new world and a bright new future. Instead, he murdered their sick relatives, persecuted gypsies, homosexuals and the disabled, and instigated the Final Solution, which saw the slaughter of nearly six million Jews. To the world he brought a war of unparalleled destruction, a war that would claim the lives of more than forty million people. Over half of them were civilians.

Adolf Hitler was born at 6.30 p.m. on the evening of 20 April 1889 in the small town of Brasnau on the frontier of Austria and Bavaria. The Europe he was born into was controlled by the Hapsburg Empire – one of the four great empires that ruled over central and eastern Europe. Hitler's family, on both sides, came from the Waldviertel, a poor, remote country district, cut off from the main arteries of Austrian life.

Adolf was the third child of his father, Alois' third marriage. Alois, a customs' official, was hard, unsympathetic and short-tempered and much older than Adolf's mother, Klara. Faithfully protective of his mother, Adolf found his father a boorish brute. He went to school where it was reported that, 'he lacked self-discipline, was arrogant and bad tempered. He reacted with ill-concealed hostility to advice or reproof; at the same time, he demanded of his fellow pupils their unqualified subservience, fancying himself in the role of leader.' But he left school without a leaving certificate. It was a failure that was to rankle for a long time.

After living at home for a while, Adolf went to Vienna and stayed there from 1909-13. He applied to the Vienna Academy of Art and the Academy of Architecture, but was rejected, so instead spent his time lounging around cafes and joining in every discussion on politics and philosophy. These were among his most formative years when his character and opinions were to take definite shape. For most of the time he lived in a doss-house near the river, making just enough money to live on, by drawing posters and crude advertisements for small shops. He was a loner with

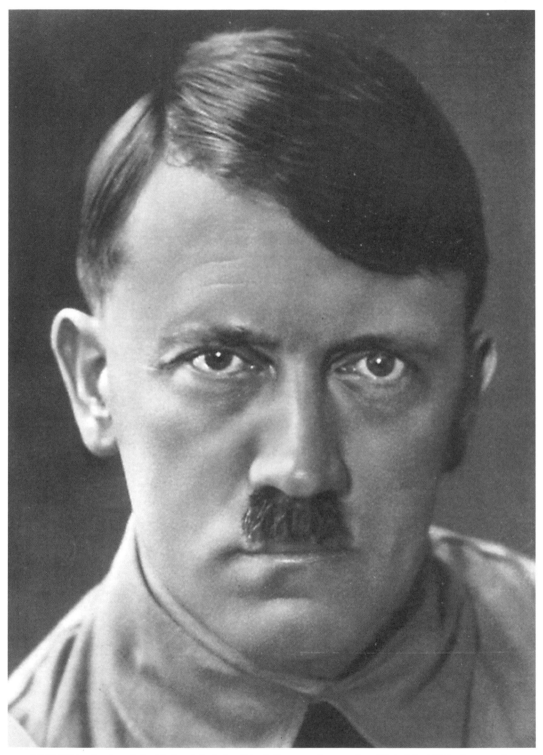

Adolf Hitler, leader of the National Socialist (Nazi) Party, a photograph published in 1934, the year after he became Chancellor of Germany. He brought upon the world a war of unparalleled destruction, upon his own people absolute and utter defeat, and upon Jews, Slavs and others he considered 'subhumans', a policy of unremitting genocide. (© The Illustrated London News Picture Agency)

few friends or acquaintances, a fringe character convinced of his own artistic talents and embittered by the bourgeois society which had rejected him.

In 1913 Hitler left Vienna for good. He was twenty-four-years-old, awkward, moody and reserved, yet nursing a passion of hatred and fanaticism, which from time to time broke out in a torrent of excited words.

To avoid conscription into the Austrian imperial army, he moved to Munich and found lodgings with a tailor's family. He was still living in a fantasy world, brooding and muttering about his theories on race and then bursting out into wild rages against the priests, the Jews, and the Hapsburgs. The Jewish people, Hitler was convinced, were conspiring to destroy and subdue the Aryan people as an act of revenge for their own inferiority. Sadly, the Jews were an easy target in the early years of the twentieth century as more and more of their peasant communities in Russia and eastern Europe were being driven west by the pogroms.

In 1914, patriotic crowds gathered in German streets to celebrate the outbreak of the First World War. Amongst them was the twenty-five-year old Hitler. Though still an Austrian citizen he succeeded in joining a Bavarian infantry regiment. War offered Hitler the chance to slough off the frustration, failure and resentment of the past few years. Throughout the war Lance-Corporal Hitler served as a *Meldeganger*, (a runner) whose job it was to carry messages between Company and Regimental HQ and he was awarded two iron crosses for bravery. The years between 1908-18 had hardened Hitler and when he emerged it was with a stock of fixed ideas and prejudices which were to alter little for the rest of his life. He had acquired an even stronger hatred of the Jews; contempt for the ideals of democracy, internationalism, equality and peace; a preference for authoritarian government and faith in the heroic virtues of war. Most important of all, he had hit upon a conception of how political power was to be secured and exercised which, when fully developed, was to open the way to a career without parallel in history. It just required a shock to precipitate it – and that came with the end of the war, the capitulation of Germany and the overthrow of the Hapsburg Empire.

The period after the end of the First World War was one of widespread unrest in Europe as the political and social structure of half a continent was thrown into the melting pot. Few towns were as sensitive as Munich – its political atmosphere was unstable and veered from one extreme to another. Such was the promising political setting for Hitler to begin his career.

Hitler got a job as an army Instruction Officer, with the brief to inoculate the men against socialist, pacifist or democratic ideas. His first task was to investigate the extremist German Workers' Party. On the evening of 12 September 1919, Hitler attended his first meeting in a Munich beer cellar where twenty-five people had gathered.

The German Workers' Party was an ideal vehicle for Hitler – it was a Party at the bottom of the pile and so he had a chance to play a leading part. He offered his services and slowly pushed the Party forward until, in 1920 he resigned from the army to devote himself to building up the Party. He had an unusual talent for articulating the most vulgar populist prejudices and the self-awareness and self-confidence of the political agitator began to take shape. He learned to lie with conviction, to dissemble with candour and his distrust was matched by his contempt. Men were moved by fear, greed, lust for power, envy, often by mean and petty motives; politics, Hitler concluded, was the art of knowing how to use these weaknesses for one's own ends.

Hitler's bloodthirsty speeches struck a chord. Party attendance first doubled and then trebled. In a short time, Hitler was able to bully his way into becoming the undisputed leader of the Party, which was renamed the National Socialist German Workers' Party, (NSDAP – *Nationalsozialistisch Deutsche Arbeiterpartei*) or Nazis for short. In the beer halls of Munich, Hitler recruited an army of thugs called the *Sturmabteilung*, (the Brownshirts) or SA. Their purpose was to spread terror, intimidation and violence on to the city streets. In meetings they would act as his bodyguard, mercilessly beating up anyone who questioned Hitler's words. While his brutish gangs ruled the streets, he began a campaign to charm respectable society.

Hitler could play the game at a lot of different levels, he had a kind of folksy earnestness that appealed to the lower classes and he moved very easily in society drawing rooms. Ladies clearly found him attractive and were amongst his most important benefactors, giving him money and jewellery to further his political cause. Hitler also encouraged his female supporters by presenting himself as a hermit-like, celibate figure who devoted all his energies to the good of Germany. But again, the image he projected was a lie for, at the time, he was involved with a number of teenage mistresses, beginning with Maria Reiter, the daughter of an innkeeper from Bertesgaden. He was thirty-seven and she was sixteen, so she was literally young enough to be his daughter. The mistress who made the biggest impression on Hitler however, was sixteen-year-old Geli Raubal. Geli was Adolf's niece, the daughter of his half-sister, Angela. In 1929, Geli moved into her Uncle Adolf's grand apartment on Munich's Prinzregentemplatz. She took a bedroom adjoining his on the second floor. Geli was a vivacious, idealistic free spirit in contrast to Hitler's controlling, strict and possessive personality. Geli soon felt trapped, but Hitler would not let her go. The longer they were involved the more she saw of his nasty side. On 19 September 1931, Geli was found dead in Hitler's apartment. She was bleeding from a wound near her heart. One arm was stretched out towards a pistol, a semi-automatic. The police recorded a verdict of suicide.

Geli was the first of Hitler's mistresses to be driven to a violent death, but she would not be the last. The actress Rennate Muller threw herself to her death from a window in 1937, and Eva Braun attempted suicide at least once before her final pact with Hitler. However it was Geli's picture that Hitler kept in his bedroom in Munich and in Berlin until his death in 1945.

Four years after the end of the First World War, Germany was still a sick, distracted and divided nation. But events were on the side of the extremists. Germany was crippled by the massive reparations owed under the Treaty of Versailles made at the end of the First World War and the nation's inability to pay meant the rapid acceleration of inflation. At the end of 1918 the German mark had stood at four to the dollar, by 1923 there were 7,000 marks to the dollar.

Nazism was a phenomenon that thrived in conditions of disorder and, in 1923 two new factors made their appearance, which brought Germany to the verge of economic and political collapse. The first was the occupation of the Ruhr by France and the second was the total collapse of the mark. The French occupation united the German people as they had never been united before, and by 1 November the mark stood at 130 thousand million to one dollar. This meant food shortages, bankruptcies and unemployment. Economic collapse reached down and touched every member of society in a way which no political event ever can.

In 1923 the Nazi Party began holding a series of rallies in Bavaria, however Hitler was convicted to five years in prison for attempting to overthrow the Bavarian government. The Party was dissolved, but not for long. At the end of 1924 Hitler was released from custody and reformed the Party.

He now set himself two objectives: to establish absolute control over the Party and to make it a serious force in German politics. The process was to prove a slow one. Germany was making an astonishing economic recovery, but fortunately for Hitler, disaster was just round the corner. In 1932 the global depression hit Germany hard. Unemployment soared to well over six million and countless Germans saw the apparently solid framework of their existence cracking. In such circumstances men entertain fantastic fears and extravagant hopes, and it was under these conditions that the fantastic demagogy of Hitler began to attract a mass following. When it came to the elections, the Germans needed a radical solution. The solution they chose was Hitler and the Nazi Party. Hitler portrayed himself as a Messiah whose role it was to lead the German people to a type of paradise on earth.

On the morning of 20 January 1933, Adolf Hitler, the petty-official's son from Austria, the down-and-out of the Home for Men, became Chancellor of the German Reich. Nazi propaganda later built up a legend which represented Hitler's coming to power as an upsurge of great national revival. The truth is more prosaic. Despite the mass support he won, Hitler came to power as a result of a shoddy political deal. He did not seize power; he manipulated his way into office by Machiavellian intrigue. Within a few weeks, Hitler had banned the Communist and Social Democratic Parties, dissolved the Catholic Centre and right-wing Nationalists and taken over the trade unions, five of the most powerful organizations in Germany. His gangster methods with the crude and uninhibited use of force in the first, not in the last resort, had produced astonishing results. Any opposition in the cabinet dissolved before the wave of violence, and by the summer of 1933 Hitler was complete master of the German Government.

In 1934 Hitler started a chain of events that led to a purge within the army and SA in Germany. How many were killed will never be known as all documents were burnt, but the figure is believed to be around five hundred. When he was asked why

The original German caption to this photograph, taken in October 1938, reads: 'Impressive in its interpretation of the Loyalty of German Youth is this picture made at the Nuremberg Nazi Party Congress. Thousands of young arms shot out in the Nazi salute with the word "Heil" as Hitler's car passed the grandstand.' When it came to dominating masses of people, Hitler had few equals.

the men had not been tried before execution, he replied that, 'I am responsible for the fate of the German people, I am the supreme Justice…and everyone must know that for all future time that if he raises his hand to strike the State, then certain death is his lot.' Hitler had with one blow removed the pressure on him from both the Left and the Right, and could proceed to deal with the problem of the Succession. When

President Von Hindenburg died on 2 August, all had been arranged. Within an hour came the announcement that the office of President would be merged with that of Chancellor and that Hitler would become the Head of State as well as Supreme Commander in Chief of the Armed Forces of the Reich. On the same day the officers and men of the German Army took the oath of allegiance to their new Commander in Chief. The form of the oath was significant because they were called on to swear allegiance not to the Constitution, or to the Fatherland, but to Hitler personally.

On 19 August 1934, Germany went to the polls and the Führer, as Hitler was now to be known, swept in with a majority of nearly 90 per cent of the votes – out of forty-six million voters, only around four million had had the courage to vote against him. The Nazi revolution was complete; Hitler had become the dictator of Germany.

But Hitler's new German paradise was not a place where everyone was welcome. From the very beginning Hitler's propaganda had portrayed the Jewish people as everything that was wrong in German society. In one film the Jews are compared to rats: treacherous, cowardly and cruel and appearing in large swarms. In 1935, at a rally at Nuremberg the Law for the Protection of German Blood and German Honour was passed. This prohibited marriages or sexual intercourse between Jews and Aryans, and banned Jews from holding public office. Furthermore, in November 1938 Hitler whipped up anti-Semitic feeling into a nation-wide frenzy of violence. Jewish shop windows were broken, and over a hundred Jews were killed, with over 27,000 being interned in camps, for their so-called protection. It was called the *Reichskristallnacht*, (the imperial night of crystal). Then he re-introduced a medieval law, forcing Jews to wear a yellow star for identification.

Hitler spread his message of hate through technical devices like the radio and the loudspeaker; eight million people were deprived of independent thought and it was now possible for him to subject them to his will. No regime in history has ever paid such careful attention to psychological factors in politics. Hitler was a master of mass emotion. At the big rallies nothing was left to chance. He used every trick and device to heighten the emotional intensity. The sense of power, of force and unity was irresistible, and all converged with a mounting crescendo of excitement to the supreme moment when the Führer made his entry. Hitler had grasped what could be done with a combination of propaganda and terrorism and, in using the formidable power placed in his hands he also had one supreme advantage over his rivals for Hitler had neither scruples nor inhibitions. He was a man without roots, a man who admitted no loyalties, was bound by no traditions, and felt respect for neither man nor God. Hitler showed himself prepared to seize any advantage that was to be gained by lying, cunning and unscrupulousness. Wary and secretive, he distrusted everyone and believed that, '…it is not by the principles of humanity that man lives or is able to preserve himself above the animal world, but solely by means of the most brutal struggle.' Everything was the result of cold calculation.

Hitler also preserved his position in the Party by allowing rivalries to develop amongst the other leaders and applied the principle of 'divide and rule'. There was always more than one office operating in any one section and he played one department off against another. Hatred intoxicated him. Many of his speeches are long diatribes of vitriol directed against the Jews, the Marxists, the Czechs, the Poles and the French. No less striking was his constant need for praise. His vanity was unappeasable, and the most fulsome flattery was received as no more than his due. He came to believe that he was a man with a mission, marked out by Providence, and therefore exempt from the ordinary canons of human conduct. Against all the odds, and appealing to man's baser nature, Hitler succeeded in releasing the pent-up energies in the German nation, and in re-creating a belief in their future. Hitler had recognized the immense attraction to the masses of force combined with success. However, he hated the routine work of government and so long as his suspicions were not stirred, he left the business of running the country very much in the hands of his lieutenants, but no one needed reminding where the final authority lay.

Now in complete control of the German political system, its army and its youth, Hitler was ready to take increasingly extreme steps towards his vision of a new Aryan Germany. Hitler was a hypochondriac and he had never been good at sports – yet he believed that the sick and the weak were an unnecessary burden on the rest of society. He ordered the sterilization of 400,000 gypsies, the disabled and the long-term unemployed; people he considered genetically sub-standard. At first the systematic killings were carried out by lethal injection, but as Hitler's list of candidates for annihilation grew, a new technique for mass-murder was developed. It was tested in six provincial hospitals, where the patients were taken into the basement and told to undress. Then they were directed to the shower room. But the drain in the floor was a fake, and the pipes didn't contain water but carbon-monoxide gas. Hitler's hospitals of death claimed the lives of over 300,000 people. The bodies were never released to the relatives in case they uncovered the truth.

Having never been interested in administration, only in power, Hitler now began using the State as an instrument with which he meant to conquer Europe. From 1935 Germany began to re-arm at an alarming rate. Hitler was well aware of the rest of Europe's extreme reluctance to engage in another war and he used this to further his own position.

On 11 March 1938 German troops entered Austria, Hitler's homeland, and two days later the country became part of the German Reich. One year later Hitler invaded Czechoslovakia and the government was placed under German protection. By 1940 Hitler's armies had swept into Poland, the Netherlands, Belgium and France and in 1941 they declared war on the United States. With Europe at his feet and all need for restraint removed, Hitler now abandoned himself entirely to megalomania and the purification of Germany using his specially chosen elite, the SS.

Hitler's vision of the SS Empire was put in hand at the beginning of the war when the SS divisions numbered only three, but by the end of the war this number had risen to thirty-five, with over half a million men. They were designed as an alternative to the army and as Hitler's personal killers. Certain characteristics were established, namely the concentration camps and the *einsatzkommandos* (extermination squads). By 1944, the extermination of the Jews, the first item on Hitler's programme, was well on the way to being accomplished.

At the outbreak of the war, Hitler had interned all German Jews in camps. In occupied territories, such as Poland, they were corralled in inner-city ghettos. Here they were to be worked to death, manufacturing material to help the German war effort. With constant hunger, cold and dirt it was very difficult to keep some semblance of human dignity.

But Hitler had other plans for Poland and European Russia; he wanted to populate them with German settlers, however first he had to get rid of the native population. Some were used to provide slave labour for the new German Empire and remained in a state of total inferiority, without rights and without education, treated literally as a sub-human race. The surplus, including all those of education, property and position were to be exterminated to make room for the new colonists, or left to die of starvation.

Before the war the concentration camps had been used for the 'preventative detention' of opponents of the German regime. During the war great numbers of Jews and members of the resistance movements were transported to them. Then, in 1942, Himmler, with Hitler's agreement, began to use the camps as a source of labour for armaments work, and the SS established its own factories. Certain categories of prisoners were ascribed to be 'worked to death'.

Concentration camp prisoners' were also used as the raw material for medical experiments by SS doctors. All were conducted without anaesthetic or the slightest attention to the victims' sufferings. They were subjected to intense air pressure, or intense cold, until the patients' lungs burst or froze to death, and a large number of investigations into racial hygiene were conducted.

More terrible than the concentration camps were the extermination camps. At Auschwitz in Poland there were four large gas chambers each accommodating 2,000 people at any one time. Here the SS used Cyclone B, crystallized prussic acid, dropped into the death chambers. It took between three and fifteen minutes for the victims to die and the Nazi butchers knew just when to move in – when the screaming stopped. But by 1944 even the vast capacity for killing of Auschwitz was not enough. In forty-six days during the summer of that year, between 250,000 and 300,000 Hungarian Jews alone were put to death at the camp, and the SS resorted to mass shootings to relieve the pressure on the gas chambers. For Hitler this was the logical realization of the views, which he had held since his youth, the necessary preliminary to the plans he had formed for the resettlement of Europe on more solid racial grounds. Himmler may have organized the extermination of the Jews, but the man in whose mind so grotesque a plan had been conceived was Hitler.

Hitler was now in his fifties. His physical appearance was still unimpressive, his bearing still awkward. The falling lock of hair and the smudge of his moustache gave his face nothing of the racial superiority he was always invoking; only his hypnotic eyes

Hitler in mid-speech, photographed in 1944. His powers of oratory were considerable, and he had been known to captivate and enthuse rallies of hundreds of thousands of people. By 1944, however, Germany was on the road to defeat, and many Germans knew it, though none would have dared admit it openly – Nazi reprisals against their own kind were as savage as they were against perceived 'enemies' like Jews and communists. (© The Illustrated London News Picture Agency)

betrayed the man himself. He also suffered from constant physical pain; his spine was irreparably curved and he was racked by severe spasms often lasting days. As Hitler's megalomania grew, he began to see himself as something more than human. He believed he was an agent of divine will like the Emperors of Ancient Rome. When he ordered the building of a gigantic Nazi meeting hall, it was based on Rome's Coliseum, but Hitler's building was to be twice as high and seat over 50,000 people.

By the end of 1942 Hitler's armies were fighting on many different fronts and the bombing of German industry and the losses of manpower and equipment began to exert a greater strain on the economy. Russia, like Poland and other occupied countries was turned into a vast labour camp to provide the human material needed for German industry and agriculture. By the end of 1943, 4,795,000 foreign workers had been recruited for work in Germany, of whom 1,900,000 were Russians, 851,000 Poles, 764,000 French, 274,000 Dutch, 230,000 Yugoslavs and 227,000 Italians. Out of nearly five million workers who arrived in Germany, only 150,000 came voluntarily. Regular manhunts were organized; men and women seized from their homes, flung into cattle trucks and transported hundreds of miles. On the way thousands died of privation.

The most fortunate were those who went to farms. Those who were sent to the heavily-bombed industrial centres were housed in terrible conditions, beaten and exposed to epidemic after epidemic. But the figure of five million did not satisfy Hitler – he demanded more and ordered increasingly ruthless measures to secure the necessary manpower.

Just under four million Russian prisoners had been taken in the opening campaign of the 1941 war and great numbers of them were deliberately left to die from hunger or cold in the cruel winter. Hitler's need for manpower reversed the policy and by the end of 1943 nearly one million Russians were working in Germany. But it could not bring the dead to life again: of more than five million Russian soldiers captured by the Germans during the war, two million are known to have died in captivity and another million are unaccounted for.

In 1943 the 270,000 men of Hitler's Sixth Army were trapped by the Red Army at Stalingrad. Hitler refused to let them retreat and, as they stared annihilation in the face, he ordered them to die like heroes. When the 90,000 survivors surrendered Hitler went berserk.

As the façade of power crumbled, Hitler reverted to his old ways. He became increasingly vulgar and his rages grew more frequent, in fact he appeared to lose all control of himself. When he screamed out abuse his face became mottled and swollen with fury and he'd wave his arms around wildly and bang the wall with his fists. Then, as suddenly as he had erupted, Hitler would stop, smooth down his hair, straighten his collar, and resume conversation in his normal voice. But when he wanted to win someone over he was still capable of an eerie charm. He was a consummate actor; able to absorb himself in a role and convince himself of the truth at the time he was speaking.

Hitler was determined that Germany would never surrender. On 19 March 1944 he issued categorical and detailed orders for the destruction of all communications, rolling stock, lorries, bridges, dams, factories, and supplies. 'If the war is to be lost, the nation will also perish. This fate is inevitable. There is no need to consider the basis even of a most primitive existence any longer. On the contrary, it is better to destroy even that, and to destroy it ourselves. The nation has proved itself weak, and the future belongs solely to the winners. Besides, those who remain after the battle are of little value, for the good have fallen.' It was to be almost his final act of betrayal which fortunately was never implemented.

As day succeeded day in Hitler's isolated world of the Reich Chancellery and its garden shelter, the news grew steadily worse. Between 12 January 1945, the day on which the Russians opened their offensive in Poland, and 12 April, when the US Ninth Army crossed the Elbe, the Allies inflicted a total defeat upon the German army. By 16 April the way to Berlin was open. Hitler had lost all control over events, and by April he could not even find out what was happening. His one answer to every proposal was; No Withdrawal. Without bothering to investigate the facts he ordered

A rare informal photograph, taken in the 1930s, of Hitler dozing in an armchair, watched by his mistress, Eva Braun. On 29 April 1945, in the bunker beneath the Chancellery in what was by then a ruined Berlin, the couple were married; on the following day, they committed suicide together, she by poison, he by shooting. Their bodies were taken outside and burnt, the last chapter in a story that had started in the ruins of Germany after the First World War. (© HULTON-DEUTSCH COLLECTION/CORBIS)

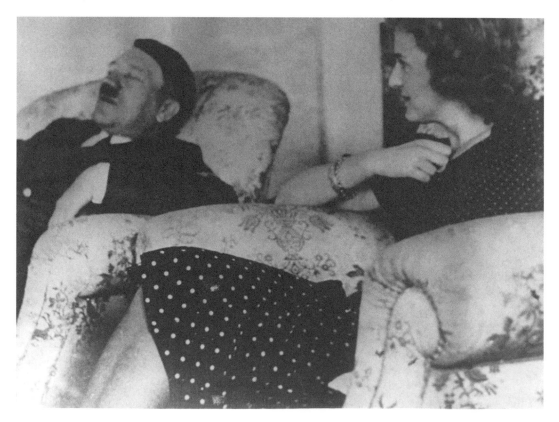

the dismissal, degradation and even execution of officers who, after fighting against overwhelming forces, were forced to give ground – even the SS were not immune. The setting in which Hitler played out his final scene was well suited to the end of so strange a history.

The physical atmosphere of the bunker was oppressive, but this was nothing compared to the pressure of the psychological atmosphere. The incessant air raids, the knowledge that Russians were in the city, nervous exhaustion and fear produced a tension bordering on hysteria, and Hitler's violent mood changes affected the lives of all those in the shelter. On the night of 26 April the Russians began to shell the Chancellery, and the bunker shook as the massive masonry split and crashed into the garden.

Facing death and the destruction of the regime he had created, the man who had exacted the sacrifice of millions of lives rather than admit defeat was still recognizably the old Hitler. From first to last there were no words of regret, or suggestion of remorse. The fault was that of others, above all that of the Jews, for even now the old hatred was unappeased. Twenty odd years had passed and taught him nothing. Hitler sat down and wrote his final testament.

Characteristically, Hitler's last message to the German people contained at least one striking lie. His death was anything but a hero's end – by committing suicide he deliberately abandoned his responsibilities and took the coward's way out. Hitler shot himself in the mouth and on his right-hand side lay his new wife, Eva Braun who had swallowed poison. The time was 3.30 p.m on the afternoon of Monday 30 April 1945, ten days after Hitler's fifty-sixth birthday.

The Third Reich outlasted its founder by one week.

ILSE KOCH

THE 'BITCH OF BUCHENWALD'

She was one of the most sadistic in the whole group of Nazi offenders. If there was a cry being heard around the world it was for the tortured innocents who died at her hands.

TRIAL PROSECUTOR, 1951

Since his accession to power, Hitler together with the Nazis had been devising ways of getting rid of all the, 'undesirable elements' from society, in order to secure his vision of an Aryan master race. These undesirables included Jews, gypsies, the mentally and physically retarded, homosexuals and intellectuals, in fact anyone who stood in his way. Initially he chose to either exile or to inter them, but as the Second World War was being fought by land, sea and air, the clinical Nazi death machine ground into action. Amongst the mass slaughter one woman saw the exterminations as much more than a job. She was Ilse Koch – the wife of the Commandant at Buchenwald. This psychotic sadist and nymphomaniac revelled in the brutal atmosphere and plight of condemned men, women and children. She would force prisoners to indulge in depraved sex acts before they were tortured and killed. Her home was adorned with shrunken heads alongside lampshades made from the skin of dead prisoners. A monster of unimaginable cruelty, Ilse Koch was known as the 'Bitch of Buchenwald'.

Born in Dresden in rural Saxony in 1906, Ilse Kohler was the daughter of a labourer. At school she was known as a quiet, well-behaved child from a loving home and she was popular with local boys. On leaving school at fifteen, Ilse started work in a factory, but soon became a librarian in a bookshop. Germany was in a period of incredible economic stagnation and the country was still reeling from their losses in World War I. Surrounded by drabness, young Ilse started to become aware of a new, energetic element around her. In the early 1930s, this element galvinized into an official branch of the Nazi Party and the young, attractive red-head fell under the spell of the macho henchmen that frequented the shop. She soon worked her way through the ranks and had affairs with several SS men.

Ilse became a Nazi secretary and was personally singled out by Heinrich Himmler – head of the SS and the Gestapo – for marriage to his top aide Karl Koch. One of the key beliefs of the Party was to create a new, perfect Aryan breed and Ilse and Karl were seen as an ideal match. In reality, Karl Koch was a failed bank clerk with a failed

Ilse Koch with her husband, SS Colonel Karl Koch, Commandant of Buchenwald concentration camp. The couple would so abuse their positions at Buchenwald that the Nazis themselves put them on trial; indeed, Koch was eventually sentenced to death, and was executed by his accuser in the yard of the camp he had brutalized, and which he and his wife had treated as their own pleasure ground. (© CORBIS)

marriage who had joined Hitler's Party at the beginning of its rise to power in 1931, but he soon rose through the ranks to become a top SS officer.

Hitler had created the SS as his own personal bodyguards and henchmen, against the power of the German military and to carry out tasks unique to his ruthless style. Hitler liked to create disharmony and launched a massive recruitment drive upon coming to power. Every pure Aryan was encouraged to join, as a path to a better life – Karl Koch was a perfect candidate. He was made colonel at the infamous Sachsenhausen concentration camp, built near Berlin, where he gained a reputation as a sadistic bully.

One evening in 1936 Karl and Ilse were married at midnight in a grove of oak trees. His new bride didn't mind his profession at all. On the contrary, she was proud that she had risen from peasant status to become the wife of a top-ranking official.

Karl Koch was a model Nazi who dispensed violent discipline. His speciality was beating prisoners with a horsewhip embedded with razor blades. He advocated the use of the thumbscrew and branding iron and the SS hierarchy soon spotted his potential. In 1939, as the Nazi *Blitzkrieg*, (lightning war) smashed through Europe,

Karl was promoted to Commandant of a new facility called Buchenwald, named after a beech wood on the site.

Throughout the 1930s, the Nazi Party had been attempting to cleanse Germany of 'undesirables'. Street shootings, starvation in the ghettos, gassing in railway coaches killed thousands, but the coldly efficient SS decided that the genocide was not proceeding fast enough. Many of the concentration camps which had been established years before, to house political prisoners, were turned into extermination camps.

Buchenwald was a labour camp where the weak were exterminated and the healthy worked to death. It also served as a feeder station for Auschwitz particularly for Jews who would often remain at Buchenwald for a short period of time before being transported to their deaths in the gas chambers. Even for those people who arrived at the beginning of 1938, before mass exterminations were ordered by Hitler, and whose stay at Buchenwald was restricted to a short period before emigration, the effects were horrific. They had been forced to leave their secure existences and were thrust into cells with only the barest of amenities.

Set up in 1937 in the rural Weimar region, Buchenwald was one of the first and largest concentration camps in Nazi Germany. It complemented the camps of Sachsenhausen to the north and Dachau to the south. Like many other concentration camps, the population of Buchenwald increased dramatically throughout the years of the Reich. In July 1937 there were 1,000 inmates, but by September 1939 this number had increased to 8,634. By December 1943 the population reached 37,319 and by liberation it stood at 80,436.

The camp consisted of 130 satellite camps and extension units, and was divided into three main sections. The first, or 'large camp', housed prisoners with some seniority; the 'small camp' contained prisoners who were in quarantine; and the 'tented camp' contained thousands of Polish prisoners sent there after the German invasion of Poland in 1939. Besides these parts there were the administration compound, the SS barracks and the camp factories.

The camp was built by the prisoners. During the entire summer of 1937, the SS forced the prisoners to use their, 'free time' to carry huge stones from the quarry to the camp. Those who had the misfortune to carry stones that were too small in the eyes of the SS were killed immediately. Later, dozens of prisoners were chained to a huge four-wheel cart and had to pull enormous loads to the camp while forced by the SS to sing. The SS referred to these prisoners as the 'Singing Horses'. Thousands of prisoners also died during the construction of the road leading from the foot of the Ettersberg Mountain to the entry of the camp and the road became known as 'Blood Street' by the prisoners.

Most of the initial prisoners were political detainees, but in the spring of 1938 the numbers rose dramatically as a result of the operation against, 'anti-social elements' i.e. the Jews, homosexuals and gypsies. A further 10,000 Jews arrived after the *Reichskristallnacht* (November 1938) when the SS and populace had destroyed a vast number of Jewish businesses in Germany. During the war years Buchenwald held up to 80,000 prisoners, controlled by over 7,000 SS guards.

There were no gas chambers at the camp; they weren't needed. Inmates were worked to death in factories and on the land, and life expectancy was around three months. The official purpose of Buchenwald was the destruction of the prisoners by work. Everyone was involved, young and old, men and women and hundreds perished every month through disease, malnutrition, exhaustion, beatings and executions.

In addition there was also another, even more gruesome aspect to Buchenwald: its ongoing medical research. The Division for Typhus and Virus Research of the Hygiene Institute of the Waffen SS was based in Buchenwald and carried out its work with horrific enthusiasm. Sterilizations without anaesthetic, injections to test new drugs and bizarre tests of human resistance to pain, heat and cold were all encouraged. The Nazi butchers conducted live vivisections on the prisoners, and conducted experiments on their livers, whilst anyone unfortunate enough to have been burnt would have poison injected into their wounds. Most bizarrely of all however, the researchers conducted a series of experiments on homosexuals, hoping to find a cure for the 'disease'. Patients were also infected with fatal diseases and closely observed; hundreds were contaminated with typhus whilst the doctors watched them die a slow, agonizing death. To the doctors and scientists, these people were guinea pigs, used to further the glorious cause of Nazi science and the protection of its Aryan people. Few were treated for their infections and, once they had outlived their usefulness, most were left to die.

Another way to kill prisoners was used in the stable. The prisoners had to enter a fake infirmary room and place themselves under a height gauge. Then an SS man killed them with a revolver by shooting through a small hole placed at the height of the prisoner's neck. The noise of these executions was masked by a radio turned up to maximum volume.

When Karl and Ilse Koch arrived at Buchenwald their first few months were spent having another child to provide them with the minimum two children required of senior Nazi Party members. It was a basic Nazi assumption that a woman's main duty was to cherish 'her husband, her family, her children and her house'; a philosophy that Ilse Koch had little intention of following. Once this formality was over, her husband was able to get on with his work and promptly forgot about her.

Now Ilse was free to begin her own work. As wife of the Commandant, she led a life of luxury and privilege whilst all around her brutality and degradation thrived. At first she began taking small liberties – she demanded all prisoners address her as 'Gunadige Frau' – a term reserved for female nobility, but she would soon move onto other activities.

Karl had an indoor arena built in 1940, at a cost of a quarter of a million marks. He paid for it with the money he had extorted from prisoners and with large scale embezzlement. He and Ilse took morning rides, which had to be accompanied by music played by the SS band standing on a special platform.

Obsessed with her looks, Ilse would take baths in Madeira wine whilst thousands

Buchenwald concentration camp in October 1945, with an effigy of Hitler hanging from a gibbet, made by the camp's former inmates and placed there as a memorial to the thousands who had died or been murdered there. By then the camp was being used as a hospital for the many inmates still suffering from the effects of starvation, disease and brutality. (© BETTMANN/CORBIS)

of prisoners starved yards from her front door. By day she would walk around the camp with a whip, lashing out at prisoners she didn't like the look of. The sight of suffering made her eyes widen and her pulse race. She would unleash her dog on pregnant women and squeal with delight at their fear while, by night she would organize lesbian orgies with officers' wives. She then moved on to her husband's junior officers, having affairs with up to a dozen at a time. Ilse became fascinated by punishment techniques and the torture of prisoners and quickly acquired a reputation as a nymphomaniac and sadist. Prisoners were forced to indulge in depraved orgies and the most horrendous sex acts, while she sat back and enjoyed the show. One of her many twisted pleasures was to stand at the camp entrance as new prisoners arrived. She would wait topless, fondling her breasts and shouting lewd remarks. If one prisoner so much as glanced at her they were beaten senseless. On one occasion, guards noticing three men looking up at her from the ground, beat two of them to death on the spot whilst the third man was suffocated by a guard standing on his neck, grinding his face into the dirt. Ilse filed a report stating that the executed men had given her lascivious looks.

As the Nazi war machine became bogged down on the Eastern Front, Ilse was treating her death camp as a playground. One day her guards began shooting prisoners as they worked. She was visibly excited and grabbed a pistol, adding twenty-four victims to the death toll.

But this was only the beginning of her campaign of terror – there was an even more gruesome side to her – which was about to be revealed. Ilse enjoyed having sick trophies adorn her home, and she ordered the heads of several prisoners to be severed and chemically shrunk to the size of a grapefruit. Dozens of these heads decorated Ilse's dining room as she sat and ate there each day with her children. Furthermore, it was around this time that she also created one of the most enduring and revolting images of the Third Reich.

Ilse had always admired the bodies of the young prisoners and had attractive men brought before her to parade up and down. She began to covet their smooth skin and hit upon a novel idea. Ilse had their skins removed and a seamstress make them into book covers, wallets, gloves and lampshades. While most German mothers were knitting woollen scarves and socks for their children, Ilse was producing handicrafts from human remains. The SS skinned and then tanned their victims' flesh in the notorious Block 2, which became known as the 'Pathological Block'. The lampshades were particularly sought after as a symbol of the superiority of the German Race. Presents fashioned from skin would be admired at dinner parties and exchanged as gifts between husbands and wives and the higher the quality of the skin, the more valuable it became. To Ilse and her circle they were like the finest leathers – rare and valuable material.

Those who deny the Holocaust have since cast doubt on the origins of these skins, but sophisticated forensic tests have left no doubt they are human. Ilse admired one thing in particular, as an inmate of Buchenwald remembers, 'During roll calls, the wives of the SS selected their victims and they did so with even more cynicism than their husbands. They sought beautiful human skins artistically tattooed. In order to please them, a special roll call was often held on the square at which the prisoners had to present, completely naked. Then these ladies passed in review through the ranks making their selections as in a fashion show. One could hear the titters, their exclamation, and their small laughter of satisfaction. They would murmur "Das ist Schon" and they would point their fingers at the object of their choice.' Ilse's preference was for the skins of gypsies and Russian prisoners of war and she would order their deaths by lethal injection so as not to damage the skin. (In line with an SS directive, human hair was also collected. The hair would be used in the manufacture of socks for U-boat personnel and for employees of the State Railway.) Ilse would have the tattooed skins made into gloves and wear them as she paraded around the camp looking for prisoners to torment.

However, it wasn't just Ilse who entertained herself with perverse acts; her husband, Karl, also took pleasure in causing unnecessary suffering amongst his prisoners for, as soon as he arrived at Buchenwald, Karl had a small zoo built. It featured a birdhouse, a water basin and room for four bears and five monkeys. Buchenwald survivor Morris Hubert remembers: 'In the camp there was a cage with a bear and an eagle. Every day, they would throw a Jew in there. The bear would tear him apart and the eagle would pick at his bones.' The bears' cages were in full view of the prisoners and the Jewish Prime Minister of France, Leon Blum, was kept in the falconer's house before being transferred to Dachau.

In fact Karl Koch was extremely soft hearted when it came to animals. The camp guidebook contains the following order given by him, '… it has been found that members of the SS have tied deer's horns to the fence and cut them loose only after a long while. In addition deer have been lured to the fence and tinfoil put in their mouths. In the future, I will find out the perpetrators of such loutish acts and have them reported to the SS Commander in Chief, in order to have them punished for cruelty to animals.'

If however, Karl Koch was soft hearted when it came to animals, this trait certainly didn't apply to his human victims and, in addition to the indignities meted out to the living, Karl also began racketeering – stealing gold teeth from the dead, ripping wedding rings from the fingers of corpses and jewelry and cash from the deceased. He then deposited the plunder in secret Swiss bank accounts.

The couple continued their regime throughout the war, but not without hindrance from their superiors. Ironically, the German Third Reich frowned upon the use of excessive cruelty in the camps, and despite ordering horrific experiments and atrocities to be visited upon their victims, they found time to discipline those they felt were unruly.

In 1941, the Koch's found themselves before an SS court on charges of, 'gross brutality, corruption and dishonour.' It was one thing to beat, torture and murder people, but it was another to actually enjoy it. The charges were dismissed, but Karl was sent to work in Majdanek concentration camp in Poland while Ilse returned to

Buchenwald. With no powerful husband to hide behind she embarked on a series of affairs with senior camp officials, and kept a low profile.

In 1944 Karl returned to his wife at Buchenwald, but his past was catching up with him. Soon new accusations were levelled at him, this time for his theft and racketeering. This was the final straw for the Nazis. Torture and murder was nothing compared to ripping off the Reich.

Unable to accept defeat, Karl poisoned a chief witness a day before the trial and murder was added to Karl's lengthy charge sheet.

On a cold morning in April 1945, Karl Koch was taken outside and shot by his accuser Von Waldeck, in the yard of his own camp, the very site of the brutality he had masterminded. One can only imagine the joy that the prisoners watching must have felt at their ex-Commandant's death. But meanwhile the Bitch of Buchenwald, his wife, remained.

Despite equal guilt and accusations that she had actually encouraged her husband, Ilse had been acquitted. However, no longer able to take advantage of her

The tattooed chest skin, with nipples, of a Jewish inmate – an example of the 'handicrafts' Ilse Koch produced at Buchenwald, and which she and her circle greatly admired. Some of these gruesome and horrific relics were produced in evidence at her trial for war crimes in 1947; when her case was re-examined by an Allied tribunal in 1951, however, they had disappeared, probably stolen – a circumstance that has given rise to Nazi apologists' claims that these and other similar human 'artefacts' had never existed.

(© CORBIS)

The 'Bitch of Buchenwald' at her trial by an Allied court, which was held at Dachau in 1947, and at which she was given a life sentence. When she was freed by a US military tribunal in 1951, she was immediately rearrested and tried by the German authorities, who sentenced her to life imprisonment without remission. Sixteen years later she hanged herself in her cell.

(© CORBIS)

position as wife of the camp Commandant, the cunning Ilse attempted to disappear and melt back into the general population. As the Russians advanced and the mighty Third Reich began to crumble, she joined thousands of others and headed westwards looking for safety from the Allies.

On 10 April 1945, the Americans entered Buchenwald. By now Ilse was staying with friends in Ludwigsburg, but the liberated prisoners hadn't forgotten her. The atrocities witnessed by the Americans were such that President Eisenhower ordered that all men from the division that entered Buchenwald be made to see the horrific scenes within camp. He said, 'they may not know what they are fighting for, but at least now they will know what they are fighting against.'

During the next few months, Ilse buried herself in anonymity, convinced that the Allies were after far more important people than herself. She was finally caught and imprisoned in 1947 and went on trial at Dachau whilst pregnant by a fellow male inmate. For weeks on end, abused and emaciated former prisoners testified about her activities. Prosecutors claimed that the blood of over 50,000 inmates lay on her hands. Ilse read out a statement claiming she was merely the servant of evil people. When shown photography of piles of bodies, Ilse screamed, 'Lies! All lies!' She denied everything and claimed the Allies had framed her. Halfway through the proceedings, Ilse pretended to go into an epileptic state, twitching uncontrollably and staring blankly ahead, but when a court physician examined her in her cell afterwards, she laughed, telling him how she was enjoying her, 'first class comedy act'. Meanwhile, crowds had gathered outside the courtroom, calling for her immediate execution. The court responded by sentencing her to life imprisonment with hard labour. But it wasn't over. In 1951, American General Lucius D. Clay, granted Ilse her freedom, claiming there was 'insufficient evidence' to support her incarceration. There was an immediate worldwide protest. Her prosecutor said, 'This is a gross miscarriage of justice. She was one of the most sadistic in the whole group of Nazi offenders. If there was a cry being heard around the world it was for the tortured innocents who died at her hands.'

However, justice was to prevail. As soon as Ilse left the prison, she was rearrested and given a retrial. More than 240 witnesses testified against her and she was given life once more and told to expect no mercy. Life would mean life.

In 1967, Ilse wrote to her son Uwe, whom she had given birth to during her first trial, from her cell in Aichach Prison in Bavaria. She bitterly complained that she had been a scapegoat for the higher echelons of the Nazi Party. There was no remorse, no sorrow for her crimes.

On 1 September, at the age of sixty-one, Ilse Koch ate a simple meal before penning a final letter to her son. She then knotted some bed sheets together, tied them to the lamp above her bed and hanged herself. In her last letter she had written, 'There is not any other way for me. Death is the only deliverance.'

POL POT

ARCHITECT OF GENOCIDE

The red, red blood splatters the cities and plains of the Cambodian fatherland,
The sublime blood of the workers and peasants,
The blood of revolutionary combatants of both sexes,
The blood spills out into great indignation and a resolute urge to fight.
17 April, that day under the revolutionary flag,
The blood certainly liberates us from slavery.

NATIONAL ANTHEM OF DEMOCRATIC KAMPUCHEA

In 1998, the world watched in disbelief as footage was released of an old man who had died in the jungles of Thailand. He had a broad, chubby face with sparkling, grandfatherly eyes and thick lips that split into a toothy, genial grin. He looked slightly comical, an impression not dispelled by his peculiar name, Pol Pot. But there was nothing funny about Pol Pot – he was a leader who showed his people no mercy. On the run since 1979, this was the one-time ruler of Cambodia who was responsible for the deaths of almost two million people, a third of that Cambodia's population. Over a period of four years, he had tortured and starved the Cambodians to death and men, women, children and babies were often brutally clubbed with hammers and buried alive.

Born Saloth Sar, in 1925, the youngest of seven children, he was brought up on a prosperous rice farm north of Phnom Penh, in a Cambodia ruled by the French. The young boy never worked in a rice field, or knew much about village life because at the age of six he was sent to the capital to train as a monk. He spent six years in a Buddhist temple and two years as a Buddhist monk. But the boy from the village only felt like an outsider in the bustling, modern city. Pol Pot didn't have a sense of the multi-cultural nature of the Cambodian cities, or if he did, he resented it. He said he felt, 'like a dark monkey from the mountains.'

In 1949 Pol Pot went to Paris as a student when he was awarded a scholarship to study Radioelectricity. Here he met his first wife, Khieu Ponnary, eight years his senior and the first Cambodian woman to be awarded the *Baccalaureate*. There his innate racism would find expression in extreme communism. During the years that Pol Pot studied in Paris, the Communist Party was probably the most hard-line, doctrine-led Stalinist Party in western Europe. He also absorbed the philosophy of another left-wing Cambodian student, Khieu Samphan, who believed that to achieve a true, rural revolution Cambodia needed to regress to a peasant economy – without towns, industry, currency or education.

After university in Paris, Pol Pot returned to Cambodia full of revolutionary ideals, and joined the underground Communist Party in opposition to the French-backed monarch, King Sihanouk and President Lon Nol. Within two years he was made General Secretary of the Party, and in order to escape capture by government forces, he fled to the hills, with his now heavily armed cadres, and preached his revolutionary doctrine to the hill tribes whilst also waging a vicious guerrilla war. Even then, Pol Pot had his sights on ultimate power and in 1962 it is believed that he ordered the execution of his predecessor as leader of the Communist Party. Initially he was extremely unpopular with the peasants, but that would all change once he was in power.

From the early 1970s, Pol Pot and his group, known as the Khmer Rouge, engaged in a savage campaign against the Lon Nol government, and by 1972 the conflict had escalated into a full-blown civil war. Pol Pot's ruthless march to power was also boosted when the Vietnam War spilled over into Cambodia. The massive American bombardments that fell on the Cambodian people between 1969-1973 supplied Pol Pot with a potent hate-object and undoubtedly delivered to the revolution thousands of recruits and sympathizers. In 1970 the Party had 4,000 members; by 1975 they had 14,000. Between 1970-75 the Americans had supplied $1.18 billion in military

*One of the very few portraits of Pol Pot, the architect of a genocidal policy that killed some three million Cambodians. This photograph hangs in the Tuol Sleng Museum, a former Khmer Rouge prison and torture centre.
(© PABLO SAN JUAN/CORBIS)*

material, and an additional $503 million in assistance, to Lon Nol's Khmer Republic. Then, suddenly America stopped all aid to Cambodia, which sent the country into a period of economic and military destabilization. Pol Pot took advantage of the government's weakness and by the spring of 1975, the Khmer Rouge was on the outskirts of Phnom Penh.

On 17 April, just after the Cambodian New Year, the Khmer Rouge entered the capital, victors of a five-year war against a government backed by the Americans. When it was announced that Pol Pot, a rubber plantation worker, was the new Prime Minister, no one had ever heard of him. It wasn't until 1978, when his picture began to appear in communal dining halls, that his own brothers and sisters realized that it was their brother who was in charge of the government.

After twenty-four years in existence, the Communist Party of Cambodia, now renamed Kampuchea, had won a stunning victory. As a political force it had been almost totally unknown five years earlier, when Prince Sihanouk, Cambodia's king had been overthrown. Now Pol Pot's regime was in a position to put in place and carry out an extreme, pure, total revolution of a sort that was more complete than any other revolution in history. The outside world reacted with amazement when the revolutionaries emptied the cities, destroyed western consumer goods, abolished money and foreign exchange markets. They established state control over all domestic and foreign trade, and then began liquidating the westernized elite.

The Central bank was demolished with explosives and bank notes allowed to flutter through the deserted streets of the capital. The Roman Catholic cathedral in Phnom Penh was disassembled stone by stone, until no trace whatever remained of the most prominent western edifice in the country.

Flushed with victory and imbued with a sense of righteousness, Pol Pot set out to implement his plans to restructure Cambodian society. The plan was to erase everything that had gone before and start again, even to the point that they declared that the year was no longer 1975, but Year Zero. This was to be the beginning of four years of murder and misery for the Cambodian people as Pol Pot began to destroy and rip apart Cambodian society, reducing it to a state of barbarity. The Khmer revolution altered completely and immediately the most basic aspects of Cambodian life such as language, religion and work habits.

Within hours of entering Phnom Penh, the new authorities ordered the city to be evacuated. Initially, they claimed this was to ensure that everyone got enough to eat, since the countryside had more food, and to ensure victory over the concept of private property, which was banned under the new regime. In reality it was because the new government could not control the towns, as their supporters were, by and large illiterate peasants, and the cities were considered to be centres of foreign domination.

Whether a doctor, lawyer, teacher, mechanic or street sweeper, everyone was forced into the countryside to labour as a peasant, where they would grow rice and build dams for the revolution. Two million Cambodians living in Phnom Penh were evacuated in seventy-two hours; soldiers marched from door to door and literally shoved people out onto the streets at gunpoint – if they resisted they were shot on the spot. The forced march of approximately three million out of Phnom Penh, and hundreds of thousands of others from Cambodia's provincial towns, meant death for around 400,000 people from heat, lack of food and water and not least, the total absence of any medical assistance. 'From noon onwards, the masses in the streets multiplied as Communist troops uprooted more and more families...there was a huge crowd of every age and condition, young, old and sick...virtually everybody saw corpses rapidly bloating and rotting in the sun. Then the water supply ceased throughout the city...No stores of drinking water, no stocks of food, no shelter had been prepared for the millions of outcasts. Acute dysentery racked and sapped life from bodies already weakened by hunger and fatigue, we must have passed the body of a child every two hundred yards.'

Through the forced evacuation of the cities, the Khmer Rouge had virtually cut off the entire population from whatever material connection it had with the old order. All homes, money, bank accounts and consumer goods were left behind. Potential adversaries were disorganized and separated from the places that might serve as centres of resistance, making Pol Pot's regime total masters. Familiar social, religious, familial and economic patterns were shattered, as all evacuees were thrown into a basic struggle for survival.

To reinforce his policies, Pol Pot declared that, henceforth, the Buddhist religion, money and personal possessions would all be banned. It was back to basics. Believing the city people to be contaminated by past lives, Pol Pot would rewrite their histories. In the idealized peasant state, they would be purified through hard labour and brutality. Elderly monks who had not done manual labour for decades were forced to do particularly punishing work, digging for very long hours. People – including pregnant women – stood in water up to their necks in the cold and rainy seasons, working on canals, with legs and feet swelling up and bleeding. If you stopped work because of illness, you did not get fed. The Khmer Rouge slogan at the time was, 'to keep you is no gain and to destroy you is no loss.' Everyone laboured in the same way. If you didn't – you were shot. Fear and the threat of arbitrary, casual death was everywhere.

Pol Pot believed that for his vision of purity to work, individualism had to be obliterated. Only by destroying every root, every vestige of individual thought would a people dedicated to a collectivist regime emerge. With this in mind the population was divided into three categories, depending on class background and political past. *Penh sith*, who had full rights; *triem*, those who were candidates for full rights; and those who had no rights whatsoever, *bannheu*. The *penh sith* received full food rations and were allowed to join any organization, including the Party and the army. Almost all of them had joined Pol Pot at an early stage and came from the poorest, most uneducated segments of the rural population. *Triems* were second in line for rice rations and allowed to hold minor political offices. Many of these were drawn from the rural population, but as time went on some of the poor who had been forced out of the cities were promoted to this status. The lowest category, the *Bannheu*, had no rights whatever, not even the right to food. Most individuals targeted for liquidation fell into this category. Those not immediately executed received a near-starvation diet and were expected to work to the point of exhaustion.

With the advent of the new revolutionary morality, husbands were separated from wives for long periods, permission to marry was only granted by *Angkar* (The Organization), and that was within strict guidelines, and premarital sex became subject to extreme punishment, sometimes even the death penalty. Drinking and gambling were banned, and by 1976 Khieu Samphan, an officer of *Angkar* declared that, 'there were no thieves, drunkards, hooligans, or prostitutes in our country.' *Angkar* also considered itself to be the parents of all Cambodian children. Young teenagers were taken away from their families and sent away for rigorous ideological training. Pol Pot believed that if they trained their young recruits on cruel games, they would end up as soldiers with a love of killing, and encouraged the young recruits to take pleasure in tormenting animals and to make their victims suffer as much as possible.

Children scarcely lived with their parents any more: those under the age of six were entrusted to 'grandmothers' who cultivated their revolutionary spirit through the narration of heroic tales. Between the ages of six and twelve the children lived in separate quarters and were encouraged to spy and report on their parents for any infractions of the rules. Once they were twelve, they were enlisted in 'mobile troops' and hardly ever had the opportunity to see their parents again. In Pol Pot's hands they were taught nothing but discipline – just to take orders and not to look for reasons.

Pol Pot was now head of the ironically named Democratic Kampuchea and would brook no opposition to his plans to restructure society. The *Sangha*, the Buddhist monkhood, the only remaining institution that might have challenged Pol Pot by representing the traditional Cambodia, was ill prepared to resist the totalitarian power of the Khmer Rouge, and was dismantled. Before Pol Pot took power, Cambodia was considered to be the most Buddhist country in South East Asia. The countryside was dotted with more than 2,500 temples, and most men became monks at some point in their lives. Immediately after victory however, the Khmer Rouge moved swiftly to expunge all vestiges of Buddhism from daily life, since its teachings and practices contradicted vital aspects of the revolutionary doctrine. They executed the leading monks, defrocked the rest, forbade the accumulation of merit through giving, and destroyed many of the temples.

The Khmer Rouge then began to identify and execute political leaders, military officers, civil servants and anyone with an education. In some instances the spouses and children of the officials were killed alongside the supposed traitors. 'The Khmer Rouge thrust each official forward and stabbed them in the chest and back. As each man lay dying, his anguished and horror-stricken wives and children were herded up to his body. The women, forced to kneel, were stabbed to death and the children were stabbed where they stood. The very small children, too young to fully appreciate what was happening, were picked up by the executioners and torn limb from limb.'

King Sihanouk was discredited and put under virtual house arrest. Pol Pot was

A pile of skulls in an abandoned Cambodian school, a hideous reminder of Pol Pot and his regime. Schools were closed after the Khmer Rouge came to power in the 1970s, part of a campaign against educated people that also saw the closure of newspapers and libraries – as well as literally hundreds of thousands of murders (© MICHAEL FREEMAN/CORBIS)

embarking on a policy of permanent purge that strove to create a society with no past and no alternatives.

According to eye-witnesses, much of the slaughter was carried out by fanatical brain-washed teenagers in red bandanas, who screamed and fired into the air while selecting their next victims. The youthful murderers were illiterate and ignorant and this made them even more violent and unpredictable. The killing was indiscriminate; the Khmer Rouge didn't need reasons. Whenever Pol Pot's troops were faced with a lack of comprehension or passive resistance, they chose to exterminate rather than take the time and trouble to re-educate.

Schools and libraries had been closed shortly after the Khmer Rouge came to power and newspapers were non-existent. The wearing of spectacles was enough to identify you as a member of the intelligentsia and therefore an enemy of the revolution. Everyone ate communally and individuals were only allowed to have two basic possessions of their own: a spoon and a bowl. Once ordinary shoes wore out, footwear consisted of Ho Chin Min sandals, improvised from pieces of rubber tyres and they were allowed one piece of clothing, a black boiler suit. All foreign medical supplies ceased in 1975 and the new government promoted the use of medicinal compounds made from local herbs. Untrained personnel performed medical operations. Even when disease ravaged the land throughout most of 1975 and 1976 Pol Pot remained inflexible – he repeatedly reminded people of the vital importance of self-reliance. If the bullet didn't get you, starvation would.

South East Asia is dominated by its staple food, rice. The average person would consume the equivalent of seven cans of rice per day. People who laboured in the rice paddies for up to fifteen hours a day, had to exist on one-and-a-half cans. Pol Pot expected rice production to treble in the first three years of his regime, believing that enthusiasm and heroism would be enough. But disastrous harvests as a result of the increased population in the countryside, and the urban people's inability to farm meant starvation. However, the Khmer Rouge refused to back down and constantly overstated its achievements. Life wasn't even cheap; it had no value at all. Cambodia became a macabre network of killing fields. Even today, the exact number of mass graves into which the victims' bodies were thrown is not known.

Pol Pot also imposed a rigid organization plan that outlined when planting, weeding and harvesting was to occur, despite the fact that the country's conditions varied from place to place. There was no incentive in the propertyless society; you worked to avoid getting killed and even in death, one's body might be used as fertiliser. A phrase evolved for those executed: 'to be turned into a coconut'. Life became a continuous process of working in the rice fields during part of the year and on the irrigation systems during the remainder, with no respite in-between. If a worker made a mistake or criticized a project, they were taken away to be flogged to death or shot. Special offenders, like those starving peasants found cannibalising dead bodies, would be buried up to their heads in the ground and left to die. Their heads would then be cut off and stuck on stakes as a warning to others.

Within two years of Pol Pot coming to power, hundreds of thousands of Cambodians lay rotting in mass graves. Summary executions, starvation and overwork had taken its toll on both the city people and the peasants. The architect of this misery controlled every aspect of people's lives, but he never accepted that he was responsible for any of their suffering, or that anyone who died did so for anything but the right reason. Terror was the chief instrument of Pol Pot's dictatorship which sought to liquidate, as quickly as possible, all officers and many enlisted men in Lon Nol's army, bureaucrats of the old regime, landowners, those engaged in commerce, skilled labourers, western-educated professionals and many Buddhist monks.

The truly extraordinary aspect of the Pol Pot revolution was the literalism with which they applied abstract political principles, without regard for the awesome costs to Cambodia, in terms of diplomatic isolation, economic devastation and massive human suffering. Other revolutionaries have talked long and loud on the subject, but have always been sobered by the responsibilities of power. The scope and extreme literalism with which Pol Pot pursued his aims of complete sovereignty and self-reliance make him unique. The Khmer Rouge leaders had been living in their own peculiar dream world, in which the human element was virtually forgotten. What they saw as a rational economic organization may have made sense in the isolation of the forest, but as an operative policy, it was cruel and unrealistic.

With the country closed to outsiders, the world was blissfully unaware of what was happening – or chose to ignore it for reasons of political expediency. Refugees reaching neighbouring countries told stories of unbelievable horrors. Yet with no diplomatic ties, no travel, not even a postal service, the nation of Kampuchea was an impenetrable armed camp, seemingly set on the genocide of its own people. When the United Nations called for a debate, Pol Pot's ministers sent their regrets that they could find no one with the time to spare to attend the hearings.

But two journalists, (one of them Elizabeth Becker) did get into Cambodia in 1978. Accompanied by the British academic, Malcolm Caldwell, they met Pol Pot, and he then proceeded to give them a lecture on the wonders of his experiments in Kampuchea. Later that night, an unremarkable meeting with Pol Pot turned into a unforgettable nightmare. Hearing gunfire coming from Malcolm Caldwell's room, Elizabeth rushed upstairs and found his body riddled with bullet holes. She still cannot work out why he died and not her.

Whilst propaganda films projected a country in the grip of well-being, Pol Pot had exterminated the majority of his class enemies and broken the old system. He now turned his attention to enemies within his own government. When Pol Pot took over in 1975, there were twenty-two members of the central committee of the Communist

Tuol Sleng prison, also known as S-21. Established by Pol Pot during his reign of terror, this former school house in Phnom Penh was used as a base for the torture and execution of over 20,000 people arrested on suspicion of spying for the KGB or CIA. Innocent children were among those murdered.
(© Kevin R. Morris/Corbis)

After being deposed in 1979 when Vietnamese troops invaded what was then Kampuchea, Pol Pot and his henchmen went into hiding in a succession of guerrilla bases. By 1997, however, the remains of the Khmer Rouge had begun to fragment. Pol Pot was captured and given a show trial by his former colleagues for being a 'political enemy'. He was sentenced to life imprisonment, but died the following year while under house arrest. This photograph was taken by a Japanese journalist in a Khmer Rouge camp near the Thailand-Cambodia border in December 1979. (© BETTMANN/CORBIS)

Party. By the end of his reign – three years, eight months and twenty days later – eighteen of those twenty-two had been executed. Murder by government under Khmer Rouge rule was in fact so systematic that a large bureaucracy was required to eliminate the projected, suspected and imagined opponents of the transformation of Kampuchean society. The nerve centre of the purge apparatus was the *Santebal*, or special branch.

In a former school house in Phnom Penh, Pol Pot established the notorious Tuol Sleng prison or S-21, as an extermination centre at the hub of a nationwide system of imprisonment, interrogation, torture and execution. Initially set up for the interrogation of counter-revolutionaries, over 20,000 people were tortured and executed here on trumped-up charges of spying for the KGB or the CIA – or simply because they knew someone who had been arrested before. Men, women and children were tagged and almost all were tortured into confessing anything they were told to confess to. Of the 4,000 who entered S-21, only 7 survived and 1 was released – the rest were buried in S-21's customized killing field, Cheung Ek, where over 8,000 skulls have so far been counted.

Anyone brought into S-21 was photographed and their crimes were meticulously recorded. The Khmer Rouge had developed their own code for recording the crimes and fates of the prisoners. At any one time, the prison held around 1,500 prisoners. The ideology of the prison was that the Party was never, ever wrong. If people were arrested they were guilty – indeed the word for prisoner in Cambodian means guilty person, rather than somebody who is being held.

A tiny rectangular notebook found in a house near Tuol Sleng contains five hand-written pages on Human Experiments on seventeen different prisoners. Deuch, the governor of S-21, recorded the effects of slashing a girl's stomach and placing her in water to see how long she would float. Similar details were recorded for, 'four young girls stabbed in the throat.' One of the problems that repeatedly emerged from the files left behind was that torture became too indiscriminate and prisoners were dying before information could be extracted from them. This represented a 'loss of mastery'. With class and political opponents out of the way, Pol Pot, compelled by the racism that was so much a part of his agenda, now turned his attention to Cambodia's ethnic minorities. Pol Pot believed there was only one pure race: the Khmer, who originated in Lower Cambodia. The Chinese were probably the largest ethnic minority in Cambodia and half of them perished in the Pol Pot regime. The Ethnic Chams and Muslims were directly targeted and ruthlessly slaughtered. But Pol Pot's most extreme persecution was reserved for the Kampuchean Vietnamese. The Khmer Rouge had been eliminating the Vietnamese in Kampuchea since 1970 but now it became a crime punishable by death to speak or look Vietnamese. Kampuchean men married to Vietnamese women were instructed to kill their wives or else face execution themselves. In excess of 20,000 ethnic Vietnamese lost their lives. Even Pol Pot's Northern Zone Secretary, Kang Chap was ordered to shoot his wife because she was half-Vietnamese. He did as he was ordered.

The Khmer Rouge publicly glorified revolutionary violence and blood sacrifice and celebrated them in the country's official documents. The blood spilt for the revolution became a sanctifying symbol. Virtually every line of the national anthem mentioned bloodshed. It was as if the revolutionaries were harnessing the darker, more violent side of their national character to give their own deplorable acts legitimacy.

By late 1978, with executions and starvation at their height, and with the Pol Pot regime seemingly invincible, the government began to self-destruct. With information only coming from its security forces, the Party fell under the spell of the counterespionage myth, consuming itself as it nearly consumed the people of Cambodia. No traditional institutions existed to check the Party authority. They had crushed any opposition by terror and coercion. Now Pol Pot's psychotic and life-long hatred for the Vietnamese would be his undoing.

After a series of violent border confrontations with Vietnam, 150,000 Vietnamese troops stormed across the Kampuchean border and by 6 January, they were approaching Phnom Penh. Pol Pot's repeated purges had broken the links of command between officers and men and shattered morale in both the army and Party. Those targeted as traitors who knew they were not, did not know what to do; die in the name of the Party or flee. However the Cambodian people themselves knew what to do – they welcomed the Vietnamese with open arms and shouts of joy. Ironically three Vietnamese Cambodians, who had escaped the purge, Heng Samrin, Chea Sim and Ros Samay, would soon head the government that replaced Pol Pot.

Pol Pot and his henchmen fled to Northern Cambodia and Thailand and the hated governor of S-21, Deuch, evaded capture by one hour. Forty-four months after capturing Phnom Penh the Khmer Rouge were swept from the capital by Vietnamese invasion forces. The intervening period had witnessed the greatest per capita loss of life in a single nation in the twentieth century. In the search for 'pure communism', the Khmer Rouge reduced a war-torn, but traditionally resilient, economy to one almost without prospect of spontaneous regeneration. The draconian rules of life according to Pol Pot had turned Cambodia into a nation-wide gulag.

As Pol Pot fled in a white Mercedes and helicopter, taking him and his aides to Thailand, thousands more Khmer Rouge cadres left a ravaged Cambodia. He continued to fight on from his power base among his dedicated followers in the countryside and formed the Khmer Peoples' Liberation Front announcing a hypocritical manifesto promising political and religious freedom. It would be another twenty years before Pol Pot was seen again – but this time he was on trial.

Finally the Khmer Rouge had turned against their former leader. They had arrested him, not for crimes of genocide or crimes against humanity, but for being a political enemy. In an interview conducted by Nate Thayer shortly before his death, Pol Pot refused to say whether he regretted having caused the deaths of so many innocent people, and said that the mistakes made by the regime were mainly in implementation of policy. Two weeks later, in April 1998 Pol Pot died of natural causes.

Twelve years after his death, Pol Pot's comrades in slaughter have still not been brought to trial. Mass grave sites have been discovered throughout Cambodia, mainly in remote areas. Skulls have been collected and piled into an enclosure to serve as a reminder of Pol Pot's evil. Evidence is still being collected for a United Nations backed tribunal, but progress is being hampered by the fact that Khmer Rouge operatives occupy posts in the new Cambodian government. When Cambodia's foreign minister, Ieng Sary finally admitted to the deaths of three million people during the Khmer Rouge regime, he claimed that Pol Pot had been misunderstood and the massacres had all been 'a mistake'.

IDI AMIN

THE BUTCHER OF EAST AFRICA

'His Excellency President for Life Field Marshal Al Hadji Dr Idi Amin,
VC, DSO, MC, Lord of All the Beasts of the Earth and Fishes of the
Sea and Conqueror of the British Empire in Africa in General and
Uganda in Particular.'
TITLE AND STYLE ADOPTED BY IDI AMIN AS PRESIDENT OF UGANDA

In 1971, the self-created General Idi Amin became President of Uganda. To the rest of the world he was a showman whose extravagance was exceeded only by his talent for comic buffoonery. But behind the grinning face was a calculating monster, who brought about a tragedy of monumental proportions. He set up the notorious State Research Bureau, who, on his orders, slaughtered thousands of innocent Ugandans in a campaign of ethnic cleansing, and executed his enemies live on television. He mutilated his wife and murdered his ministers, keeping the head of one in his refrigerator as a warning to others. By the end of his reign over 300,000 people, one in sixty of his population had been murdered.

Uganda is a landlocked country in East Africa. Covering a total of just over 93,000 square miles, it is slightly smaller in size than Great Britain. It is bordered by the Sudan to the north, Kenya to the east, Tanzania and Rwanda to the south and the Congo to the west. A former British colony, Uganda gained independence on 9 October 1962. Under British rule, economic power and education were concentrated in the south, whilst the majority of the armed forces, police and paramilitary forces were drawn from the north. This imbalance would help to shape the savage history of Uganda.

Idi Amin Dada was born around 1928 in Uganda's West Nile district. His father was a Kakwa Muslim and his mother a Christian Lugbara, a neighbouring tribe of the Kakwa. Both these tribes are generally defined as Nubians, renowned for their sadistic brutality, lack of formal education and ability to poison their enemies. His parents separated when Idi was very young and the young boy moved from one army barracks to another with his camp-follower mother, who was purported to be a witch.

After only two years of primary education, Amin joined the King's African Rifles in 1946 as an assistant cook. His service record shows that he was always in trouble. Despite this, he was the physical type that the British liked best in their ranks – he was six-feet-four-inches tall and uneducated, characteristics his officers believed would ensure bravery in battle whilst making him more amendable to orders. Rising quickly through the ranks, Captain Amin was sent to England in 1962, to undertake a Commanding Officers' course in Wiltshire, but he returned in 1964 having failed to complete it. He was then sent to Israel on parachute training – again he failed to finish his training, but the Israelis gave him his wings anyway. By 1966 Amin had returned to Uganda and become Deputy Commander of the Ugandan military – he was now an indispensable ally to any politician wanting to rule the country.

But even before his return to Uganda it was reported that Amin had been exhibiting signs of sadism. As a corporal fighting the Mau Mau uprising in Kenya in the 1950s he was said to have made members of the Karamajong tribe place their genitals on the table. He threatened to cut them off with a machete. It was also said that early in 1962 he was directly responsible for the murders of innocent Turkana tribesmen. His behaviour was reported to Obote, then Prime Minister of Uganda, via the British Governor, but Amin was one of only two black officers in the whole Ugandan army on the eve of independence, so the incident was apparently hushed up and Amin was promoted to Colonel. He had been saved by the political winds of change; it was an error that Obote would come to regret bitterly.

It was not long, however, before Amin was in trouble again: this time it was his greed that led him there. In 1966 he was investigated for corruption, when it was discovered that within a month, he had deposited £20,000 in his bank account – more than a Ugandan colonel could earn in a decade. Amin suceeded in having the charges dropped.

By 1966, the political situation in Uganda was becoming increasingly volatile. Milton Obote had become the country's first Prime Minister in 1962 and his first priority had been to forge some sort of unity among the fourteen million Ugandans who owed more allegiance to their tribal chiefs than to any government in Kampala. Obote, a professional lawyer, came from the minority Langi tribe and, mindful of this, he appointed the powerful ruler of the Buganda tribe, King Freddy, as President. The Buganda tribe, largely anglicized by colonial commissioners and missionaries, was the largest single ethnic group in Uganda. They considered themselves the elite. But in placating them, Obote earned the growing distrust of all the other tribes.

Obote began to limit the power of the President and Buganda tribesmen started agitating for Obote's overthrow. Realizing that he needed to pit some military muscle against them, he chose the new Deputy Commander of the army, Idi Amin, to help him keep control of the country.

Amin's response to the call was both swift and energetic. Using a 122mm gun mounted on his personal jeep, he blew gaping holes in King Freddy's palace. The president, warned of the danger just before the attack, fled into hiding and eventually made his way to Britain, where he died in lonely exile.

For the next four years, Amin was the Prime Minister's trusted strong-arm, and Milton Obote was calm and relaxed when, in January 1971, he flew off to Singapore to attend a Commonwealth conference. However, on 25 January, Radio Uganda

President Idi Amin Dada takes the salute in Kampala, February 1975. To a physically imposing presence Amin added a capacity for brutality and terror made all the more sinister by the fact that, to many Western eyes, he often appeared to be little more than a figure of fun; in fact, as thousands learned, to cross him was to invite torture and death, often without the slightest provocation. (© BETTMANN/CORBIS)

In January 1971, Amin orchestrated the coup that overthrew President Milton Obote and his regime. Here the then Major-General Amin drives his own jeep into Kampala, to be greeted joyfully by thousands of cheering Ugandans. Almost at once, however, he embarked upon a campaign of slaughter, murdering those who had supported Obote, as well as most of the army's officers, whom he replaced with his own corrupt placemen. (© BETTMANN/CORBIS)

started playing martial music throughout the morning and at 3.45p.m. Wilfred Aswa, a warrant officer (destined to die three years later at the hands of Amin), read an announcement stating the reasons for the military coup. Amin was not mentioned in the first broadcast, but thirty minutes later it was announced that he had been asked by the armed forces to take over the country. His first words were: 'I am not a politician but a professional soldier. I am therefore a man of few words.' But now he was Uganda's President he would not stop talking.

Initially there was great jubilation among many sections of the population at the birth of the new regime. Following his overnight coup, Amin promised to return the country to democracy. It was a lie. Many of those who welcomed him were to suffer later at his hands. Foreign newspapers, particularly in Britain, hailed the event as a new era in Uganda. Amin's first move was to pacify tribal enemies and buy valuable breathing space. He persuaded Bugandan tribal leaders that he had actually tipped off King Freddy, giving him time to flee to safety, and he organized for the deceased President's body to be flown back and buried with full ceremony. Amin was said to be deeply affected by the ritual outpouring and lavish expense of the funeral, but the experience was to be put to hideous use later on.

Encouraged by adulation and euphoria, yet quite unable to transcend the severe limits imposed by his lack of formal education, Amin now chose a course which was to take his country back down the dark tunnel to an era of barbarism and internecine slaughter.

Amin and his henchmen embarked on a campaign of genocide against the tribes who had supported the previous government. He purged the army, killing the members of Obote's tribe and his supporters. The West Nilers and Nubians were filled with a desire for vengeance, and Amin fuelled their passion with his own paranoia and blood lust. Soldiers started appearing at universities. They would look at the names on the doors and take away women with certain names, principally Bugandans, but not only from that tribe – these women would be dragged, screaming out into the night. They were culling women from various tribes and many of them were never seen again.

In March 1972, Amin announced a restructuring of the army and began by ordering thirty-six army officers to report to Makindye prison in Kampala, the capital of Uganda, for training in internal security. Disgruntled, but seduced by the thought of forming part of a government of military men rather than politicians, the officers arrived at the prison. They were placed in the cell called Singapore – both the prison and that cell in particular would become bywords for terror and torture. Through a spy hole in the door, the prisoners next door watched a hideous scene unfold. Some of the officers were crawling, screaming in pain because their arms and legs had been broken. Military guards prodded them with bayonets and knives to hurry them up – splitting their stomachs open, cutting their throats or beheading them. The blood lay half-an-inch thick on the floor.

The former army Chief-of-Staff, Brigadier Suleiman Hussein, was arrested and taken to another prison where he was beaten to death with rifle butts. His head was severed and taken to Amin's palatial new home in Kampala, where the President preserved it in the freezer compartment of his refrigerator. In two widely separated army barracks, at Mbara and Jinja, the elite of the officer corps were lined up on the parade ground to take a salute from an armored column. The tanks swept across the square, swung into line abreast formation and crushed most of the officers to death. Those left alive were used for target practice. At another barracks, the remaining staff officers were herded into a briefing room for a lecture by Amin. As they saw his gleaming Mercedes sweep into the square, the doors were locked from the outside and grenades were lobbed through the windows.

Within five months, Amin had killed most of the trained, professional officers in his army. Yet news of these events was kept from the Ugandan people, who were simply told that a few disloyal officers had been court-martialed and executed. To make up the gaps in the ranks, Amin promoted fellow Kakwa tribesmen. Cooks and drivers, mess orderlies and wireless operators became majors and colonels overnight. During the greater part of 1971, the up-country areas, where the majority of killings took place, were sealed off from foreigners and those attempting to find out the truth, such as the American journalist, Nicholas Stroh, who soon fell victim to Amin's wrath.

Stroh and his colleague, Robert Siedle, had been asking questions about the army massacres. At Mbara barracks they were granted an interview with the new commander, Major Juma Aiga, a former taxi driver who had gained an instant army commission. When their persistent questioning became too much, Major Aiga telephoned Amin. His reply was said to be a terse: 'Kill them.' Two days later Aiga was seen driving around Kampala in Stroh's Volkswagen. The two Americans were never seen again.

Amin had now broken the back of the Ugandan army and decided to set off on his first foreign trip as head of government. The trip was seen as the act of a man of peace, anxious to consolidate the security of Uganda on the world stage, but the reality was very different, Amin was looking to buy weapons to further establish his reign of terror in Uganda.

His first visit in July 1972 was to Israel, where he met with the Prime Minister, Golda Meir, but apart from a vague offer to supply training for his troops he left empty-handed. Then Amin decided to give his old colonial masters a surprise. The first that anyone knew of his visit was when the pilot of his plane radioed to the control tower at Heathrow Airport, announcing his arrival. The Queen was in residence at the time, and she was prevailed upon to give a luncheon at Buckingham Palace. When the Queen asked Amin for his reason for visiting Britain, he replied it was to shop for size fourteen shoes.

At a meeting with Edward Heath, the Prime Minister, Amin was more frank about his intentions. He wanted guns, aeroplanes, and ammunition, but he had no money with which to buy them and he was turned away. Furious at being rejected by his supposed allies, Amin returned to Uganda. Soon, both countries would feel his wrath.

Meanwhile in Uganda, Amin's rages were becoming legendary. One hot August night in 1972, dinner guests at Amin's palace, State House, were shocked and revolted when he left the table and returned with the frost-encrusted head of Brigadier Hussein. In a ranting fit of rage, Amin screamed abuse at the severed head, throwing cutlery at it, before ordering his guests to leave.

When Amin had seized power in 1971, Uganda was by far the most economically viable state in East Africa. There were no shortages of essential commodities and hunger and abject poverty were unknown. Tourism was booming and had almost replaced cotton as the prime foreign exchange earner. At the beginning of 1971 Uganda's foreign reserves stood at twenty million pound sterling, but by the end of the year they had dwindled to three million. Within a year of Amin coming to power Uganda was virtually bankrupt. The President's response was to order the Bank of Uganda to print millions of worthless banknotes to pump into the economy. All that remained of the reserves of US dollars were made available for his personal use.

In Kampala the price of a bar of soap rose to £6, two weeks' wages for the average worker on the coffee plantations, which were among the country's few remaining

Like many treacherous men, Amin was obsessed with loyalty. This photograph, taken in 1975, shows a group of thirteen white men and one woman, five of them British, being sworn in to the Ugandan Army, a ceremony which required them to kneel before the President and swear to fight South Africa. Hitler, whom Amin publicly admired, demanded similar oaths of allegiance from his troops. (© BETTMANN/CORBIS)

economic resources. Temporary salvation was offered by one other extravagant dictator, Libya's Colonel Gadaffi, with whom Amin met on 13 February 1972. The price was one Amin was only too happy to pay for their newly-formed alliance. As Libyan money poured into Kampala to keep the country barely afloat, Amin kept his side of the bargain.

Amin declared he was now against the State of Israel and backed the Palestinian cause, and on 27 March 1972 he ordered that all Israelis had to leave Uganda. His accusations became increasingly wild – he claimed they had been intending to poison the Nile and kill all Arabs in Sudan and Egypt. In an interview with *Arab Week* he said that he would lead the Arab troops to conquer Israel. The contradiction that wearing Israeli paratrooper wings on his uniform presented when he was depicted on the new Ugandan currency later that year, was lost on Amin. Angered and hurt, the Israelis pulled out. The documents they took with them included one slim volume which would help to make history – the plans of Israel's last gift to Uganda – the new passenger terminal, control tower and runway layout for Entebbe Airport.

Amin, anxious to prove to Gadaffi that he was a worthy protégé, opened an office in Kampala for the Palestine Liberation Organization, with full diplomatic status. He declared his admiration for Adolf Hitler and drew up plans for a memorial to the Nazi dictator to be erected in the middle of Kampala. When, in 1972, Palestinian terrorists massacred the Israeli Olympic team in Munich, Amin sent a telegram to the United Nations stating that: 'Hitler and all German people knew that the Israelis are not people who are working in the interest of the people of the world and that is why they burnt over six million Jews alive with gas on the soil of Germany. The world should remember that the Palestinians, with the assistance of Germany, made the operation possible in the Olympic village.'

By August 1972 Amin was in deep trouble inside Uganda. The economy was under intense pressure because of excessive military spending and his claims that the hundreds of people who had disappeared, had been murdered or spirited away by Zionists and imperialists, were no longer believed. There were fewer jobs than ever and violence and murder had become institutionalized. The civilians were complaining and even the army personnel were looking to Amin for a solution. Amin needed a diversion, and he needed money – the Asian population in Uganda were to be his next victims.

The Asians had originally come to Uganda to construct the railway as indentured labourers. Thousands had stayed and more had joined them later. Britain had used them to establish and consolidate its rule as middlemen – political and economic – between themselves and the Africans. They owned and controlled approximately half of Uganda's wealth, and were the focus of much internal jealousy within the African community.

Some early indicators of the coming harassment of Uganda's Asian community had already surfaced during 1971. Amin had ordered a head count and started to accuse them of currency racketeering, smuggling and isolationism. In January 1972 he warned that any Asians holding political meetings would be summarily shot. Then on 5 August he dropped his bombshell. He gave the 80,000 Asians ninety days to leave Uganda, claiming the idea had come to him in a dream from God. The expulsion opened the way for the state to acquire the Asian community's assets, without payment, for Amin to dispose of as he saw fit. Amin had given his answer to the masses and the greed of his soldiers.

For the next three months, Amin's voice could be heard on Uganda radio, making a daily countdown to the deadline. Although most of the Asians had lived in Uganda for generations, forming the backbone of the nation's commerce, they now fled in terror leaving behind their houses, offices, shops and plantations.

The Asians were treated brutally as they left Uganda. Some were killed by Amin's marauding troops. At airports, border posts, railway stations and road blocks they were harassed, manhandled, robbed and raped. They were forced to leave all their property behind with their businesses, which were being allocated to Africans. Amin gave away the choice businesses to his friends and cronies. Pharmacies and surgeries were handed over to motor mechanics from the infamous State Research Bureau; textile warehouses were given to Research Bureau telephone operators and army corporals. Within weeks the shops were deserted, their stocks sold and the shelves never filled again. Africans, with no retail experience, fixed the prices of expensive foreign shirts in Kampala shops according to their collar size, thinking that it was the price tag.

Amin knew that in expelling the Asians he was causing difficulties for Britain as the majority of Asians with British passports fled there. But he had not finished with Britain yet, and on 17 December, in a midnight radio and TV broadcast, Amin announced that he was taking all property belonging to British citizens in Uganda. The Ugandan government was to take over all the tea estates as well as Uganda Television and the British Metal Corporation. Any Briton remaining would be accused of spying and would have to suffer with the consequences.

But Amin was creating a monster that needed to be fed constantly. The infamous State Research Bureau was a state within a state, run by men who did not seem to possess the hearts and feelings of human beings. He bought their loyalty with lavish gifts of money and expensive luxuries like video recorders and whiskey, and clothes imported from London and Paris.

Once the Asian and British businesses had been given up, the men of the State Research Bureau wanted to be paid again. With no money or property left to meet their demands, Amin gave them the only asset he had left, the lives of his fellow Ugandans. It was the most bestial mass murder contract in history. Amin had given his followers the licence to kill for profit.

He knew the custom of Ugandans, their deep reverence for the last remains of dead relatives, and that they would spend every last Ugandan schilling, and part with everything of value to recover the body of a loved one for burial. In many of the tribes, 'body finders' will earn their rewards by tracking through the bush to find the corpse of a father or son who has died in some remote area. Now the State Research Bureau became both the killers and the body finders.

Cruising through the streets of Kampala in their imported cars, wearing their uniform of gaudy shirts and bell-bottom trousers, they openly arrested ordinary townspeople. And at their headquarters, only a few hundred yards from Amin's home, they ruthlessly butchered their victims.

One of Amin's ministers later compiled a list of the tortures that they inflicted. They are as follows:

Slow killing was common practice. A man would be shot in the arms, chest and legs and left to bleed to death.

There was a technique for cutting a victim's flesh and force-feeding it to him raw until he bled to death.

A man's flesh would be cut, roasted and he would be forced to eat it until he died.

Certain prisoners were kept in very deep and dark holes. These holes are filled with ice-cold water in which the prisoners were kept and tortured to death.

Amin's house after the liberation of Kampala by the Tanzanian Army, April 1979 – a building made more sinister by its innocent air of a respectable suburban villa. In fact, it was next door to the headquarters of the euphemistically named 'State Research Bureau', where over 100 prisoners were slaughtered by Amin's secret police as Kampala fell. The State Research Bureau, with the army, was one of the principle instruments of Amin's policies of repression, extortion and genocide. (© BETTMANN/CORBIS)

Sticking bayonets through prisoners' anuses or genitals.
Women were raped or had their reproductive organs set on fire whilst still alive.

As the corpses piled up in the basement cells of the three-storey building, other Research Bureau investigators were dispatched to inform grieving families that their loved ones had disappeared after being arrested and were feared dead. For a body-finding fee of £150, or every last possession the family owned, the state-sponsored murderers would drive the widows and weeping sons and daughters to a lush forest on the outskirts of Kampala.

Almost every gulley and bush concealed a dead body. Night after night as many as a hundred families made the trip. The bodies not reclaimed were thrown into Lake Victoria, useless assets written off as a business loss until they floated through the sluiced gates of the Owens Fall Dam or the hydroelectric generators.

The dimming of the streetlights on the warm, tropical nights in Kampala now became a barometer of the morale of the people of Uganda. Visitors, arms salesmen and foreign diplomats in the two showpiece hotels would grumble loudly when cocktail bars were plunged into darkness and the elevators jammed between floors. But the uncomplaining residents of Kampala would leave the unlit streets and go home behind their barricaded doors. Fitful blackouts were a sign that President Amin had just completed another busy day of butchery. The drop in the voltage could only mean one thing – that the hydroelectric dam at Owen Falls, forty miles west of Kampala, was once again clogged with rotting corpses. Time after time the generators had to be shut down and the water inlets cleared of the day's toll of death, which usually numbered forty to fifty corpses. But despite the constant boat patrols on Lake Victoria, the maintenance engineers couldn't hope to spot every dead body. Luckily for them they had allies: crocodiles who would scavenge, eating the evidence. But even these voracious creatures had become bloated and lazy. The pickings were too rich for them.

By now, the executions by firing squad at the Research Bureau were becoming a problem. The neighbouring French embassy staff complained directly to Amin about the constant gunfire through the night. Amin, sinking deeper and deeper into depravity, discussed a solution with the head of the Bureau, Lieutenant Isacc Malyamungu.

Malyamungu, a gatekeeper at a textile factory before Amin made him a government official, was a notoriously sadistic killer. After executing the Mayor of the town of Masaka, he had paraded the badly mutilated man through the streets carrying his amputated genitals in his hands. Now he and Amin calmly came up with a solution to the problem of maintaining the horrendous flow of very profitable killings without the disturbing, continuous rattle of gunfire.

Each murder victim would be kept separately in the basement, while another prisoner was offered the promise of reprieve, if he would batter the solitary man to death with a sledgehammer. Terrified, and pleading for their lives, few prisoners were brave enough to refuse the offer. But once they had carried out their grisly deed, the roles were changed. The unwilling executioner, usually sobbing and demented would be left alone. He would become the solitary man, while in the cell next door another Ugandan was being given the sledgehammer and the heartless promise of life if he would repeat the procedure.

Even Amin's own wives were not safe from his insane paranoia and rages. In March 1974 he decided to divorce three of his four wives. He accused them of meddling in his affairs and ordered them out of his home. Three months later, one of the young ex-wives, Kay, died in an apartment in Kampala as the result of a clumsy abortion attempt. She had been four months pregnant. Amin, in a state of fury, rushed to the mortuary to see her body. Shortly afterwards, having barked a few orders at the hospital staff, he left.

Two hours later he returned and satisfied himself that his orders had been carried out. His youngest wife, Sarah, and Kay's young son, Aliga Amin, accompanied him. 'Pay close attention to what you see', he roared, 'Kay was a wicked woman and you must see what has become of her.' His ex-wife's mutilated torso lay on the operating table. Her head and all of her limbs had been amputated and her head had been reversed and sewn onto her torso face-down. Her legs had been sewn onto her shoulders and her arms attached to her bloodstained pelvis.

But Amin was about to reap the reward of his swaggering arrogance. On 28 June 1976, an Air France airliner, hijacked by a group of Palestinians, arrived at Entebbe Airport. The plane had been en-route from Tel-Aviv to Paris when it had been taken over near Athens. It carried some 300 passengers, most of whom were Jewish.

In the heart of an African country governed by a Hitler-worshipper, far from any hope of rescue, the Palestinians confidently drew up a list of demands while Amin looked on, gloating and basking in the world's limelight. Amin helped to draft the blackmailers' demands stating that all the passengers would be killed within forty-eight hours, if fifty-three imprisoned Palestinians in Israel and Europe were not released. As international tension mounted, the deadline was extended until the early hours of 4 July, and non-Jewish passengers were allowed to leave.

Two days before the deadline, as terrified hostages huddled together in the passenger terminal, one elderly Londoner, Dora Bloch, who held dual British-Israeli nationality, choked on a piece of food and was driven the twenty miles to hospital in Kampala. But as Idi Amin was being seen world-wide on television, badgering the hostages in the passenger lounge, Israeli engineers unlocked a filing cabinet and began to pore over the vital blueprints of the airport they had helped to build.

Shortly after midnight on 3 July, a task force of Israeli Air Force planes, filled with commandos, swept down over Lake Victoria and landed at Entebbe Airport. They taxied to the precise spot where the hostages were being held. In less than one hour they took off again with the rescued hostages, killing twenty of Amin's troops and all seven hijackers. They also took with them the bodies of two of their own men who had been caught in the crossfire.

But elderly Dora Bloch remained behind in Kampala Hospital, frail and barely able to breath – Amin decided to vent his fury on her. After she had received reassurance from the British High Commissioner, Peter Chandley, two of Amin's henchmen from the State Research Bureau crashed through the doors of the hospital. They pistol-whipped the frail widow and dragged her down three flights of stairs. Half-an-hour later they dumped her bullet-riddled body in a field on the outskirts of Kampala. When the High Commissioner went to see her, Amin informed him that she had been returned to the airport before the raid had taken place and was therefore with the other rescued passengers – a palpable lie since the commissioner had seen Mrs. Bloch after the raid had taken place.

And so the situation drifted on until the late 1970s. Violence and murder became endemic. Citizens lived in spite of, and not because of, the existence of the state and individuals and communities found themselves without protection against humiliation, violence and dispossession.

Amin assassinated the Anglican Archbishop, Janani Luwum and this was followed by the banning of all twenty-six Christian organizations working in Uganda. There was now an unprecedented out-pouring of exiles of every ethnic and political background. Amin received worldwide condemnation, even from those who had hitherto been his allies, and America's House of Representatives passed a resolution condemning his gross violation of human rights. However, Amin remained undeterred, and people began to believe that their President was indestructible and that they would never live to see another leader. It seemed as if the people's prayers were not being heard, and that God had forgotten the ill-fated people of Uganda.

But God had not forgotten. Amin was still vulnerable – especially from his own army. He could never totally eliminate those against him, in addition to which, other forces were now coming into play. Civilian groups were forming and troops were preparing in Kenya and Tanzania. Amin's excesses had galvanized the opposition, especially the exiles living abroad.

Idi Amin's last desperate gamble to hold onto the reins of power collapsed in April 1979. In a moment of over-confidence bordering on insanity, and to scare the Ugandan people into submission, he claimed that the country was threatened by bloody invasion from its southern neighbour, Tanzania.

To give substance to his fantasies, Amin ordered small contingents of his troops to cross over to Tanzania on raids against the 'invaders'. Such provocation was too much for the Tanzanian President, Julius Nyrere. His soldiers repelled the attacks and then pressed on deep into Uganda. They were welcomed with open arms by the long-suffering Ugandans as they advanced towards Kampala, arriving in April 1979.

In his final television broadcast, Amin urged his troops to join him in a last stand at the town of Jinja, but the soldiers never turned up, but then again neither did Idi Amin. He had fled in his personal aircraft to the safety of Libya to seek sanctuary with his one remaining ally, Colonel Gadaffi. The brutal reign of Idi Amin was over and today he lives near Mecca, in Saudi Arabia, a guest of the royal family.

BIBLIOGRAPHY

CALIGULA

Barber, Stephen and Reed, Jeremy, *Caligula – Divine Carnage*, Creation, London, 2001

Barrett, A. A., *Caligula – The Corruption of Power*, New Haven, New York, 1989

Ferrill, A., *Caligula – Emperor of Rome*, Thames & Hudson, London, 1991

Gibbon, Edward, *The Decline and Fall of the Roman Empire*, Everyman, London, 1993

NERO

Bishop, John, *Nero – The Man and The Legend*, Hale, London, 1964

Griffin, Miriam T., *Nero – The End of a Dynasty*, Routledge, London, 2000

Holland, Richard, *Nero – The Man Behind the Myth*, Sutton, Stroud, 2000

ATTILA THE HUN

Howarth, Patrick, *Attila King of the Huns – The Man and The Myth*, Robinson, London, 2001

Nicolle, David, *Attila The Hun*, Osprey, Oxford, 2000

KING JOHN

Appleby, J. F., *John, King of England*, Knopf, New York, 1959

Norgate, Kate, *John Lackland*, Macmillan, London, 1902

Warren, W. L., *King John*, Yale University Press, London, 1997

TORQUEMADA

Baigent, Michael and Leigh, Richard, *The Inquisition*, Penguin, London, 2000

Edwards, John, *The Spanish Inquisition*, Tempus, Stroud, 1999

Kamen, Henry, *Inquisition and Society in Spain in the 16th and 17th Centuries*, Weidenfeld & Nicolson, London, 1985

Peters, Edward, *Inquisition*, University of California Press, 1988

Roth, C., *The Spanish Inquisition*, R. Hale, London, 1937

VLAD THE IMPALER

McNally, Raymond T. and Florescu, Radu, *Dracula: Prince of Many Faces: His Life and Times*, Little, Boston, 1989

Treptow, Kurt W., *Vlad III Dracula*, Oxford, 2000

FRANCISCO PIZARRO

Bernard, Carmen, *The Incas – Empire of Blood and Gold*,
    Thames & Hudson, 1996

Innes, Hammond, *The Conquistadors*, Collins, London, 1969

Kirkpatrick F. A., *The Spanish Conquistadors*, Black, London, 1946

Wachtel, Nathan, *The Vision of the Vanquished – the Spanish Conquest of Peru through
    Indian Eyes*, Harvester Press, 1977

MARY I

Erickson, Carolly, *Bloody Mary*, Robson, London, 2001

Prescott, H. F. M., *Mary Tudor*, Eyre & Spottiswode, London, 1952

Ridley, Jasper, *The Life and Times of Mary Tudor*, Weidenfeld & Nicholson,
    London, 1973

Tittler, Robert, *The Reign of Mary I*, Longman, London, 1983

IVAN IV

Graham, Stephen, *Ivan the Terrible: Life of Ivan IV of Russia*, Archon,
    Connecticut, 1968

Hosking, Geoffrey, *Russia and The Russians: A History from Rus to the Russian Federation*,
    Belknap, Harvard University Press, 2001

Troyat, Henri, *Ivan the Terrible*, Phoenix Press, London, 1984

ELIZABETH, COUNTESS BATHORY

McNally, Raymond T., *Dracula was a woman: in search of the blood countess of Transylvania*,
    Hale, London, 1984

McNally, Raymond T. and Florescu, Radu, *In Search of Dracula: A true story of
    Dracula and vampire legends*, New York Graphic Society, Greenwich, 1972

RASPUTIN

Lincoln, W. B., *The Romanovs*, Weidenfeld & Nicolson, London, 1981

Moynahan, Brian, *Rasputin – The Saint Who Sinned*, Arum, London, 1997

Radzinsky, Edvard, *From Wastrel Monk to Political Power – Rasputin: The Last Word*,
    Weidenfeld & Nicolson, London, 2000

Xenofontova, Lyudmila (trans.), *The Romanovs – Love, Power and Tragedy*,
    Leppi, Italy, 1993

JOSEF STALIN

Conquest, Robert, *The Great Terror – A Reassessment*, Pimlico Books, London, 1990

Conquest, Robert, *Stalin – Breaker of Nations*, Phoenix, London, 1998

Figes, Orlando, *A People's Tragedy*, Pimlico, London, 1996

Sema, Robert, *A History of 20th Century Russia*, Penguin, London, 1997

HITLER

Bullock, Alan, *Hitler – A Study in Tyranny*, Penguin, London, 1962

Kershaw, Ian, *Hitler – Profiles in Power*, Longman, London, 1991

Kershaw, Ian, *Hitler – Hubris and Nemesis*, Penguin, London, 2001

Maser, Werner, *Hitler*, Bechtle, Munich, 1971

ILSE KOCH

Hackett, David A. (trans. and ed.), *The Buchenwald Report*, Westview, Oxford, 1995

www.jewishgen.org/ForgottenCamps/Camps/BuchenwaldEng.html

POL POT

Chandler, David P., *Brother Number One: A Political Biography of Pol Pot*, Westview, Oxford, 1999

Jackson, Karl D., *Cambodia 1975-1978 – Rendevouz with Death*, Princeton, 1989

Kiernan, Ben, *The Pol Pot Regime*, Yale University Press, 1996

Martin, M. A., *Cambodia – A Shattered Society*, University of California Press, 1994

IDI AMIN

Jamison, Martin, *Idi Amin and Uganda: an annotated bibliography*, Greenwood, London, 1992

Listowel, J. H., *Amin*, IUP Books, Dublin, 1973

Martin, David, *General Amin*, Faber, London, 1974

Mutibwa Phares, *Uganda Since Independence*, Hurst, London, 1992